MEMORIES FROM BOSNIA
Nadžija Gajić-Sikirić, M.D.

Translator: Edina Jerlagić
Editor: Bonnie Granat

Copyright © 2006 by Nadžija Gajić-Sikirić, M.D.
All rights reserved.
ISBN: 978-0-557-06176-1

"It seems to me sometimes that life is only a series of various experiences. In that series sometimes only one atom of reason is needed for us to avoid the things that could make us sore and dissatisfied in ourselves."

About the Book

Zijada Djurđević-Alidžanović, M.Sc. Arch.
(Architect and designer at the National and University Library of Bosnia and Herzegovina, Sarajevo)

We have the book MEMORIES FROM BOSNIA in front of us, the memoir of Nadžija Gajić-Sikirić, M.D., composed of 35 chapters—the life sequences. There are not many people who can say they had a meaningful life, both private and professional. Nadžija Gajić-Sikirić, M.D., belongs to the group of people whose life and professional experience deserved to be written down. In MEMORIES FROM BOSNIA, we follow a long time period within two centuries, starting from the thirties of the twentieth to the beginning of the twenty-first century. In that period, while reading MEMORIES FROM BOSNIA, we witness the important historical events that significantly influenced the private and professional life of the author. In addition to the historical events, the author familiarizes us with many people who were important to her (her family, work colleagues, patients).

The book presents us a remarkable woman, who dedicated her life to the medical sciences (pediatric surgery) and to her family. Reading this book, we meet a brave woman who managed to overcome the prejudices of her environment. The majority of the successes she achieved have a special dimension because she is a woman. MEMORIES FROM BOSNIA shows us a woman with remarkable energy, a person who has had visionary ideas her whole life, and a person who has always lived in advance. MEMORIES FROM BOSNIA is an impressive record of the author's dedication to her professional vocation and of her significant contribution to the development of pediatric surgery in our area. Someone whose life was really meaningful, someone who found her life's meaning in helping other people, can really say, "I am a lucky woman, I carried out my mission ..." And Nadžija Gajić-Sikirić, M.D., can say something like that.

Amra Rešidbegović, M.Sc.
(National and University Library of Bosnia and Herzegovina, Sarajevo)

The book MEMORIES FROM BOSNIA of Dr. Nadžija (Nadja) Gajić-Sikirić is an interesting and original book, written in the form of a memoir. It covers a tempestuous period of Bosnian-Herzegovinian history, starting from the thirties of the last century and ending at the beginning of the new millennium.

Memories make a testimony about the life of a surgeon having remarkable energy and enthusiasm, about her temptations and escapes, about her struggle against impossibilities and about her victories, about her interests as spread out of her basic vocational field and surroundings. Accordingly, *Memories* makes a testimony of an unusual period when two wars occurred within a very short time and caused great changes within the social system, ideology, culture, habits, way of living, and system of values—from the one to another and a completely new one.

Although in *Memories* we see her zealous dedication to her professional work and her optimism, the author did not emphasize her obvious contribution to development of pediatric surgery in our region, where she opened many roads toward its advancement.

The book tells us about a modern woman who enlightened a time and place from the perspective of a doctor. *Memories* can be used as a source and an inspiration, and fills a gap in our memoir literature.

About the Author

Nadžija Gajić-Sikirić was born on April 13, 1927, in an intellectual family from Sarajevo. Her father was a university professor born into the famous and talented intellectual Sikirić family, while her mother was from the well-known Kasumagić family, which owned real estate in and outside of Sarajevo. She spent her childhood, until World War II, in that upper-middle-class family. The changes that occurred during, and especially after, that war influenced personal, professional, and family life significantly.

In MEMORIES FROM BOSNIA, she presents to us the society she lived in as well as herself—unwavering in her thirst for knowledge and human progress.

As a doctor, she gave her contribution to the field of pediatric surgery, where she was engaged for many years, from the pioneer era in this medical field to its later higher development.

MEMORIES FROM BOSNIA will be equally interesting to her contemporaries and those who belong to the new generation.

Contents

Part I

1	Oglavak	13
2	School	23
3	Old House	31
4	New House	39
5	War	43
6	War Atrocities	57
7	Liberation	65
8	Wedding	71
9	Graduation	79
10	Gračanica	83
11	Child	89
12	Field Work	97
13	University Enrollment	105
14	Student Life	117
15	University Degree	131

Part II

16	Surgery	143
17	Chief Editor of *Oslobođenje*	153
18	Changes	163
19	Childbirth	169
20	Pirkko	175
21	Specialty Board Exam	179
22	Belgrade	183
23	Loss	187
24	Switzerland	191
25	Return	205
26	Success	211

Part III

27	Illness	227
28	Recovery	233
29	Loss Again	243
30	Mother	249
31	Conferences	253
32	Retirement	261
33	Dissolution	269
34	Besieged	273
35	Exile	295

Part I

1 Oglavak

"Waaah!! Waaah!!" A baby was crying, and a little girl was standing at the door and watching some women dressing the baby in a striped gown on the bed where the mother was lying. The little girl was amazed that the baby did not choke, for its head was under the coverlet. I think that this is my first memory, sometime shortly after the birth of my youngest sister who is three years and nine days younger than I am—I was born on the thirteenth, and she was born on the twenty-second of April. There is a superstition about the thirteenth day in a month being an unlucky day, but I have never thought it was the case with me.

Another image comes to mind: I was with my grandmother in a room with a dim electric light. I watched her preparing herself to go to bed and wrapping herself up in her scarves. I fell asleep. I woke later and went down a dark staircase and entered the room where my parents and two younger sisters were sleeping. "Where are my toys?" I cried out. My father jumped out of his bed and turned the light on, while my mother said, "You are a big girl, and you still want to sleep with your parents." They put me in bed with my sisters. This memory is much less clear than the one from the first grade of my elementary school several years later, and I was a "big girl" then.

A macadam road that ran along the field adjacent to the Fojnica River connected Kiseljak and Fojnica.[1] On that road you could hear the river's sometimes higher- and sometimes lower-pitched roaring. Halfway down the road, the river had hills on both sides, and on the right side of the road, going toward Fojnica, the hills were so close together that the top of one hill hid the foot of the next one. The peaks of these hills were small plateaus that were at the foot of the even higher hills of Vranica Mountain. Those small plateaus and hills had scattered villages in which Muslims and Catholics lived. You could reach these villages either by walking through the forest or by taking a narrow, dusty, uneven road that was very difficult for horse- or ox-drawn carts to use.

The village of Oglavak was at the top of one of those hills. Each year on the first of July we (my parents and I, and my two sisters) left Sarajevo by bus and traveled on the macadam road up to the foot of that hill. Then we all climbed up through the forest to the village and to our summer house there. The road was quite steep, so we took frequent breaks in order to rest. During those breaks we would sit by a small stream in a deep cleft of the hill and watch as the stream murmured softly and jumped over the small stones. When we finally left the forest, we could see the vista of large plowed fields on the gently rounded hills. Finally, a small, narrow road through a meadow brought us to our first view of the village's house roofs, which were covered by darkened boards. Oglavak was so peaceful—only the cackling of a hen disturbed it. Soon we were embracing our Aunt Zahida and her daughter Dika at their house, and the first thing we did after that was take off our dresses and shoes and run barefoot over the soft grass of the field in front of the house. My two sisters and I enjoyed being with Dika, who was our age. As we played on the grass, our mother and father chatted with Aunt Zahida.

---

[1] Two small old towns in Central Bosnia, about 30 miles from Sarajevo.

MEMORIES FROM BOSNIA

The houses in Oglavak were laid out in such a way that they surrounded the field, in the center of which stood livestock sheds and stables. The grain threshing floors were next to the stables. Most of the houses had two floors—kitchens and pantries were on the first floor, and bedrooms and other rooms were on the upper floor. The houses were painted white, and they had windows that opened vertically made of a light-colored wood, possibly oak. The doors were made of the same wood, were nicely polished, and had doorknockers. The houses looked very different than those in the surrounding villages—more like houses in a Bosnian provincial town. There were toilets in the houses, too, both on the first and second floor; each toilet had a deep fenced pit underneath it. From the lounge in every house you could see beautiful vistas far away—over the fields toward Kiseljak and Sarajevo and also toward Zenica and Travnik. Only the backs of the houses in the direction of Fojnica faced the forest-covered hills, the foothills of Vranica Mountain.

Next to the village was a vehicular road that was partly even and dusty, and partly uneven, with stones and some grass. On one side above that road was a turbe[2] with a silver roof and large and beautifully carved tombstones around it. On the other side of the road was a tekya[3] with two rooms, one for praying and the other for meeting with visitors. Between the two rooms was a hall paved with large boards, and at the front of the tekya was a roofed porch with a wooden railing. On the opposite side of the road was a public drinking fountain consisting of two metal pipes on a stone wall. The pipes were plugged with wooden rams. The water was drinkable and soft, not too cold, and if you came very, very close, you could hear the resonant pouring out and filling up of the reservoir.

The tekya was built by my great-great-grandfather.[4] He grew up in Fojnica, and his well-educated teacher had persuaded him to build the tekya there. He also built a small burial chamber, a few hundred yards from the tekya, in memory of Hussein-baba, a highly honored man who had come with the Turkish Army in the fifteenth century when the Turks

---

[2] Burial chamber.
[3] Dervish house.
[4] Sheikh Sirry.

arrived in Bosnia, who had died there. His teacher had learned about this fact while traveling throughout the Turkish Empire, reaching even the Caucasus, where Hussein-baba was born.

My great-great-grandfather found the land on which he was asked to build a tekya neglected and overgrown with forest, and he had a hard time clearing it. It was said that he used to work very hard. He was well educated and had received some education in Constantinople. He was also a poet. Some of his poems, mostly mystical and religious, have been preserved in the private libraries of his descendants.

At the beginning in that spot there was only my great-great-grandfather's house and the tekya; his sons and his grandsons later built their own houses there. The village, which was down the road from the tekya, had no more than eight houses. The men remained there and continued to live in the village, but the women got married and moved to nearby provincial towns and cities with their husbands. The tekya, however, served as a spiritual center and an educational institution not only for the surrounding villages but also for pilgrims who came from the wider area of Central Bosnia. The responsibility for managing the tekya was passed on from father to son or brother, and only the third generation of my great-great-grandfather's descendants, which included my father, went to the cities, got an education, and stayed in the cities to live permanently. After the death of my great-great-grandfather, his burial chamber was built next to the tekya, and to this day many pilgrims visit there.

Oglavak remains the most wonderful memory from my childhood. In the mornings after breakfast I used to go from our house to see Aunt Zahida. Shadows of varying sizes made by the surrounding houses could be seen on the sunny grass. Some hen was always cackling and disturbing the complete peace that was otherwise in that place. We preferred to go to her summer kitchen, which faced the yard and had a constantly lit fire. Above the fireplace hung a kettle with boiling water. Aunt Zahida, a tiny woman, was making popcorn, swaying a griddle back and forth above the fire, and she was always glad to see us. The griddle was soon full of popcorn, and I always wondered how you could get so much popcorn from only a handful of corn. We would sit on low benches, and I liked the smell of the fire, and especially the soil and stone, when I came into the summer kitchen. My aunt often made a zucchini pie in an iron baking pan, and we would sit around the table and eat with regular spoons while Aunt Zahida used the wooden spoon she preferred. In the evenings I often sat on the threshold of her stable with the cows and watched her milk them, pressing each teat of the udder one by one while milk sprinkled into the milk bucket. She would usually let a calf suckle first so that the cow would let her milk go, and she never let a calf milk as much as it wanted but instead gave it a little bit from each teat.

Our house was located across the road from the only drinking fountain in our village. Everyone took water home from there in copper jugs and cans. Evenings were the busiest times, because many people came to get water then, which greatly diminished the supply all of a sudden. Because it was just across from our house, very often we went there in the mornings and washed ourselves with cold water. Our father bought us a huge copper tank with a faucet at its bottom that we filled with water from the fountain across the road. This tank was set on a wooden stand in our yard, and in front of it, below the faucet, there was a sink. Our father demanded that we be clean and stressed that we always had to wash our hands before meals and after going to the toilet. In one of the bedrooms we had a fenced concrete space we called "banjica," which was a small bathroom where we could have a bath, pouring warm water from a copper jug.

Two of the three pipes of the main drinking fountain across the road were plugged with rams; the third one did not have a ram, and water would flow away after the reservoir filled to the top. The whole night we could hear the water running—a resonant murmur that had a magic power to make us fall asleep. In front of our house was a big silver linden tree that flowered and smelled for the whole month of July and had lots of bees around its high crown. After lunch, when my parents took a nap, I often used to sit on the sunny threshold of our house and listen to the buzzing of the bees, a lovely music in that peace.

We spent two months (July and August) of our school holidays in Oglavak, and our father wanted us to be free and without too much control while we were there. Together with the children from surrounding villages, we took care of cattle and sheep. Sometimes we would ride an oxcart full of grain ears to be threshed. We forced horses to tread on ears in a circle so that grain could be separated from the stalks. The horses were running in circles over and over again, rolling up and unrolling the rope with which they were tied to a wooden pole, and I was sorry for the horses, because they had wet spots on their skin, probably resulting from sweating. When resting, the horses would drink a lot of water from the drinking fountain and would eat some oats from a wooden manger in the shade. The best part was in the evening when the men put the straw into the stable and we, the children, would jump into it. We climbed up the beams to the ceiling hundreds of times and jumped into the hay. By doing that, the straw was compacted and much more of it could then be stored—that was the reason the adults wanted us to jump on it.

Sometimes we went too far from home, and we hid those adventures from our parents. Together with our cousin Dika, we would go far from our house and light a fire on a hill or make mud cookies that we baked on a fire near a creek. We picked hazelnuts, put them in our blouses, and peeled them later. We climbed up large wild cherry trees. Strangely enough, we were never seriously injured any of the many times we fell out of those trees. We picked other people's apples and early plums, because our own orchard was young and we did not have any of those trees in it. Sometimes the orchard's owner threatened to tell our father what we had done, but luckily that never actually happened.

Our adventurous life in the country was wonderful. The best thing was when our parents allowed us to go swimming in the river. We would take some flatbread and go down quickly through the forest to the river. In the middle of the forest, we would begin to be able to hear the noise of the river, which became louder and louder as we got closer and came out of the forest. We then had to cross a field, a macadam road, and then another field to reach the river.

MEMORIES FROM BOSNIA

Fojnica River was crystal clear, because it had a stony and pebbly bottom. In some places it was shallow and in others it was deep, with rather big bends where we could swim. The river was good for swimming only in the afternoon, because the water was too cold in the morning. So we went swimming there only in the late afternoon hours. We would occasionally go there in the morning when our mother wanted to wash our clothes in the river. That happened when water in the Oglavak reservoir was low because of high consumption. We would go to the river with baskets full of clothes. There was a girl who helped our mother, and so some assistance was always there for her. My sisters and I would help by washing small items. The day was clear, transparent, as it could be in the morning hours. The clothes were boiling on the fire, and later we scrubbed them and rinsed them out in the river. We put the clothes on bushes and low willows around the river, and it was wonderful to see their flash of whiteness in the sun. We usually had lunch there as well, swam afterward, and then came back home in the evening with dry, clean clothes.

I made my first attempts to swim and to do handstands at the Fojnica River. I also learned to dive there. Diving and doing the backstroke were much easier than doing the breaststroke for me, but still, with great effort I managed to do the breaststroke for a few yards.

We caught small fish and crabs and put them inside small areas near the riverbank that we fenced off with pebbles in the water; in the tiny enclosures that were just a few feet wide, we watched the fish move quickly and the crabs move backwards. We fed them with breadcrumbs and we spent many summer hours on the river, which sometimes roared and flowed up to and over the banks and reached clusters of low willows along its edge. At some points on the riverbank there would be a rock that provided easy access to the river. Part of the river was diverted to a water mill nearby. If you followed that branch of the river, you could hear noise and see a big wheel turning around under the waterspout. It was extremely noisy, especially when we entered the water mill. Both the miller and everything around were covered with the white of flour, and the scent of flour permeated the entire mill.

My father often organized picnics for the people in the village. We would go to some faraway glade or forest and bake pumpkins, and very often we had picnics on the riverbank. Everybody brought some food, flatbread, sponge cakes, egg and flour pastry, and halvah, a special dessert made on a fire that people ate with coffee. Children usually swam until evening, and after many mothers' calls and almost freezing, we put on our dry clothes and enjoyed eating flatbread and pastry. I can remember that warm feeling when I put on my undershirt after swimming.

Oglavak sometimes—maybe due to its geographic location—had very strong winds. The village was on a plateau and open on three sides; on the west side were the smaller peaks of branches of Vranica Mountain. Oglavak was thus open to winds that even forests could not stop. In the summertime we would have hailstorms, and those storms were so strong that people were afraid of them because sometimes they ruined their crops. One day we were swimming in the river and our father was sitting in front of a small coffee bar on the nearby road with two cousins. Heavy, dark clouds came in from the side of Vranica Mountain and the hail started to fall. Fortunately, we managed to run to the small coffee bar for shelter, and when the time came to go back home, our father and his two cousins put each of us on their backs and brought us back to Oglavak, walking barefoot through the flooded fields. The village looked terrible—the hail had cut the grain in the big field, and the orchard trees lost some of their branches. We could still see the leftovers of the hail, nut-sized irregular pieces of ice scattered on the road as we went home. When we arrived, we found our mother very worried about us, because she did not know where we were during the hailstorm. Those storms were so fierce that sometimes they would even kill an animal as large as a sheep or ox that had the misfortune to be outside of the shelter.

During our summer stay in Oglavak we enjoyed nature, friendship, and games. The village had very little of its earlier character, which was described to us by my grandmother, my father's mother. My grandmother would tell us about the very quiet, prayerful way they used to all live there and about the many visitors who came to Oglavak for religious retreats and talks. I learned that from my grandmother and not from my father, who never told us about the history of the religious past of Oglavak and the village's original mission to be a religious center. For my father, a modest and moral life based on universal principles was more important than prayer. The only thing that remained of the religious life in Oglavak was ezan[5] in the evening, when one of the men called for prayer standing on the big stone in front of the tekya.

When my school holidays ended and I had to return to Sarajevo, my heart was full of sadness. Usually it rained then, which made my bad mood even worse. In the summer, our father bought us each a lamb, and it was very difficult for us to leave them at the end of the summer. The lambs ran after us all the way up to the forest, which was fenced. We could see wet tracks from their eyes to their little muzzles. I thought the lambs cried. I wasn't able to find out if a lamb can really cry, and I still do not know what those wet tracks on their faces were that we saw only when leaving Oglavak.

Upon our arrival back in Sarajevo, we cleaned our house, and the mild autumn sun came through the trees into our yard. The sun's rays also spread in our rooms through the windows. I watched it all with my heart full of sadness. I sat on the stairs and cried. My mother, who had understood I was crying because I missed Oglavak, would try to encourage me to see that it was no use to cry anymore. But I still felt so sad, so I got up and went to some other place on the stairs and cried there. My sadness lasted several days and then slowly disappeared. Buying new books and school supplies, and picking apples and fallen walnuts in the yard brought some new joy to me.

---

[5] The call to prayer.

2 School

When I entered the first grade, there was a family celebration in my honor. I remember the pink dress I had on. My aunts and other relatives came and brought me gifts—dresses, scarves, stockings, and school supplies, and some of them gave me money. They were mainly women, and when my father came home, some male relatives came, too. Even today it is not clear to me why my parents celebrated my first day of school, and I do not remember if they did it for my sisters also. Maybe it was my father's idea—he was always very enthusiastic about learning and education. And with good reason: My father was a highly esteemed teacher—a professor at the Islamic Theological School in Sarajevo. He later was rector of that school, also.

The first day of school was cloudy, dark, and rainy. I was afraid. I climbed up the wooden stairs to the first floor, which had only two classrooms. I entered the classroom timidly, and five or six girls were sitting there. It was dark in the classroom, too, just like it was outside. The day matched how I felt. The teacher, a slim young woman, came into the classroom. We stood up and greeted her with the traditional "I kiss your hand."

"My name is Mirjana Bajac, and I will be your teacher," she said. "There are not a large number of you here today, but tomorrow some other students will come too. You do not need to say to me 'I kiss your hand'—it is enough for you to stand up when I or some older person enters the classroom. If you meet some of the teachers outside the school, you will greet him or her with 'I kiss your hand.'"

That first school day lasted only for a short time, and we soon went to our homes.

I loved my teacher, and she loved me. She told me many times, "You will have the best grades." I do not know why she would tell me that so openly. Unfortunately, during the second semester, our teacher got sick and died. The new teacher, a chubby woman, did not have as good of a rapport with us. We practiced mathematics, repeating the multiplication table all together, loudly. The words of my first teacher, "You will have the best grades," did not come true. I got a B in both mathematics and in the Serbo-Croatian language.

The second grade was difficult for me. We had a new teacher who chose Šeka, a tall, dynamic student, to be a student monitor. Šeka immediately asked our teacher if I could be a monitor together with her, and the teacher agreed. This is how my school nightmare began. The nightmare lasted until the end of the school year. I wish I could just totally erase that entire year from my memory and to forget that awful child and the suffering she caused me!

Our monitoring duty started. We had to tell each student who made noise before the teacher came to be quiet. If a student did not heed our warning, we had the right to place that student's name on a list of disobeying students. However, in a short time, when I warned a student, Šeka said, "Do not listen to her, because she has no right to warn or register you—our teacher chose *me* to be the monitor." I did not know what to say to that, so I said nothing. Šeka talked to me again that day like nothing had happened, and we came back home together because we lived close to one another. She often did such things to me, turning on me and then pretending nothing had ever been said by her that humiliated me in front of the other students. I suffered through these things she did to me and frequently came to school with hard feelings toward her. But I did not dare to say anything to our teacher or to Šeka about it. One time, though, I burst into tears in the classroom and told Šeka, "I do not want to be a monitor at all!" When the teacher entered the room, we were all silent. Šeka sometimes tormented me by cutting some page of my book or make a little hole in it while were sitting in class. I told no one but my grandmother about my problems with Šeka. I asked her to ask my father to visit my teacher and talk to her about it because I was afraid to. She did it, but my father did not help me. And I never found out why. So the school year ended, we had our holidays, and then my third grade began.

We moved to a bigger and nicer building with a lot of classrooms, large halls, and yards for my third grade. Boys' and girls' classrooms and yards were separated. We also had a new teacher who remained at my school until I finished the elementary grades two years later. Her name was Bera Djunio. On the first day of school, when she introduced herself, she asked the class, "Who is your best student?" The children shouted my name, and the teacher looked at me and said, "You will be a monitor and watch these children." On my way back home after school, Šeka caught up with me and said, "Will you ask our teacher for me to be a monitor with you? You remember that last year I asked the same for you?" I do not know what I thought then, whether it was scorn or anger I felt, but I only remember that I told her, calmly and gently, with no trace of whatever inner turmoil I was experiencing, "No, there is no need, I can do it myself." She then tried to talk me into doing what she wanted me to do, but my attitude toward her was a reflection of all the suffering I endured at her hands in the previous year at school, and I did not waver in my decision. But I was not unkind. I was just firm.

After that, I did not have any contact with Šeka. I avoided her, but when I would notice holes and cut pages in my old schoolbooks, I was reminded, painfully, of her. Many years later I met her accidentally. I was at an exhibition of paintings and my cousin introduced me to a couple, a lady and gentleman. He was good-looking, with blond hair, and she was tall, with shiny black eyes and black hair. We recognized each other, and our faces reflected a cold discomfort, although she smiled. I don't remember if I smiled or not. After a short greeting, we separated. I later learned she was married to a gentleman from a renowned family of intellectuals.

Because our school's classrooms and yards were separated into boys-only and girls-only, we did not have much contact with boys. But on the way to and from school, the boys made a lot of different comments as they passed near to the girls. I remember taking a roundabout way just to avoid a group of boys who used to wait for me and then, when they were sure I was close enough to hear them, say to a red-faced fat boy who was with them, "There is your girlfriend." I had to pass by those boys, and that fat boy was really disgusting to me. But there was another boy, pale-faced and likable, who was coming back home with a group of boys and girls toward a poorer settlement in the town outskirts. I followed my girlfriends, climbing up to their houses, in order to get closer to that boy. He would sometimes smile at me, and he became even cuter for me when he did that. I came back home after school later than usual for many days after that, but my parents did not notice. I liked that smiling boy, and I do not know how long it lasted, but even to this day I have a charming picture of that sweet pale boy in my mind and how I wished we could be friends.

In the third and fourth grades, our teacher tried to teach us many things. My father used to tell me, "You have a good teacher." She was also quite interested in music and would often bring her violin to school and play for us while our choir practiced. She thought my singing soprano was not a good choice for my voice, because it was a bit deeper than a usual soprano's voice, so she put me among the altos. I found that alto was too low to sing comfortably, but I tried anyway, and thanks to our teacher's efforts to help me continue singing, I enjoyed many good things later in my life from that time in the choir singing those beautiful songs.

My elementary school education was coming to an end. I had to decide on my further education, or at least my parents had to decide what I would do. My father said that I would attend the high school for girls, the eight-year school from which one could go on to the university. I was eleven years old.

Most girls wanted to attend only the four-year high school, from which one could not go on to the university, in order to learn sewing and homemaking. Some wanted to go to yet another four-year school, which provided a general education along with a few additional subjects but from which one could only go to the technical or medical middle schools, not the university. Many girls, however, ended their education right there in the fourth grade, at the close of elementary school. This was because there were a lot of poor students, and although education was free, the school supplies and various taxes were often too much for their parents to afford.

I was, in fact, the only girl from my whole class to attend the pre-university, eight-year high school. My father insisted on that, while my mother wanted me to attend the Islamic religious school, the madrasah, instead. My mother had been given a religious education and also attended a sewing and embroidery school, but her older sisters taught her everything else. My father studied Oriental languages at the University of Budapest and earned the degree of the doctor of philosophy in that field. However, he greatly appreciated my mother's skill as a homemaker and her impressive talent for sewing, knitting, and embroidering. She also was very skilled at cultivating flowers. But my father loved my mother not just for all the things she could do well: She was very beautiful, too, and he loved her for that and for her beauty of spirit, also—for her wisdom and her extreme generosity. In terms of religion, my mother was very religious, while my father recognized the moral principles and tradition but did not practice what he called "blind religious obedience."

I had to pass an entrance examination in order to be admitted to the eight-year high school, from which I could go to the university. My father accompanied me as I went to take the test. From our home, which was located in the old part of Sarajevo, we went through Baš-čaršija.[6] Then we walked beside a low stone wall to the fourth bridge over the Miljacka

---

[6] Picturesque merchant center of Old Sarajevo.

River. On the other side of the river, over the bridge, was a big three-story building in the Austro-Hungarian style. It had the kind of façade that reminded me of a barracks building where soldiers stayed—there were a lot of windows in the front. This building was the school I wanted to attend. It had a rather large yard with an iron fence that was on the very edge of the river. The bridge we went over was made of wood and was called Drvenija.[7] Everyone who came for the test that day was seated in the separate forms in the classroom. The test covered mathematics, Serbo-Croatian grammar, and other subjects. I especially remember the dictation test of Serbo-Croatian language. The slim male teacher, smiling at a younger female teacher, read a chapter from a book, and we had to write it down. I followed him well for some time, but then I fell behind a little—it seemed to me he was talking too quickly. I had to skip part of a sentence and just go on, though. I was afraid afterward that I had done badly because of that. But my worry evaporated after a few days when I went back to the same building and read my name on the board near the school's entrance. This meant that I had been admitted to the high school. I was relieved.

There were sixty students in my class, 1-C. We had to wear black school uniforms—actually, dresses with long sleeves. They had two different styles of the dress, with or without white collars. I had to make that rather long trip every day to and from school. I could take a tram for about half of the way, but my parents did not think it was necessary and did not buy me a monthly tram card.

I listened carefully to my teachers, most of whom were women. It was interesting to learn about a variety of different subjects. The most interesting to me was geography, because we also learned about celestial bodies and their movements, and about the Earth as a celestial body with meridians and parallels. It was all so new to me. I did not have any one particularly close girlfriend, but I had a few close friends who were girls. With one of them, I used to slide down the banisters on the stairs from the third to the first floor of the school building. With another one, I used to come back home, because

---

[7] "Woodily."

she lived close by. I was intrigued by one of the girls, because she was tidy and always gave good answers. She wore glasses and spoke in the Ekavian dialect. During breaks, she often used to talk to me and two other students. While eating her snack, she would talk about serious topics such as school and religious instruction. I remember her saying, "Children, the Islamic religion is very similar to the Christian religion." At the end of the school year, the four of us were named as the students who completed the school year with the highest grades.

During that first year of high school and later as well, my stockings were a source of much embarrassment for me. My mother insisted that we wear long stockings year-round. According to her religious understanding, the bare legs of girls must not be seen. My embarrassment would start at the end of April each year. All of the other students had knee socks or ankle socks on, and only I had to wear stockings. Sometimes other students asked me if I had rheumatism, and I replied that I did—because it was easier to say that than to tell them the real reason I wore stockings. I begged my mother many times to buy me knee socks, but she remained firm in her decision. After some time, however, she bought me knee socks, but they were for picnics only. I was not allowed to wear them in the city. Those socks saved me from that horrible embarrassment! I kept them in my school bag, and I put them on in the hallway of a building near my school that I stopped at on my way there. On my way back home, at the same building, I would put my stockings back on.

3 Old House

We started building our new house during the springtime when I was in that first year of high school. It was an addition onto the house that my mother's sister Aiša then lived in; we would share only the entrance to the building. My mother's two brothers also lived on the same site in the larger main house, which had been the home of my mother's family.

My aunt was a widow and had two daughters close to our age and an older son who was in school abroad. My father and mother worked on our house design for months, changing and adding to it, and when the building process actually began they were quite enthusiastic about it, especially my father. I wasn't sure how I felt about it all. I cannot say that I was especially happy about it. In the fall, when the new house was finished, we moved some things from our old house there every day—everything that we, the children, could carry. From one house to the other we went, crossing several streets, and because the houses were each on a hill, we had to climb down one and then up another. We moved many things that way, especially those that needed to be transported with great care in order to avoid damaging them.

During this process, my two sisters and I began regretting that we had to leave the old house where all three of us had been born. One day my middle sister sang a farewell song in each room and hall of the old house. I walked around our yard and looked at the big walnut tree under which every autumn I used to find nuts in broken green shells, especially after windy and rainy nights. I looked around at the huge pear tree that brought us the sweet yellow fruit, then at the two smaller apple trees that bore us sweet and sour apples each year, and finally, at a white mulberry and a few plum trees. We had a swing hanging from a branch of the mulberry tree. I would spend hours there on a hot sunny day. We were saying a sad goodbye to the home of our birth that held our memories. I have a vivid memory of my grandmother, my father's mother, who had lived with us when I was younger. She walked slowly, and her legs were bent a bit. She had small blue eyes, and we loved her stories from the old days—we kept asking her to tell them again and again. In the evening, when my parents were out visiting their friends, my grandmother liked to put potatoes in the oven. While they were baking, she would tell us stories. I remember especially the story about the black and the white grapes: The Emperor asked the Empress which grape she preferred, black or white, and when she answered "black," each night thereafter he would break ten sticks, beat her with them, and say, "You love Arabs more than me!" One day, another emperor visited him and heard him beating his wife. When the visiting emperor was told in the morning why the Empress was beaten, he advised the Emperor about what to do instead. He gave him a pin and told him to put it in his wife's head. The Emperor did so, and his wife turned into a bird and flew away. Another bird with a pin in its head came back. When the emperor removed the pin, the bird turned into a she-ass, on which you could read, "An emperor deserves an empress, and an ass deserves a she-ass." I do not know how many times I asked her to tell me that story; although sometimes it was hard and boring for her, she told that story over and over.

My father was very tender with my mother. Every morning, when she saw him off at the door, he would kiss her softly on her cheek. She had gallstones, and sometimes she would get attacks at night. The next day our house had to be very quiet so that she could sleep. I also could not sleep during the nights my mother was ill, and I felt sorry for her as I heard her sobbing from the pain. My father was tender with us children, too. He was always interested in our school achievements. He taught us by heart some old songs we liked, such as, "You are beautiful, white Sarajevo, whoever sees you begins to sing to you. If it is early, or it's late, you are happy, white Sarajevo." He liked funny stories and laughed so much at them that his blue eyes would become full of tears. His eyes were also wet sometimes from tears, when he spoke about poor people not having wood for a fire and freezing in the winter or not having enough bread to eat. He and my mother often sent us to bring a basket of wood and a lunch to poor people. And every day we brought lunch to an old aunt.

Our father often took us children for a walk at the outskirts of the city. He taught us about natural phenomena, plants and animals. He recognized each plant we saw on our way. He showed us red sumach (Ruj) and told us that September was named "Rujan" after it. He taught me that mistletoe is a parasite herb that lives on a tree. One day we found three horned vipers. It was a snake nest, and my father showed us they had small horns on their heads and said they were called jumping vipers because they can throw themselves up to several yards in pursuit of an animal that accidentally stepped on them.

In the month of Ramadan, my father used to bring us some special pastry that looked like a small copper kettle. We did not fast during Ramadan, because, as he used to say, "Children do not have to fast," but on the fifteenth night of the Ramadan fasting, he took us to the city. Everything was very solemn, and he bought us different things.

When the fasting ended, we celebrated our holiday, Bayram. Children would get presents, usually some clothes, and for me the best present was patent-leather shoes. We visited our aunts and other relatives on the occasion of Bayram and got money from them. Our parents also gave us money in addition to presents. On the first day of the holiday, my father was visited by friends who stayed only a short time and came just to wish us a Happy Bayram. We served them coffee and Turkish pastries. I have always remembered the smell of the coffee served during our holiday. My father had his best clothes on and was constantly coming and going with his guests, looking very young to me. Women paid their visits on the second and third days of Bayram, and younger ones visited the elderly.

In spite of all the great things our father gave us and showed us, I was often afraid of him. We children always expected him to be angry with us if we disturbed the order of things, if we broke something at home or forgot something. He would yell at us then. We could not be disobedient—ever. In one such situation, he slapped my face several times, and I still think, without a proper reason. He ordered me to do something, and I was joking and laughing at his order. It made him mad. Our maid tried to defend me, but he pushed her away. Finally, he told me to go to the yard with our maid. Shortly afterward, he came to see me, and I was pale and shivering. I think he was sorry, but he didn't say anything. He slapped me another time when we made a fire in Oglavak, although he forbade it, and then another time when we peeked at some children swimming naked in the river. Although my sisters were wrong also that time, he beat only me, because I was the oldest child.

My mother was thought to be a very beautiful woman. She had a very pleasant shape and lovely dark brown eyes. She sewed clothes for us and dressed us in dresses, and people in the street stopped and looked at us with admiration. She was also very ambitious. She showed her ambition in various ways, not all of them as admirable as sewing well. Sometimes during lunch she would raise her voice and say to our grandmother, "You slander me around," and our father would immediately yell at our grandmother. "I swear I did not," my grandmother answered in her timid voice. When I went to her she was crying and her body trembled. Our grandmother was weak; she would often crush the green little leaves of the ruta plant and take it for her heart.

Except for sporadic incidents like that one, our mother was peaceful and full of dignity. She walked slowly, never ran, maybe because she was afraid of having a gallstone attack. My father really loved her and was never seriously angry with her. He used to say to us, "Your mother is a remarkable woman."

She really had warm feelings for everybody; somehow she was compassionate to all people, to the poor, to foreign people, and to people of other religions.

My mother also defended us whenever our father was angry with us. But sometimes she used to lightly discipline us with a cane on our legs. That sort of thing was rare, and we probably deserved it. Although my mother liked to cook meals that we liked, such as meatballs and pies and other sweets, in general we had to eat everything she cooked whether we liked it or not. I did not like many of her meals, so I would secretly give them to our maid. One day I vomited when my father forced me to eat. Because I did not eat enough and was thin, sometimes my father would give me something special and say to my sisters, "She is a bird." My middle sister once replied: "A thief bird." A doctor told me I had slightly enlarged glands in my neck and prescribed fish oil. It was sweet, like thick white syrup.

One day I came back from school, sat by the stove, and vomited. I was very weak. In the morning I felt even worse, and my parents then called the doctor. He told me I had diphtheria. Because it was found very early, and only in my throat, he told me I did not have to go to the hospital and that he would give me injections of serum. In our home, certain precautions were necessary. I was lying in an "isolation room" on the upper floor, where only my mother and the doctor were allowed. My sisters were to always stay on the first floor. My mother put a note on the outside of the door of the house: "Contagious disease, no entrance." After a few injections, I started getting better quickly, and I soon went back to school. A few years earlier, my youngest sister had a case of diphtheria that was much worse than mine. She was rushed to the hospital because she was choking. Because she was a baby, our mother was in the hospital with her. My father, middle sister, and I visited them once, but we could only see them through a window into the room. My mother held my sick little sister in her hands. We knew she had a very dangerous disease. When she came back home with our mother, we were so happy that we hid ourselves under the table and stuck out and touched our tongues while our parents talked. Because my little sister was already well by then, nothing happened to us for carrying on like that.

One winter night while I was still recovering from my own case of the disease, our father promised to take us to the seaside in the spring. Our joy was immense, but in fact we knew neither what the sea was nor what it looked like. My father told us it was a vast body of water without end. I could not imagine that—"without end." I imagined the sea with ships sailing on it and some of them disappearing in it. The sea from my grandmother's stories was something mysterious, full of wonders and dangers, where the ships in the stories often disappeared. One evening the following spring, we went aboard a narrow-gauge steam engine train. We traveled the whole night and half of the next day. We traveled in first class in a compartment that had comfortable armchairs covered in a plush red fabric with white embroidery that could be turned into beds. My father always traveled in first class. Because it was night, we slept a bit, but we stayed awake because of our excitement. We heard the train whistles and the voice of the railroad employee who called out the name of each station. We heard the noise of the train quite loudly at one point and felt the rhythmic movement of its wheels, and my father said then that we had just passed through the tunnel called Ivan, which was very long. It took us fifteen minutes to pass through it. I could hardly imagine a tunnel so long. When dawn came, we looked out the window curiously. The landscape was full of stones and almost no grass, and an ass browsed a green bush. In a moment, my father said, "There's the sea." We saw a blue surface of water shining in the sun, at first far away and then closer and closer to us. Large white birds flew over the water, and my father told us they were sea gulls, birds that lived only near and on the sea. There were many boats with masts and sails. A large ship with two levels and a lot of small windows was arriving. From its narrow chimney rose black smoke. When we stopped, we heard the railroad employee's voice again, this time announcing Dubrovnik.

During our several days in Dubrovnik, we could not swim, because it was April and the sea was quite cold. We walked on the shore in the shallow water and collected seashells. We went by boat to a small island, Lokrum, and walked through its resin-scented forest. We found there a children's camp that belonged to nuns. My parents thought about my staying there for some time to recover even further, because I was still eating poorly. My heart was joyful at the idea, because I would be in that wonderful place with a lot of other children. In the end, my parents finally decided that I would stay there with my mother for about ten days, which they thought would be sufficient for me.

One day while my sisters and our father were still there, we played with some girls we met there. Their names were Nela, Nada, and some other names I do not remember. They asked us about our names and when we told them, they asked us, "Are you Turkish?" "Yes," we answered. Actually, we did not know the meaning of that. We thought it was due to our Muslim names, although in school they taught us we were not Turkish, but South Slavic, as were the others in our country, and that our ancestors adopted the Muslim religion from Turks who were the rulers in our region.

From Dubrovnik we went to Herceg Novi. We sailed on a wonderful large ship, the Kraljica Marija (Queen Mary). The day was sunny, the sea was calm, and we enjoyed playing hide-and-seek on the deck. Herceg Novi was located on a hill and not in a flat area like Dubrovnik was. We did not have girlfriends there, but we met a shoe-shine boy, really a young man. He was sitting on the side of the street with brushes and his shoe-shine stand. We watched him as he polished people's shoes. We asked him if he would like to polish our shoes, and he said the price was one dinar each. We did not have any money, so each of us offered him a boiled egg that our mother had given us for a snack. He accepted our offer and cleaned our shoes perfectly. It was now time for my father and sisters to return home to Sarajevo, but I stayed there with my mother for about ten days. On sunny days we walked next to the sea, and I collected seashells and pebbles. I was rather bored to be there with my mother, but we came back home soon. My mother later told me that after that trip I started to eat better.

Not long after we returned home, elections were held. I did not understand their meaning at the time. I just saw my mother whispering to her sisters. A carpenter was doing something around our house when I ran outside and cried, "Our father will vote for Maček." The man put his finger on his mouth, looked very fearful, and said, "Silence, you must not say that." I learned years later that at the time of this incident, on the eve of World War II, the political climate was very turbulent. After a previous election, the Croats had received some autonomy in the Croatian Dominion Province, but now they wanted to have a completely separate Croatian territory. That territory would become the "Independent State of Croatia" under the rule of Nazi Germany.

Years earlier, when I was still in elementary school, a tragedy had occurred. Our king, Aleksandar Karađorđević, was killed. An unknown man shot him in Marseilles during his visit to France. It was written in the newspapers that he had said, "France, a wonderful country, did not know she had a hidden enemy inside." They also quoted his last words, "Take care of Yugoslavia!" Each house had a black flag on it. Our father bought one for us and we put it on our window. Our father wore a black armband during that time. All employed and many other people had black cloth either on their sleeves or on their lapels. I did not see much of Sarajevo during those days, because I went only from my home to school and back, but what I remember was this: Everything was in black. They even changed the photograph on our classroom wall, and put up one of the young prince. But we knew he was too young to rule and that others ruled instead of him.

4 New House

We moved into our new house at the beginning of my second year in high school. My school was a bit closer to the new house than it was to the old house. My father showed our house to his friends; it was large and modern, and smelled of fresh paint. We shared our room with our grandmother, but she did not disturb us. She would mainly sit on the sofa by the window and look at people passing by, always praying with beads in her hands. Sometimes we were so restless and jumped around her so much that she would call for our father and mother, who usually were not at home. I remember her saying, "Please do not do that, children, I am very weak!"

In the new house we had a big yard where we played games with Diba, the younger daughter of our aunt Aiša. She was in the same grade as my middle sister, that is, the first year of high school. She looked like a Japanese girl, with an oval face and small eyes. Our yard had a wall surrounding it, and we played there and bounced a ball off that wall. Diba was especially skilled in playing with a ball and also was an excellent student.

In the second year of high school I had almost the same teachers and classmates as I had had in the first year, except for the students who were repeating the second year. We were all very afraid of our new Serbo-Croatian language teacher, Ljuba Djurić. She would suddenly interrupt a student saying, "Enough!" if the student's reply was not complete. However, somehow she liked me, so she told my father, "Never, never have I had such a student." Nothing special was going on, except that we knew Hitler invaded Czechoslovakia and Poland. Our father listened to Radio London and to Hitler's speeches, and he talked about Hitler with a lot of antipathy.

I started my third year of high school amid great changes taking place around me. The German invasion advanced, and it was clear that the war would be expanded even more. At that very moment, I got sick. I got some stomach disease and had a temperature and diarrhea all the time. Dr. Ševala Iblizović and her husband were treating me. They thought it was typhoid, but my blood and stool testing did not show anything like that. The symptoms lasted two months, and I was on a severe diet, eating nothing but ladyfingers and a lot of lemonade. After I got a bit better, the doctor gave me calcium injections on a daily basis. However, since they were expensive, and I already felt much better, my mother told me to tell the doctor that I did not want to get injections anymore—she wanted me to say that I was afraid of them. So I did what she told me to do, and the doctor said angrily, "Each of your notebooks should have the word coward on it." I was ashamed—it was hard for me, and it had not even been my idea, anyway.

Just before the very end of the first semester of that third year of high school, I went back to school. Due to the large number of students, the school had been divided into two high schools, the First and the Second. Many of the old teachers left, and some new ones came. I had to quickly learn the curriculum I had missed during my absence from school. A classmate showed me mathematics, and because they had already started learning algebra, I was confused about how A and B were numbers. Somehow I was able to learn it, and at the end of the semester I had a grade of B instead of my usual grade of A. My father insisted that I try to get as good a grade as I could that semester, even though I had missed a lot of school and was trying to catch up. Early in the next semester, our school was closed because of the war and the creation of the new

"Independent State of Croatia," and at the end of that school year we learned that students would get the grade they had earned at the close of the first semester. So that year I got a B instead of an A. It was the best that I could do under the circumstances, because it was a lot of material to learn in a very short period of time, and I was glad my father had pushed me to try my hardest after being sick.

MEMORIES FROM BOSNIA

5 War

Something happened on March 27, 1941. Confusion spread through the school that day. They told us suddenly the school would be closed and we should join demonstrations. I was 14 years old. Our art teacher, whose class was under way at that moment, was silent and anxious. He took us outside and we joined a large number of people marching and carrying signs with slogans like "Better war than pact." We also chanted in a procession. It was a nice, sunny spring day. We knew that the young king had come of age and had assumed the throne and that our country had rejected a non-aggression pact with Germany. The war soon started. We could not even imagine, at least we teenagers could not, how big of a danger lay behind those proud words, "Better war than pact." We did not know that disintegration would follow for our country, which for a short time had kept the fragmented South Slavic peoples together.

In a few days, my father came home and said that we should go to Oglavak while he and our grandmother stayed at home. The Germans will bomb Sarajevo, he said. We prepared food, we bought flour, oil, butter, marmalade, and other things, and in two days we left Sarajevo by bus. My mother took her cousin and her children with us, a daughter and son who were near to us in age. Their father was a physician, and he had asked our father to allow them to hide in Oglavak too. We climbed up the familiar forest toward Oglavak, and it seemed to me that the forest was thin, because we could see the sky. The leaves had fallen, and since we used to come to Oglavak only in the summertime, the forest looked completely different to us.

We settled in our house and made a fire in the stove. We did not have enough blankets, and my mother had all of us sleep under the same blanket. She then put an old ragged quilt on top of the blanket. We—there were five of us—yelled, "We do not want a rug, we do not want a rug!"

The weather was crystal clear then, and it was nice and warm in the sun. There were many children who found shelter in Oglavak, as we did, and we played all day in Barice, a wonderful field a few hundred yards away from the village. We played different games and were very happy playing. We looked with admiration at the planes we saw that were shining brightly in the sun and flying toward Sarajevo. A hollow sound was heard from the direction of Sarajevo, and although we knew it had just been bombed, somehow we were not worried about our father and grandmother who stayed there.

A few days later it started snowing, and the village changed. Our field and everything around it was covered with snow. It did not snow for long, and it was cold. Thick icicles hung from our roof. In a few days, though, it was sunny again and the snow started to melt. The sunny reflection off the snow was so intense that we could hardly look at it. Our father and our cousins' father visited us and said the war was over and that the Germans had come to Sarajevo. My father told us that many buildings in the city had been destroyed but that our house had not been hit. Some of our friends were killed, though. Especially painful was to learn that my father's good friend, a doctor, and his whole family, the wife and two daughters, had died. One of my classmates was also killed with her family. We packed our things immediately and left for Sarajevo by bus early the next morning. Passing through Kiseljak, I saw for the first time the Germans in their green uniforms, a bit lighter than our own soldiers' uniforms. Driving over Kobiljača and the U-shaped curves toward Sarajevo, we were sad to see the traces of tanks that hadn't follow the road as it curved and had damaged the clean edges of the winding road as they cut across the land in straight lines. We met more and more German vehicles and tanks as we traveled toward Sarajevo, and we saw a lot of Germans with helmets on their heads.

When we arrived in Sarajevo, we saw a lot of German soldiers in the streets. We took a tram home and curiously looked through the windows to see the results of the bombing. I found our grandmother sitting by the window and looking at people outside. Groups of German soldiers passed by our house and looked at our windows. Our grandmother told us about horrible detonations of bombs and about the city being empty because the people had run away to the outskirts. She pointed out especially that our father was worried and silent all the time, because he was a strong opponent of Hitler, although he appreciated German discipline and order. When he visited Professor Obrad Vukomanović, who was Serbian and was very worried, my father told him, "Dear Obrad, you should know that these tanks hurt me the same as you." My father's mood remained the same as he carefully put thick cloth on our windows when we got there that our mother had sewn for use during the blackout. He told us sad stories about people looting Jewish shops. He warned us not to look at the people wearing yellow stripes on their sleeves, because they were our Jews who were being persecuted by Hitler. And for centuries, he told us sadly, the Jewish people were at home in Sarajevo with their districts, shops, and synagogues.

Our father bought some other newspapers instead of the *Politika*, the newspaper we used to read. In the other newspapers, you could read about the "Independent State of Croatia," which was going to be the name of our new country. The newspapers often had a picture of Ante Pavelić, the head of the state. He spoke about Bosnian Muslims as the purest Croats and the "flowers of the state of Croatia." One day he appeared in the newspaper with a tarboosh on his head, because many Bosnian Muslims wore tarbooshes. That kind of politics toward Muslims was understandable, because Bosnia and Herzegovina was included in the newly created state. The

Croatian euphoria could be seen in the processions, meetings, and speeches that were held in the former King Alexander Street, which was renamed after the Croatian leader, Ante Pavelić. Because of the war, and in honor of the new state, our school year had finished early, and we got the same grades we had at the end of the first semester. My father's efforts for me to obtain as good a grade as possible at the end of the first semester, after my illness, proved to have been very well justified.

That summer, we went to Oglavak earlier than usual. There were no changes in our village games. Sometimes we would hear about some sensational news, such as, "Moscow fell." We knew the Germans had come close to Moscow, in Russia. A relative, who was in the Yugoslav Army when the Germans attacked, told us that some new units were established as a result of the disintegration of the Yugoslav Army. The soldiers in those new units sang, "Chetniks, get ready, get ready, we will make a powerful army." We learned that song and sang it until they finally told us it was forbidden in the Independent State of Croatia.

I attended my fourth year of high school the next fall. At the beginning of the third year, when the high school had been divided into two groups, I had belonged to the first group, and I stayed in that group. My sister Fadila (we called her Dila) was one grade behind me, and my other sister, Maksuma (we called her Suma), started her first year in the same school. Our teachers changed in my fourth year—some of them had already left when I was in my third year—and there were no teachers now who spoke the Ekavian dialect. Instead of the Serbo-Croatian language, we studied Croatian. However, the other subjects remained the same, but their names were changed into their Croatian equivalents, such as "kemija" instead of "hemija." The German language was introduced in the first year in place of French, and French was introduced in the third year in place of German. I liked my teachers, and we studied seriously, as before. We did not like the geography teacher who yelled if some student used the wrong language version—Serb instead of Croatian. "Ocean" she yelled, "Okean went away over the Drina River." We did not like her, and we laughed at her when she could not see us. We still had the three confessions in our grade, the Orthodox, Catholic, and Islamic, but the name of Orthodox was changed to Greek-Eastern. Our Jewish classmates, Sephardim and Ashkenazim, of whom there had been several in our class, had disappeared.

One day a week we went to the Young People's Ustasha[8] headquarters. A woman named Zora told us about the war and about Chetniks[9] slaughtering Muslims in Eastern Bosnia. She did not speak about the slaughter of Serbs by Ustashas in Croatia and Bosnia. She had an Ustasha uniform and a cap with the letter "U" on it. There were many soldiers in the city wearing Ustasha uniforms, greeting each other with the phrase "Ready to fight for home" and lifting their right arms in the Nazi manner. Each of our classes began for us in the same way, with that phrase and the Nazi salute. Sometimes we went to a gathering or special parade, and we marched in front of a grandstand where German military officers and Croatian statesmen were standing. One day, after such a parade, I went to see a dentist who was a Croat. He was very enthusiastic about what was going on, saying, "Sarajevo has never seen this before." I was thinking about our former celebrations of Vidovdan[10] and the demonstrations held at the stadium. For that, we did not march through the city as we now did.

Food shortages were becoming more frequent. We still had flour, marmalade, and apples that we had brought from Oglavak. Our mother remodeled our old clothes and we wore them instead of buying new ones. She darned our stockings too much, though, and I was ashamed of my big darn going from my heel to my lower leg, whenever I had to do mathematics on our school blackboard. The value of money decreased a lot. Dinars were replaced with kunas,[11] and devaluation was so extensive that our parents managed to pay off our house mortgage very quickly, something that previously would have taken years. We, teenagers by then, glued some little mirrors. We usually got together at our uncle's and glued little mirrors for hours. The mirrors were sold later by a relative of ours, especially to soldiers. That's how we earned a little money.

---

[8] Croatian extremists.
[9] Serbian extremists.
[10] Serbian holiday.
[11] Croatian money.

Even then, in the peak of the war, we had times of joy. That year, the winter was cold and there was a lot of snow. We would slide down from the top of Sagrdžije Street to Baščaršija,[12] especially at night, under the streetlights. Our father wanted us to be joyful. There were no cars and very few people, so the atmosphere was really nice. My cheeks were red as blood when I looked at a mirror after sleighing.

Due to the very dangerous bombing of the German positions by the Allies—Great Britain, Russia, and the United States—our school program was often disturbed. The sirens announced when the Allied Forces were flying over Sarajevo, stopping our classes, and we had to go to the school shelter. Almost every house had a shelter. We would often go to our cousin's shelter next to our house. Thick wooden beams were on a low ceiling, and wooden benches were placed next to the wall in this very small space. Some people were always the first ones in the shelter, depending on the level of their fear. A young girl, living opposite to our house, was always the first one there, sitting in the corner, sometimes shivering and talking to no one.

We spent the next summer again in Oglavak, all the time playing, riding in an oxcart, swimming in the river, climbing up cherry trees, and picking hazelnuts. The village people went to picnics and baked pumpkins. In the midst of all that normalcy, something terrible happened—my grandmother died. She always wanted to die in Oglavak, because my grandfather and her two children were buried there. Each year, my grandmother went to Oglavak and stayed in my uncle's house from mid-spring to mid-autumn. She was there by herself, and Aunt Zahida, my father's first cousin whose house was next to my grandmother's, helped her a little. She liked going to Oglavak a lot, and my mother was also pleased when her mother-in-law was there.

That summer, a Jewish physician used to come to Oglavak on Thursdays with his wife and his son, who was close to my age. The Croatian authorities did not imprison him because they wanted him to visit surrounding villages and help people.

---

[12] The old marketplace in Sarajevo.

He was slim, of medium height, and his wife was buxom and freckled. Their son Hans was handsome, with a bright face and nice black hair. They had little rucksacks and heavy hobnailed boots on, because they always took long walks to remote villages. They lived in Polje Brestovsko, on the road to Travnik, in the house of my cousin and his wife Lidija (we called her Litka), who was a Czech woman. Our cousin married her when he was in the Austrian army in Czechoslovakia. My father, keen on talking to a fellow intellectual and feeling much sympathy for Jews, always invited them to stay, and my mother made a good lunch for everyone.

One morning, when my father visited my grandmother, he found her unable to walk. He told us that her left hand and leg and a part of her face were paralyzed and that she could hardly speak. The Jewish doctor—Prohnik was his name—came the next day. He gave her some injections and medicines, and I do not know what he said to my father. My father and Aunt Zahida were helping my bedridden grandmother while my mother was preparing meals. I visited my grandmother only after a few days. She was sitting with a pillow behind her back, bent, diminished. She looked at me and said, "So girl, only now you are coming to see your grandmother?" I tried to defend myself; I told her I did not know she was so sick, but my feeling of a shame and pity toward her, so bent and diminished, left a deep wound in me. Doctor Prohnik visited my grandmother one more time, and then, one evening, my father, mother, and Aunt Zahida hurriedly went to see my grandmother. In half an hour, Aunt Zahida came back and told us that our grandmother had passed away. Her funeral was held the next day. I remember very clearly when they carried her under the windows, and I had a hard feeling of death. Previously, I had very little contact with death. I was a few years younger when my mother's mother died, and I did not remember much. It was hard for me to witness my mother's sadness, and I did not go to my grandmother's funeral because children did not go to Muslim funerals then. After my grandmother's death, my parents' days were mournful. Every day my father spent hours sitting alone in his bedroom and crying. His eyes became swollen and red. I had never seen him cry before. It was so unusual to me. My mother started to smoke cigarettes at that time; she would frequently sit thoughtfully and just smoke.

In September 1942, I began the fifth of my eight years of high school. I went to school on those nice sunny days that year with an exalted feeling of a student who has entered the upper high school grades. We studied some new subjects that year, such as Latin, trigonometry, and German literature. Thanks to our teachers, when we were in school we felt like it was peacetime. Maybe that illusion of peace was a reflection of our teachers' fears that the war horrors were going to become even more and more apparent. The Germans furiously advanced on the front lines, bombed incessantly, and took and killed the Jews and partisans in the concentration camps.

Still, I remember that year and that grade as one of the most joyous times of my life. I see a teenager in a dark-blue school uniform, with her hair styled smartly, standing at the blackboard and solving a difficult mathematic problem. I carefully obeyed our teachers, as usual, by doing my homework regularly, but now it was so easy for me, as if the knowledge I had gained was just naturally coming out of me. I could solve any mathematics problem we were tested on. The teacher of mathematics, Georgina Huša, once told my father, "She knows more than she needs to."

My father boasted of my successes to our cousin, who had a nice goldsmith's shop. He gave me an arithmetical problem to solve that dealt with his shop, thinking I could not solve it. And I managed to solve it using "the rule of three." Afterward, my father gave me the coins of 50 or 500 or more kunas, I do not know exactly how much it was because we had devaluation. In any case, it was a big reward. With regard to the Latin language, I could decline four adjectives and a noun of a different declension at the same time, and the reciting of old Latin verses was easy for me. A few students once complained to our homeroom teacher and asked the teacher not to take me as a judge of how well other students ought to be doing, because, they said, my father was a professor and was certainly helping me. Our father helped neither me nor my sisters with our studies; he was only enthusiastic, in fact, when I told him I had successfully solved some mathematic problem.

He was also enthusiastic about the wonderful German literature we studied for our homework. I read him the story about a marvelous dog, our required reading, and he listened to me with tears in his eyes. I accidentally learned the beginning of that story by heart and later, at an appropriate time, I would often recite it. The story begins as follows, "Vorliebe empfindet der Mensch für allerlei Gegenstande, aber Liebe die echte, unvergängliche, die lernt er, wenn überhaupt, nur einmal kennen." In English: "A person feels strong love more than once in a lifetime, but true and lasting love, if ever, is only felt once. That is, at least, the opinion of Mr. Hop." "Wie viele Hunde hat er schon gehabt und auch gern gehabt, aber lieb, lieb und unvergesslich ist ihm nur einer gewesen—Krambambuli." In English: "So many dogs he had already had, and he loved them all, but dear, dear and unforgettable to him, was only one—Krambambuli."

Further in the story, this wonderful devoted and intelligent dog suffered a tragic death. Another story from German literature was my father's favorite: A fair was organized in a city. People had fun, bought different things, while an old man wearing a worn-out suit played a violin. He played it all day, and people passed by, but the hat he had on the ground in front of him remained empty. In the evening, a gentleman came along and asked the violinist to lend him his violin for a moment. The violinist agreed, and then beautiful sounds came out of the violin and drew the attention of an audience. People started to fill the violinist's hat with money, and the old man had to empty it several times. This story ends this way: "It was the famous violinist Alexander Bouché." One day we had to learn by heart four strophes of the poem "Des Saengers Fluch" (A Singer's Curse) from Uhland, and my father encouraged me to learn it all, that is, about ten strophes. I did it, and several times later I recited that beautifully written legend.

April 10 was the day of the establishment of the Independent State of Croatia. Each year on that day, our teacher's council rewarded the best two students in the school, one from the junior and one from the senior grades. Everybody thought it would be somebody from her own class, but the teachers were silent. So that big day finally came. We now attended classes in the boys' school building, which was located on the other side of the bridge, because the refugees from Eastern Bosnia had been living in our school building. At a modest ceremony, our high school rector gave the prize to me as the best student from the senior grades and to Nada Bilbija as the best student from the lower grades. I was awarded a set of six books, *World Writers*, and each book had "For the Best Student from Senior Grades" inscribed on the first page. After that ceremony, on my way back home, an orchestra played marches and patriotic songs in front of the House of the Army, and I was followed by a group of students. One of them, smaller than I was and with long blonde hair, said to me, "They play this in your honor," but she added immediately, "But be careful—a fall comes after a success." I memorized that sentence, although at that moment I could not think of any fall.

My fifth high school year was coming to an end, and we increasingly felt around us the terror of war. One day our father took us by tram to visit our uncle, who was in the hospital in Pofalići, and when we were crossing Marin Dvor, Sarajevo's largest avenue, he told us to look only at the left side of the street. On the right side, some fifty people, members of the resistance movement, had been hanged on the trees. More and more often, one by one, the senior students were leaving school, to join the partisans, people said.

One day I accidentally stood by the open window of our bedroom with my youngest sister. We were watching some passers-by in the evening of a beautiful September day. On the other side of the street, a young man was at the window of our cousin's apartment. Our cousin had married a pilot, and they previously lived in Skopje and Belgrade. After the fall of Yugoslavia, they moved to Sarajevo and rented an apartment on the opposite side of her father's (my uncle's) house. We guessed about who that young man could be, and my sister got very serious. I laughed at my sister, who had an increasingly serious look on her face. My hair fell onto the edge of the window. A few days later, our cousins, our uncle's daughters, whose house was next to ours, invited us to get together in the evening. There were a lot of girls there, all between fifteen and nineteen. I was sixteen and half then. I was surprised to see the young man I saw earlier at the window. They introduced him to us. He was from Gračanica. One of my aunts was married to his uncle. He attended technical school and rented a room in my cousin's apartment. We all had a good time that night, and suddenly he took a nice pencil with six different colors, gave it to me, and said, "This is for Nadja." I blushed. A handsome young man, with a bright face and nice black wavy hair, had just given a present to me! In a few days, one of my relatives told me that Kasim, which was the young man's name, would like to have a date with me. I accepted. We met behind City Hall, on the road to Bentbaša. We climbed up the serpentine road to Jekovac and sat on the fence. He took a photo of me sitting on the fence with a book in my hand.

We went on with our dates. I was happy because that handsome young man liked me so much. He said I was the most beautiful girl of all. He was so good-looking that I fell in love with him. I was in the sixth year of high school, and we met every day after school. One day he invited me to go dancing. He told me that my cousin, who was two years older than I was, would join us. I knew how to dance because I had learned during school breaks with my girlfriends. He was an excellent dancer, and I was floating in happiness. I had never danced with a boy before; my parents did not allow that. One day a friend of my father's, who was also a professor, visited him. I served them something to eat, and he said, "Oh, what a big girl, dancing will begin soon." My father frowned upon his saying that, put his head down, and said, "School is the most important thing."

Because we lived close to one another, Kasim often came to my school on his way home, and we returned home together. One night we were near my house when my father suddenly appeared from the dark street crossing ours. "Who is that with you?" he asked severely and continued to walk, in a hurry. I followed him without saying a word to Kasim. He yelled at me at home, "You can sell your books, you are not going to school anymore." He did not slap me, and I did not know which was worse for me—the yelling or the slapping. When his yelling was over, he went to another room to stir some marmalade my mother was making. After an hour, my mother came to me and said, "Go to your father, kiss his hand, and tell him you will not see Kasim again." I was shocked, especially because of what he said about school, so I went downstairs and told him,

"Please forgive me, I will not do it again." I kissed his hand. My mother wanted me to keep my promise and break up with Kasim. She was also against my dating him. A few days earlier, she had entered my room and saw me talking to Kasim at the window. She pulled my hair and said, "What are you doing with him? His father is a real unbeliever!" My father accepted my promise, because he believed that we were well aware that we should not disobey him.

As far as I was concerned, I knew what the meaning of a promise was. Our father taught us about moral principles, and I remember especially the words our grandmother spoke. She had said modestly: "Never do to anybody what you would not like to happen to you. Everything you do to others, both good and bad, will come back to you." She also would say frequently, "Do not speak bad of anyone, because even the walls have ears." My grandmother said these and many other things in order to teach us to live honorably. In my heart, though, it was impossible for me to keep my promise and to break up with Kasim. The reasoning of my parents was not convincing me of anything. Kasim was open-minded, and that was attractive to me. From our earliest childhood, our father had taught us about a more open-minded approach to life and religion than the traditional way of thinking in our country. So the things like my mother's pressure to wear stockings—things from the traditional way of life—were difficult for me to accept. I felt easy and relaxed with Kasim, by contrast; he was the kind of person I liked to be with.

These feelings resulted in my secret dating of Kasim, usually in the city outskirts. It was the worst year of the war, with constant arrests and famous people joining the partisans. Many of our older students left school and joined the partisans. Italy capitulated. Kasim told me once that he was also about to join the partisans, together with his friends, but he changed his mind and stayed because of me. Our love was strong, adolescent—only we were important. He bought various things for me—slippers, sandals, purses, which I did not have due to the war. He had a lot of money because his father had a shop in Gračanica. He liked to wear different suits, and was very good-looking. We liked to take photos, and the best photos from my youth are from that period. He was two years older than I was, and had many girlfriends before me. One day he showed me his album with girls' photos. There were many of them; some were from Gračanica and Banja Luka[13] (while he attended school there), and some were from Sarajevo. I was sad and jealous about his past, so he tore up all those photos to show me how much he loved me. My parents somehow found out that I did not keep my word. My father became rude with me, and my mother acted like she hated me, all because of Kasim. My father was very disappointed; he could not believe I could be so stubborn in spite of his prohibition. He told me he was disappointed in my intelligence. Sometimes I felt so sorry, because I knew they had a hard time because of that, but I simply could not break with Kasim. Kasim suggested that we get rings made with our initials engraved on them, and after we did that I considered myself to be his fiancée.

---

[13] A large city in Krajina, in western Bosnia.

6 War Atrocities

We attended school even during the war atrocities. We continued to have our classes in the boys' building, alternating shifts with the students from the boys' high school. Constant sirens and bombing disturbed us. At the same time, we studied more serious subjects than in prior years. Mathematics with trigonometry, physics, chemistry, and then Latin, Croatian literature, and wonderful German literature. I also continued to study French, which I had begun to do in my first year of high school. That year as well, on April 10, two students, one from junior and the other from the senior grades, were awarded the "Best Student" prize. That year I was occupied with Kasim and the problems involved with hiding that from my parents, but I guess my previous knowledge was enough for me to have been again awarded the prize as the best student from the senior grades. For this honor, I received a book entitled *Selected Documents of Ante Starčević*, the nineteenth-century Croatian writer and politician. My father was secretly happy, but his happiness was disturbed by his suspicion that I was continuing to date Kasim. I did not show the book to Kasim on the day I got it, but I did show it to him the next day, and a bit reproachfully he asked, "Why did you not show it to me earlier? I am also happy for your success."

That summer there was no peace in Oglavak. Partisans came closer to us, from Vranica Mountain, and Germans and Ustashas bombed Oglavak from the Kiseljak and Travnik roads. Sometimes partisans would break through to Oglavak and stayed there for some time. Our daily obligation was to make them bread and give them milk, while rich people gave them cattle and chickens. On some days, Germans would suddenly break through and the partisans would withdraw. One day a young partisan showed us a photo of his girlfriend, whom he planned to marry immediately after the war. He had a barber shop in Prijedor. After a calm period, our young maid Hetka, who could hardly stand all the bombing and shooting, entered our house and cried out, "I saw, I saw!" "What did you see?" we asked her, and she pointed to the village road. There, lying dead, we too saw our young partisan friend, the barber, who an hour earlier had been happily showing us his girlfriend's picture and talking of marriage.

One day the cannons shelled us heavily from the direction of Travnik road. All the villagers hid in Aunt Zahida's cellar, which was built of thick stone. Some people had children in their arms, some had jewelry hidden in their breasts, and others had other precious things with them. Some of them prayed from the Kur'an. We were waiting to see what was going to happen. The Germans suddenly entered our yard and opened the cellar door. They ordered us to come out, one by one, pointing heavy machine guns toward us. There were about ten of them. So we came out of the cellar, one by one, about forty of us. The Germans clearly had expected to find partisans among us and to kill us all. But there were no partisans with us, and upon close inspection of the cellar, with the heavy machine guns in their hands, they left us.

The next day it was calm, with little bombing that we could hear. Our father wanted us to leave Oglavak immediately. "Get ready quickly, we will walk to Visoko," he said.[14] There was no bus to take now. We took things we needed and started toward Travnik road, carrying bags and bundles, and we wore soft footwear, which eased our walk on the soft grass. We passed next to the field in which we used to

---

[14] A town halfway from Sarajevo to Oglavak.

play and the small burial chamber that was our family cemetery. We then continued toward the road, walking for about two hours. Crossing the main road, our father urged us to hurry. We could hear some gunshots. Fortunately, it was early morning and there was less fighting. We had to climb up the other hill opposite Oglavak. We followed the soft village road and in two more hours or so we arrived in Svinjarevo village. Our father found the house of Mehaga, who used to often visit Oglavak. Mehaga and his wife welcomed us joyfully, and later his wife went to prepare meat for our lunch. Of course, they also invited us to stay overnight, giving us new blankets. We really felt great there. Our father talked a lot with Mehaga, who had a serious look on his face and talked very slowly and calmly. As a young man, he had served in the Austrian army throughout Europe. My father greatly appreciated his intelligence and common sense.

The next day, after walking for several hours, we arrived in Visoko. Our father found his cousin's house there, and we visited her unannounced. She was happy to see us. We looked so dusty and had so many bundles in our hands that she offered us the best food and drink she had. We stayed there overnight and in the dark morning we walked toward the railroad station, where we could get the train to Sarajevo and home. We walked through the dark and empty streets, and all the time we heard the "Halt!" of German soldiers. My father replied to them, "Wir gehen zum Bahnhof" ("We are going to the railroad station"), so we passed through. It was hard to be on the train to Sarajevo; the people were hiding themselves from the windows because the partisans had been shelling the train from the surrounding hills.

We hadn't rested for very long in our house in Sarajevo when the news came from Oglavak that the Germans came and took all the men with them. Three cousins of my father and many more people from the surrounding Muslim and Catholic villages were taken away. They all vanished later in the German concentration camps. Only one cousin, who was a teenager when they took him away, survived the Mathausen camp and returned home after the Americans nursed him back to health at the end of the war. If we had stayed only a few more hours there in Oglavak, our father would have experienced the same fate and he would be gone. Providence saved him and us, the children, whose lives could have easily have taken a completely different direction.

I met Kasim near The Lion, the old stone statue in the graveyard next to the hospital. It was a pleasant autumn day. I was happy to be with him again after two months of separation. We talked a lot; I talked about Oglavak, the partisans, and the Germans, and he talked about Gračanica and the war situation in Gračanica and Tuzla, where the partisan movement was powerful.

One day the bombing started without the sirens having warned us. Our house shook violently, and the windows clattered shut. Our father pushed the door shut in the kitchen, where we were hiding, as if he were struggling with some attacker on the other side of the door. My mother and father soon decided after that for us to go to my mother's cousin in the city outskirts, near Koševo Hospital, to rent two rooms there and to return home only periodically.

Life was obviously very dangerous in that last year of the war. My parents, in response to an appeal from a humanitarian organization, decided to adopt two children at about that time, boys of three and five who had lost their parents in Eastern Bosnia. My mother also took in a girl from Travnik to be our maid, because her parents had also died. This was Hetka. She was younger than we were, and she could not help our mother much while we were at school. She had a full-moon face and was all round, naive, and a bit odd in her behavior. She spoke the Ikavian[15] dialect. Because we laughed at the way she spoke, she tried to change her dialect, so she said my sister Dila's name like Dijela. She did not go to school in her village, and she could not read or write, so our father taught her. Every day upon coming home, he would sit and listen to her read; he was patient while she was learning to write her first letters. One day he bought her the same shoes he bought for us and enough fabric for our mother to sew the same dresses for all of us girls. I did not like that very much. I was merciful toward poor people, and I always thought a lot about the less fortunate ones,

---

[15] Dialect spoken in parts of Herzegovina and Dalmatia.

either in our neighborhood or at school, but I disliked being equal to that girl. I do not know why. I wanted to see the difference between us. All three of us sisters complained because we did not want our mother to sew the same dresses for us as for Hetka, and finally we succeeded. As a compromise, from the same fabric our mother sewed Turkish trousers for Hetka and dresses for us.

We moved to our mother's cousin's place, our mother and all the children, while our father stayed in our house. We had two rooms in a side house next to their big house. They had a huge orchard with cherry trees, and our mother bought one cherry tree for us children; if she hadn't done that, we would pick their cherries, and nobody wanted that.

Kasim visited me occasionally, and we sat on a blanket under a cherry tree. Because the orchard was large, we could hide ourselves from my mother, and our father did not come at all, because he stayed in our house and hadn't come with us to my cousin's. Near the orchard was a narrow macadam road that passed next to a hospital wall. Sitting under the cherry tree in the evenings, we watched couples, German soldiers in uniforms with German nurses in white-striped uniforms with long skirts and white caps on their heads. The nurses had soft, light-colored skin and hair, and were embraced by the soldiers. Every day we heard a funeral march played by the orchestra at the old cemetery near the large stone lion statue, because the Germans turned it into the cemetery for German soldiers. Much worse for me was to listen to the troubled songs of a woman hospitalized in the psychiatric ward that was located in our neighborhood. Sometimes she screamed and called to somebody, and I could imagine her poor life.

During my seventh year of high school, Sarajevo was full of grayness and constant fear. Young people were arrested, and the infamous house of the war criminal Luburić was the place where our schoolmates who were accused of illegal political acts were tortured. A dear friend of mine was tortured and killed there; they burnt her beautiful body with a hot iron.

More and more often I saw two teachers speaking in secrecy before class began. One day a bomb fell diagonally in the shelter of the building where the Public Employment Office was located. It was thought to be the best shelter, but the people were killed in the shelter while the building remained untouched. Another dear girlfriend from my childhood was killed there. I met her several years earlier in Kiseljak, where we used to go because my mother had recently had a gallbladder attack and was drinking the famous Kiseljek mineral water every day. Next to the house we rented was a little creek where we played for entire days. A girl, two years older than me and thus much older than my sisters, would come to the creek and play with us. We fenced the creek bends. One day we saw a rather large fish there. We tried to catch it, but it always managed to get away. It swam elegantly in the creek. That girlfriend, Nidžara, was persistent and ran after that fish the whole day but still failed to catch it. The next day she continued to try to catch the fish, and she finally caught it with her hands. We admired her because the fish was bigger than her handspan. We lost contact during the war because we did not go to Kiseljak, and we later found out she got married after finishing high school. During the bombing of the Public Employment Office, she was in the shelter together with her husband and a small baby. They were all killed, and she was so beautiful and noble.

I continued to go to the city outskirts with Kasim, usually to Kovačići, an area in the city outskirts. Bombing began one day when we were on Skenderija Street. We ran into the nearest building and hid in the shelter, expecting the worst. Everything was crashing down above us, followed by terrible detonations. In the late autumn we often encountered muddy German tanks entering Sarajevo in an endless line. German soldiers walked tiredly, with muddy shoes and overcoats. We heard they were withdrawing from Greece. The news that Belgrade was free and that partisans entered it gave us hope the war would end soon, but we felt more and more afraid of mad Ustashas and Germans. The people were very hungry, and only because of my uncle, my father's brother, did we have any flour. In an extremely dangerous situation, he managed to bring flour from Oglavak not only for his family but for us too, so we had enough for winter. To tell the truth, it was barley and unprocessed wheat flour, but it was excellent compared to the bran people had to eat. I once tried the bran bread and it seemed to me I would choke. It was like eating wool. My uncle was a very good man, and funny, and thanks to his witty remarks he was able to pass through dangerous sentinels of Ustashas and Germans. He always told us about his experiences, and we laughed a lot. One day he had an accident, though, that changed his good humor as well as his family life. He was coming back from Oglavak on a truck loaded with flour. His wife's younger sister was with him; she went to Oglavak with him to make marmalade and to dry fruit for winter. He was sitting by the driver, and she was sitting on his other side at the window. On a curve in the road, the door suddenly opened, the woman slipped out and hit the road with her head. In the evening my uncle appeared to us with blood on his shoulders and sleeves, pale and confused. We were horrified when he told us what happened. He kept the woman on his shoulder all the way to Sarajevo, where she passed away. From that point on, his humor disappeared, which took a terrible toll on his family life.

7 Liberation

In the evening of April 5, 1945, we heard some gunfire that got louder and louder. We could not determine where it was coming from, because we heard it come from all directions. During the night, we heard more and more shelling by heavy machine guns and cannons. It was clear that the partisans were in Sarajevo. Our fear increased as we sat in the dark room waiting for the Germans and Ustashas to withdraw from the city. We had tea and dry cakes that my mother had made. Nobody slept. I knew Kasim was with my uncle, so I went to the yard, to the window of my uncle's house where Kasim was sitting. The night was not cold and it was bright, so I could stand under the window and talk to him. I was afraid in the same way as when I was in the shelter during the bombing. My mouth was dry, my body became numb, and I had a hopeless feeling in my head. Then I went home, and the hours passed. Soon it was day. Suddenly, at dawn, the ground under our house trembled and there was a terrible sound of an explosion. We thought they would blow our whole city up. Later we found out that the Germans blew up the old stone fortress on Hum Hill that was full of explosives. Afterward, because it had already dawned, we saw some partisans going down the street with their machine guns pointed outward. We could still hear the fighting down in the Valley of the Bosnia

River as the Germans and Ustashas were running away. Many patriots died that day defending the electric power plant that the Germans wanted to destroy, and they saved us from living without electricity and probably from a lot worse. A lot of young people died pursuing the Germans and Ustashas. Three of my relatives died then, each one leaving a small baby and a wife behind.

When it was announced on the radio that Sarajevo was liberated, we were relieved, and April 6 became the Day of Liberation we would merrily celebrate every year after that. The euphoria lasted several months. As soon as a few people gathered somewhere in Sarajevo, they immediately started wheel dancing, most often to the song "Kozara,"[16] but also to some others, as they do in Montenegrin wheel dancing. I was in the city two or three times, and I could not resist and joined the Kozara wheel dancing. The soldiers in their military shoes, young people, and old people danced while singing the partisan songs. We could hear on the radio the partisan ballads as well as revolutionary songs very similar to Russian songs. My father often looked gloomy when I turned on the radio, because he knew I liked those songs very much. My parents felt antipathy toward partisans because they were afraid of communists. During the war, there was horrible anti-communist propaganda that told people the communists would take away everything from people, even their own wives, so the people were afraid of what would happen if the communists were successful and took power. My father listened to Radio London and hoped Yugoslavia would not become a communist country. I remember him brutally jumping on me and turning off the radio when I listened to partisan songs. He was embittered after his friend, who owned a sawmill on Pale, was arrested and his plant confiscated. Also, my mother's cousin, in whose house we found shelter during the war, was arrested because he owned a goldsmith's shop with modern machines for the processing of gold. His shop was confiscated, too. The husband of my mother's sister, my uncle, lost a large farm in Gračanica, and my father was very unhappy about it.

---

[16] Partisan wheel dancing from western Bosnia.

One day my father was arrested, too. Upon completion of his university education and doctoral examination in Budapest, my father had worked as a professor and later the rector of the Islamic Judges School, and later, when it was turned into the Islamic Theological School, he became its rector. He was able to maintain that position in the Independent State of Croatia. After the war, the partisans closed that school and my father was retired when he was only 51. But he was not only retired; he was also arrested.

He spent three weeks in prison, and one day he came home laughing, in high spirits. He told us how he had spent all his time in prison having interesting conversations with a German from our region who was arrested for simply being German. My father was enthusiastic about the conversations he had with that man. There was no reason to have held my father, so they let him go. Although he had a high university position during the time that the Independent State of Croatia existed, he was also famous for his anti-Nazi and anti-Hitler attitude, so his arrest lasted a very short time in that period of massive retribution.

Our school was stopped in the second semester and we had to attend the same grade in the summer. So I attended classes for my seventh year of high school (the next to the last year of high school) during the four summer months that year. There were many changes then. We had some old and some new teachers. Two teachers were arrested. The teacher of the Croatian and German languages was not convicted because she was not an Ustasha, while the teacher of geography was convicted for having an Ustasha affinity. Young girls, especially those becoming members in the Young Communist League, were very active, and they put up wall newspapers and organized group activities and social gatherings. I also wrote for wall newspapers, and I admired some very nice articles and paintings done by my classmates. The classic relationship between pupils and teachers was also changed. Students approached teachers more freely and coordinated the teaching process. Some teachers behaved in a comradely manner, while others were serious and worked only in the scope of their subjects. We addressed our teachers by saying "comrade." I was so excited to learn some completely new things. The teacher of biology taught us about evolution. I accepted the concept of the evolution of life, and it remained my permanent friend in later life.

I liked the other classes, too. Instead of German, we studied the Russian language, and there was also French, which I had studied since my first year in high school. At the end of that semester, all my grades were excellent, too. I was not that good in social activities, though. I did not join dancing or other social gatherings. I considered myself a fiancée and wanted to be faithful to Kasim. One day, when my schoolmates asked me to go to a social gathering with them, I told them I was engaged. One of them replied, "We do not want fiancées, we want students." I felt bad about it. I still often listened to dance music from my garden window, because frequent evenings dances were organized in a young people's center near our house. I wished that I could join those young people, but I became immediately mindful that my father had forbidden me from dancing.

Upon liberation, Kasim was immediately drafted. He stayed in the barracks and had training in Sarajevo. He was supposed to go to Eastern Bosnia where some Chetnik units were still present. He was allowed to leave the barracks, so we met almost every day after my school classes, not in Kovačići but in Podhrastovi, in the upper part of the city, because it was summertime. I fasted because it was the month of Ramadan, but I went up the streets easily, and I was neither too hungry nor exhausted. Of course, Kasim did not fast. I did not want to eat secretly, because I considered it a desecration—not of fasting but of my parents' belief that I was fasting.

During that whole summer we went to Oglavak only once, during the day, because we did not have a place to sleep. The Germans took everything they could take from our house, even the furniture and all of our furnishings. The tekya was also looted, and the carpets, prayer rugs, and valuable Eastern antiquities were taken away, as was one huge ostrich's egg that was either artificial or stuffed, I am not sure. The cannons ruined a wonderful building called the konak[17] as well as two

---

[17] A temporary lodging for dervishes and visitors.

of the oldest houses, one belonging to my great-great-grandfather and the other to his oldest son. Oglavak looked very bad, and its shine was lost forever. Only one house was inhabited, where my father's relative, a farmer, lived. All of the other people had left Oglavak. One relative allowed a man whose house was destroyed in a neighboring village to move into Oglavak with his family. So the privacy of Oglavak was lost. Many years later, when Oglavak was restored, it disturbed my great-great-grandfather's descendants, who remembered the village as it had once been.

Sometime toward the end of the summer, Kasim was about to go to Eastern Bosnia with his military unit. I did not hear anything from him for a period of time, but one day a woman brought me a letter from him. I was so happy. He wrote me that he was stationed in Ustikolina[18] but that they often moved between Goražde, Foča, and Višegrad. He missed me a lot, he wrote, and asked me to send him my letter by that same woman. We exchanged letters that way because the postal service within Eastern Bosnia was not yet established. His letters were full of love and keen desire, and I was not aware then how dangerous his life was while they fought against the remaining Chetnik units.

I started to attend the eighth and final year of high school a little bit late that year (as we all did), because the seventh year lasted until autumn. It seemed to me that we did not have a break at all that year and that there were the same students and teachers there as in the summer. I remember dark and short December days. I was not especially excited to enter the last year of high school. It had been almost three months since I last saw Kasim, and my thoughts were with him.

---

[18] Small towns east of Sarajevo.

8 Wedding

I received a letter from Kasim one December day that had a depressed tone and content. He asked me to visit him in Trnovo, because it was not far away from Sarajevo. His letter was very sad; if I do not come, he wrote, he didn't care if he lived or died. He gave me instructions about the truck I could take to go from Sarajevo to Trnovo. I took his depression seriously and planned to go to Trnovo. I had to be at the truck's departure point early in the morning. I asked my youngest sister to join me and she agreed. The day was foggy and cold, we were in the open truck, and a cold wind was blowing. When we arrived in Trnovo, I was very eager to find Kasim's military unit, but I was disappointed to learn it had left for Bistrica on Jahorina Mountain. My sister and I walked through the cold and foggy streets of Trnovo and in the evening we returned home. That night I decided to go to Bistrica the next day. I learned in Trnovo that I had to go there by train, by way of Pale.

I woke up early, and it was still dark outside. I woke up my sister and asked her to join me again, but she fell back asleep. I left our house slowly, climbed up steep Bistrik Street in the darkness, and reached the railroad station. I bought a ticket for Pale and found my seat on the train. The train passed through countless tunnels, and the day slowly broke. When I got off the train in Pale, everything was covered with snow. I tried to find the way to Jahorina Mountain; somebody told me which direction to take. There was nobody on the road for some time, but then a man in an officer's uniform appeared. He asked where I was going, and when I told him I was going to Bistrica to visit my fiancé, he told me he was headed there too and that we could go together. We went through a forest, climbing upward, hearing the noise of our shoes in the snow. I do not remember the topic of our conversation, and the road to Bistrica was almost six miles long. I lost my strength about halfway through the last mile, so he offered his hand to me. I preferred to take the belt of his uniform's overcoat instead, and so he simply dragged me out of the forest to where the road ended.

A small house on a hill sat at the crossroads of Trebević and Jahorina Mountain. It was being used as the barracks for the soldiers. Dense smoke could be seen coming from its chimney, and there was the strong smell of burnt firewood. I was very hopeful when I entered the house, but I was soon disappointed again because the officers said to me that Kasim had been ordered to move to the top of Jahorina Mountain. However, they promised to call him to come to Bistrica.

A fire was burning in a large iron stove, and it was very warm in the small room, so my cheeks were flushed. There was a table with a few chairs there, and a wide bench with military blankets on it. Two or three officers and several soldiers were entering and leaving the room and curiously watching me. They brought me some military-style, soupy meal and a big piece of a fresh bread heel. I was extremely hungry, and I ate it all with great relish. They told me to lie down on a sofa and covered me with a blanket. I was eager to sleep, but I was too excited to sleep as I waited to see Kasim. Two officers played chess at the table, and I watched their serious faces, supported by their arms, attend to the game. A soldier brought more firewood and put it into the stove. Hours later I could hear outside the sound of military shoes moving toward the house and the stamping of feet in front of the door. Two or three soldiers came in, and one of them was Kasim, who looked so handsome to me in his uniform. I could see his black wavy hair under his cap. We embraced each other, and I felt so happy to be with him again. He talked to the senior officers, who promised to allow him to take a leave. They told him that he could wait until they called for him to come back. We had to go to Pale before dawn, because the train left early. I slept on some straw in the lower part of the house, and during that night I had mixed feelings of love, tiredness, and fear from the uncertainty I felt inside about what I was doing. A soldier on duty woke up Kasim, and we then had to leave quickly to get to the train. We took the same way back that I had come, the road through the forest. The whiteness of the snow on the ground showed us the way through the forest, and the sky was full of stars.

When we got on the train, it was full of people sitting on the benches on both sides and standing in the aisle. We were standing side by side in the aisle. It was still night, we did not talk, and it was only then that I felt fear about coming back home. Going down Bistrik Street, the day broke and I came home. Kasim went to my cousin's apartment across the street, where he used to stay. I rang the doorbell at my house, because in my excitement I had forgotten to take my key with me when I left the previous morning in the dark. My sister opened the door, and I noticed that she looked distracted. My mother was pale, speechless, and my father had left the house to avoid seeing me, as I learned later. I remember that day as gloomy, and I did not know what they thought of me. But that day, one of the most important decisions was made in my life. My mother told me that Kasim and I would get married. Kasim's father will come and the wedding will be in a few days, she said.

In a few days, Kasim's father came, along with his brother, who was my aunt's husband. They agreed for our wedding to be organized on December 26 in our house. When I said at school I was getting married and stopping my education, everyone was astonished and shocked. Some teachers said, "Why she, the least expected one?" My homeroom teacher, who taught us Serbo-Croatian and French, and my teacher of mathematics, both advised me to pass the grade at the year-end test by taking a private test. So I promised to do that. The students knew I was engaged, so maybe it was not surprising for them that I was getting married. I became somehow numbed about the whole thing, and it was in such a state that I spent my last day at school.

Everything that happened afterward brought neither happiness nor sadness but only grayness, just like the gray of those late December days. Our wedding was organized in our big, wonderful living room. A religious representative was there, because in that era the weddings were based on the Islamic moral and legal code. Kasim's father and his brother were the witnesses. I was sitting in a long white dress, which had been sewn quickly for me. I was as slim as a cane. I was always slim, but then I was even more so. Kasim was sitting next to me, while the registrar and two witnesses were sitting opposite us. My father was sitting alone. The registrar asked us if we agreed to be husband and wife, and afterward he asked Kasim, "Do you agree for your wife to be also allowed to request a divorce, if necessary?" I was not turned toward him, but I did not miss his subtle physical reaction to that nor the look he gave to his father. His father was sitting with his head down, and because he did not respond to Kasim's look of indecisiveness, Kasim answered on his own and said, "Yes." I did not know the meaning of that, but later I learned that in Islamic marriages, a husband has the right to request and to obtain a permission to divorce, but a wife does not have that right at all herself. But my father knew there was an exemption whereby a wife could obtain that right if a husband accepted it at their wedding, when specifically asked. My father thought I should have at least that privilege in that very sudden and premature wedding. Kasim's light jerk and look at his father confused me a bit, because I would have agreed with anything Kasim had wanted—that's how I felt at that moment.

Kasim was informed by the military commanders that all soldiers who completed their education would be demobilized. He needed to finish the last year of technical school. His and my father both agreed for us to live with my parents. Kasim would attend the last year of school and I would pass my last year of high school from home and graduate at the end of the year. His father would send money for food for both of us. And so our marriage began.

My father and Kasim used to smoke a cigarette together after dinner or on Sundays after breakfast. My father did not smoke earlier, but during the war he pledged to start smoking when Hitler disappeared. So he lit his first cigarette on the day Germany capitulated. But he smoked no more than one cigarette daily. Kasim smoked, but not in front of his father, so he did not want to smoke in front of my father either. It was a kind of respect he wanted to show to his father. But my father asked him once, "Kasim, do you smoke?" And when the answer was indefinite, my father said, "If you smoke, do smoke, you do not need to hide it from me."

In their conversations, my father was joyful and laughed often, and sometimes, when I watched them, I remembered how my father was repulsive with him when we were dating. There is also one mystery for me about when my father came home and saw me for the first time after my wedding had taken place. I was somehow ashamed it all happened like that, but he was very pleased, and his attitude toward me, while it was changing, reflected some relief on his part. I wanted to see at least a little sadness in his eyes, because everything turned out so differently than he or I had expected when we had both been proud of me and my academic achievements.

I do not know about the experience of other people in the first months of marriage, but mine was not particularly promising. Kasim attended school; I could not attend school—because I was married. Married people weren't permitted to attend high school. He also kept it a secret from people at his school that he was married, so he did not want to show up with me anywhere and told me that he could not go out together with me at all. We didn't even go to the cinema. By nature, Kasim was rather timid, but it seemed too much for me, as if that was not the only reason for his behavior. I even thought that maybe he was tired of me. So now I was stuck at home, and we did not go anywhere. It was the first time for me to be at home without any school obligations. I had not begun to study at home yet, although my father warned me to start preparing for my examination and graduation. I would be doing all that completely on my own, without help from anyone. When I started studying, I was sad and found no joy in it at all. I cried often. My mother was angry when she would see me crying and was often severe with me. One day she actually slapped me when I did not want to meet some guest because my eyes were red from my earlier crying.

Soon after our wedding day, Kasim and I did go together, however, to visit his parents in Gračanica. His mother prepared a small celebration. I met Kasim's relatives and friends, and they were all looking at me with admiration—they liked me and I liked them. Kasim's mother was a funny and very active woman, who wished to please us; she was about my mother's age, around forty. I had met his father earlier, on our wedding day. He was young, also, just two years older than his wife. Somehow, Kasim's father was not interested at all in what happened and why we had to marry. Kasim's father and mother gave me some valuable old gold coins. I got presents not only from them but also from his uncles and his grandmothers. I got seven or eight quite valuable gold coins. His mother also gave me expensive jewelry, and his father gave me very lovely and quite expensive fabric for a suit. Regrettably, because I was inexperienced, I had the suit sewn by a tailor who was good at his work for men's clothes but not women's clothes, and the suit was not acceptable to me. It hung off me most unattractively, because I was very thin, and I felt as if I was wearing a suit of armor. I had it on when I passed my graduation examination, but whenever I put it on I felt very uncomfortable.

With respect to the wedding presents that I had to give to Kasim's family, I found the practice quite funny. From our childhood, my mother had been buying antique embroidered shirts and undergarments called boshchaluk.[19] I gave about seven or eight boshchaluks to Kasim's family. Giving such presents was old-fashioned and was no longer done by most people at that time, and that is why I was amused.

Two important things happened to me during those several months we spent with my parents; one was good and the other was not very good. One day I went with my mother to visit my aunt. When I returned, I saw the books that I had received for

---

[19] Very popular in the nineteenth century, these items were embroidered with golden thread.

twice being the best student in the senior grades lying on the table. Kasim told me he tore to pieces the pages with inscriptions on them because he was afraid that those books, referring as they did to the Independent State of Croatia, were in our house and would come to bring harm to us. I was surprised and utterly speechless. I attempted to say, "It was my school reward." I could not react too angrily, though, because I loved him a lot. I opened the books and saw the traces of the torn-out pages; the books were wounded. I could never again read those dear, beautifully written pages because of that.

The good thing that happened was that I became pregnant. Kasim had begun to persuade me to have a child, telling me he would like to have a baby. I did not want a baby just then, because I was just about to graduate from high school, and I was in general uncertain about whether I would be able to continue my education or not. I told him it was not the right time for that, and he replied emotionally, "The baby will be ours." When I got pregnant, I was secretly happy, like every mother is, I think.

9 Graduation

I had about three months to study for my graduation examination. I had to pass two tests: The first test was the test for the eighth year of high school, and the second test was the final test. We called the second test the "matura." The matura included subjects from each of the eight years (grades) of the high school. I borrowed school notebooks for the eighth year from a classmate, and I prepared myself for that examination. Several hours a day I studied in our guest room, with the books scattered on the big table, reading, comparing what I read with what was contained in the notebooks, and memorizing things. I picked up some early apples in the yard belonging to my mother's cousin, the goldsmith; their yard was next to ours, with a small door between them. Our cousin allowed us to pick up his apples, which I ate greedily, maybe because of my pregnancy, which had already become visible. My stomach could be seen under my cherry-colored housedress. I remember my graduation by green apples and my cherry-colored housedress.

It took two days to take the eighth-grade examination; the first day was the written part, and the second day was the oral part. My father brought me a sandwich during a break. I did the written part well. All teachers whose subjects I had to pass were present at the oral part of my examination. Those were the teachers I knew, and they looked at me sympathetically; some of them were sad when they noticed my pregnancy.

I had to pass subject by subject with only one break, and except for the three excellent grades I got for mathematics, French, and biology, all of the other grades were very good. My report showed a series of B grades instead of the previous A grades that I used to get. My chemistry teacher, trying to give me an excellent grade, asked me a question from a chapter at the end of the book that had not been taught in regular classes. I failed to give her a correct reply. I got a B, though, because my other replies had been correct.

My second test—the matura—was scheduled a few days later. I walked down the hall in my "armored suit," rejecting all my fear, like I always did prior to taking my examinations. I just hoped not to be asked about Djura Jakšić,[20] because I was not well-prepared to speak about him.

Except for my old teachers, the commission included a new, handsome Serbo-Croatian language teacher who was very kind. He spoke the Ekavian dialect. The question for the Serbo-Croatian language test was about Djura Jakšić—the very one I did not want. I spoke about his biography and everything else of no importance, but when I was supposed to analyze the song, "Na Liparu," regardless of how hard I tried, I failed. The teacher's face, which was smiling previously, became serious. I gave good replies on other questions and was successful in mathematics, French, and other subjects, too. Leaving the classroom, I was broken, and I felt terrible. I thought how I often had the most difficult situation of all. I felt ashamed and I was sorry to disappoint that teacher, who showed a special kindness to me, I guess because I was pregnant. I also had stings of remorse before that wonderful poetry of Djura Jakšić.

I was walking through the narrow streets of Čurčiluk[21] and Kazandžiluk[22] a few days later on my way back home. It was

---

[20] A famous Serbian poet.
[21] The furriers' district in Old Sarajevo.
[22] The coppersmiths' district in Old Sarajevo.

late in the afternoon and the streets were empty. My steps echoed as gloomily as my thoughts. In my hands I had my final certificate—with only a C grade. The D grade I got for the Serbo-Croatian language exam was on the first line—and it had brought all my other good grades down. This was supposed to be the crown of all my school certificates! I felt lost in terms of my education and my marriage. I walked and walked and walked, with my head down. When I came home, I showed my graduation certificate to my father.

Kasim and I were sitting the next day on a train to Gračanica, each of us thinking about something. In Doboj, our train took on passengers from another train—young people going to a voluntary work drive. Young girls in their short pants joyfully sang songs about the reconstruction of our country. I did not know what Kasim thought about, but I looked at them eagerly, longing for something I did not have. I have always remembered the scene of those joyful young girls going to a voluntary work drive.

10 Gračanica

We moved to Gračanica and had our room in Kasim's parents' house. Kasim immediately found a job as a construction technician at a school construction site. His mother was happy about my pregnancy. She had a dress sewn for me right away, because I had nothing I could wear. The dress was made of light-blue silk and was the only thing I wore during my pregnancy, besides a housedress I wore inside the house. Because it was summertime, I did not need more than that.

The summer of 1946 was very hot and very good for watermelons, so you could see them a lot at the farmers' market. Each day Kasim's father brought a huge watermelon home, which he carried on his stomach. Because I was pregnant, I enjoyed not only fruit but various pies, casseroles, and baklava that Kasim's mother made so well. I remember the rich farmers' market, a delicious clotted cream that I never tried previously, and eggs of different sizes. But by nature I was not a gourmet, and the food could not really make me happy. I thought that God was giving me what I did not especially want to have. What I really wanted then, I did not have. The dreams I had while I was dating Kasim, to be happy in our living together, did not come true. Kasim's father was like a guest in the house. He would come home at lunchtime and late in the evening, leaving home early in the morning, so I almost did not see him at all. Kasim was the same. He would have a short lunch at home, and in the evening, when daily work at the school construction site was finished, he would go to a small coffee bar near our house and spent hours there with some white gypsies from Gračanica. Kasim neither drank alcohol nor enjoyed it if he did drink some, so I did not know why he liked to be there so much. During my pregnancy, we never went out to the cinema, shopping, or just to have a walk together. At first he did not want for his schoolmates to find out he was married. Now, this reason did not exist anymore but he still did not change his attitude. We were young and maybe he was weary because he had showed too much of his love earlier. His mother told me he used to have many girlfriends, and she thought it would not be easy for him to be married. I thought that some of his friends might have given him bad advice about how to "keep authority" over his wife in order to avoid being henpecked. Anyway, I accepted it and instead of going out with him, I was going out with his mother and her companions. I was still dissatisfied, and I often cried, so his mother told me once, "You will cry, but you will stop with that one day, as I also cried and stopped doing that."

I had some joy during my visits to my aunt, my mother's sister, who married Kasim's uncle. She looked like my mother, and I was happy to see her. She was always very kind to me and gave me presents. Her husband liked me too, and he was a very clever man who I respected a lot.

I also had fun talking to Kasim's youngest brother, who was fifteen. He was a blacksmith apprentice and would come home for lunch. He usually ate alone; his mother cooked him a special meal in small pots and baking sheets, and he would eat it all. I sat by him and watched him eating, and he would joyfully tell me different boyish experiences. He always invited me to sit by him while having his lunch and was happy to be with me. That fifteen-year-old boy remained forever as a pleasant memory of that period when we lived in Gračanica. Kasim had another brother, who was an army officer and lived in Belgrade.

Sometime at the end of that summer, I had a chance to visit Sarajevo. My mother-in-law suggested that I go there and then come back in a few days. I think she wanted me to visit my home city and to break my depression a bit. So I left. My parents and sisters were in Oglavak. I stayed two days in Sarajevo with my aunt, who had a house in our joint yard. My aunt and other relatives who saw me said I was very beautiful as a pregnant woman. I did not go to Oglavak; I do not remember the reason for that, if it was embarrassing for me due to my pregnancy, or because I did not miss my parents that much. I walked the city streets alone, without a special aim, thinking that I did not belong to it anymore. I encountered a gymnastic competition held in the open area that later would become a soccer stadium. Young girls performed difficult parallel-bar and balance-beam exercises, and I watched them with admiration. I remembered gymnastic classes in our school, but these exercises were more difficult.

One day Kasim said he would like to continue his education at a university. He would stop working at his current job. He asked me to travel to Belgrade and enroll him in Belgrade University, because he could not get days off from work to go there himself. His mother and father were skeptical about it, and my mother-in-law was especially worried about me traveling to Belgrade at the end of the eighth month of my pregnancy. She said, "You can give birth to your baby while traveling." I was happy. First, I was happy because he was about to study at the university; second, because I would at least shortly have a contact with school; and third and finally, I thought about how I might also study at a university one day.

I started my trip with a bag and some food that my mother-in-law prepared for me, and after two changes in Karanovac and Doboj, I was on the train to Belgrade. It was late afternoon, and I watched the low-lying landscape that I had never seen before. We traveled the whole night, too, and I may have slept a little, and at around nine o'clock in the morning I found myself in front of the wide white stairs of Belgrade University. I had Kasim's documents with me, and I was very hopeful. But soon the administrator gave me the disappointing news that Belgrade University did not accept students who had technical school certificates—they only accepted high school certificates. When she saw my disappointment, the secretary told me that Ljubljana University accepted students who had either a technical school certificate or a high school certificate.

I was thinking. To come back home with a job unfinished would be a defeat, and we would lose our only chance for Kasim to go to a university. So I went to the railroad station and bought a ticket for Ljubljana.[23] The train was going to leave at midnight and arrive the next afternoon, so I walked through the streets of Belgrade, looking at the wonderful large buildings. I passed through various parks, but everything was clouded by my thoughts. I walked down a wide and pretty boulevard that looked very beautiful in the sunlight. I walked slowly due to both my pregnancy and to my concern. I then noticed all of a sudden my former classmate Zdravka Bralić, who was walking toward me. It was a surprise for both of us, and we talked to each other with great pleasure. She said she had a scholarship to study engineering in the Soviet Union and was very happy about that. I told her about my intention to enroll my husband in the university. She was glad to see me pregnant, as if she wanted to show it was as valuable as her leaving to study in the big Soviet Union. We shared similar grades during most of our high school years. She was an excellent student, never intrusive, and always gave the correct replies. She had A or B grades at the end of all her school years. She was very kind and beautiful, with a great smile. I remember her sitting somewhere in the middle of the classroom. I liked her. When we parted, I thought about how happy I was during my high school years, the same as she was happy now, and I thought about how I felt so sad about my current situation.

That night, waiting for the train to Ljubljana, I was sitting at the railroad station leaning on my suitcase. The scene around me was such as I had only rarely seen before. People were sitting on the floor with many suitcases around them, with baskets and bundles, half asleep, half loudly calling each other, many of them looking for a place to sit. I was also sitting on the floor; the benches were either occupied or there just weren't

---

[23] Capital city of today's Slovenia, about 500 miles west of Belgrade.

enough of them. The train left on time and I was lucky to have found a place to sit. I slept. When day broke, I watched the beautiful mountainous landscape of Slovenia go by the window, and I looked at the clean railroad stations and the high poles with properly tightened wires that appeared as we approached settlements. I arrived in Ljubljana in the afternoon and immediately began to look for a hotel room. I do not know why, but I failed to find an available room. I walked and walked, and it was almost evening when, walking on a wide avenue toward the city outskirts, I met a middle-aged woman with bleached-blonde hair. I stopped and asked her to tell me where I could stay overnight. I told her that the next day I was going to enroll my husband at the university. She looked at me and said, "It is very hard for you—you are pregnant and your legs look very distended. Come with me, you can stay at my place." She told me her husband died with the partisans and that she lived with her mother. When we came to her small apartment, she explained to her mother why she had brought me home with her. They brought me a wash basin with warm water for my legs. I slept with her in her double bed, which had clean linen. Although it was very comfortable in the bed, I kept waking up all the time and thinking about the next day. She went to work earlier, so her mother saw me off and I gave her a marmalade made by my mother-in-law for me, because I did not have to pay anything. I later sent her a card expressing my gratitude for what they had done for me. From that day forward, whenever I would hear someone talk about Slovenian women, I had a picture of this great blond-haired, middle-aged woman who took me, a stranger, to her home so generously and kindly.

After I showed Kasim's documents at the university office, I was allowed to enroll him in the Technical Sciences University, and I had to fill out many forms. They knew I came from the Republic of Bosnia and Herzegovina, and they made sure I could finish everything in one day. Very relieved, I sat at the table and started to fill in the forms. A professor, as addressed by the secretary, passed by and leaned over my papers. I asked him if I could write in Serbo-Croatian instead of Slovenian and he said so pleasantly to me, "We are the same people, it does not matter which language you use for writing." I never forgot that sentence and his smile. It was all so simple, and I soon found myself on the evening train heading back to Belgrade, where I had to change for Doboj and Gračanica. I was sleeping so soundly on the train, with my head leaned on the small ledge next to the window, that I almost missed Bosanski Brod station where I was supposed to change trains. The shaking of the railroad car and the noise of the hammer strokes woke me up. It was still night, and I looked through the window and saw a lot of people. I asked someone what that station was, and they replied, "Bosanski Brod." I quickly got off and looked for my connecting train. I found it, and after several more hours and two more changes of trains in Doboj and Karanovac, I arrived in Gračanica around noon. They were all happy to see me—Kasim, because I enrolled him in the university, and his mother, because everything was all right with me during my trip. They were very surprised about my traveling to Ljubljana.

Soon it was time for Kasim to go to Ljubljana. I packed his suitcases, and we agreed that at the beginning, the source of his finances would be the gold coins I got from his family as wedding presents. I gave him seven gold coins, enough for the first and maybe even the second semester, and then he could try to look for a scholarship. Besides, he could earn some money from a summer job. So he left and I stayed, waiting to give birth, which was supposed to happen in two weeks.

11 Child

One night, seven days after Kasim's departure, I changed my position in the bed and felt the water coming out of me. I got up, knocked on my mother-in-law's door and informed her of what had happened to me. She told me to go back to bed immediately and sent Kasim's brother for a midwife. That midwife assisted all childbirths in Gračanica except the complicated ones, when a doctor was engaged or the woman was sent to the hospital. At that time, Gračanica did not have a maternity hospital. A tall, slim midwife came and told me that the birth had started. It was around four o'clock in the morning. The midwife was sitting and waiting, and my mother-in-law brought some warm sheets and they wrapped me in them. I patiently suffered from the pain, not knowing anything about childbirth. The pain became more and more frequent and stronger, and finally, when it seemed to me I would explode, I lost my strength and I felt like I was going to faint. But my baby started to cry soon, a little boy, and everything, all my pain, suddenly vanished. A bit later, lying down and watching my wrapped baby by my side, with black hair and red cheeks and mouth, I saw the sunrise. That picture was wonderful and I felt a kind of blissfulness.

They moved me to the guest room, because relatives and friends started to come to congratulate us. My mother-in-law told them I delivered my baby while sleeping, and I explained to them that I did not have the strength to open my eyes and used all my powers to deliver my child. Many years later, when I was present at births in the hospital, it was strange to me that women used their strength for loud crying when they actually needed that strength in giving birth to their babies. My mother-in-law wanted to immediately inform Kasim, as well as my parents, who we were certain intended to visit us.

My mother came. My father did not come; actually, he had visited us a month earlier, when he met his friend, my uncle, and me as well. I started to cry when I embraced him, and he said, smiling at me, "Why did you leave me?" My mother-in-law invited him two or three times for a special lunch and he was delighted. Because he liked mountain climbing, he organized some hikes together with my uncle around Gračanica. My uncle's son and his wife, who was about my age, went too, as did Kasim and I. Kasim's mother was worried about how I would manage to walk so much, because I was close to the delivery date that had been predicted for the arrival of my baby. However, everything ended well; I was behind them a bit, and my uncle's daughter-in-law followed me. It was very interesting to pass through different villages previously unknown to us. We walked about twelve miles. I have great memories about that hike, because it was the only time I was able to go out with Kasim during my whole pregnancy in Gračanica.

When my mother came alone with a huge parcel, she brought with her the quilt my aunt had given me as a wedding present. The quilt was made of red silk and was embroidered with golden and silver threads; it was really an antique. The presents for my baby and me were modest, a small pullover and cap made of gray wool for the baby, which seemed to me to be inappropriate for a newborn. But my parents had hard times then—my father was retired, so I guess they could not afford different gifts. The wonderful quilt compensated for any deficiency, though, so I was appreciative overall.

It was good to spend a few days with my mother. She slept with me in the same room and helped me when my baby woke up at night. She was gentle with me, and I was happy to have somebody there with me. She told me to breast-feed my baby every three hours, or in any case not more frequently than that, even if he cried. That advice was the prevailing view of pediatricians, who thought that three hours were necessary for an infant to digest the previous meal and that a child had to learn that schedule from the moment of birth. My mother-in-law was skeptical about it, though, because she said she had found that a baby has his own feeding rhythm and should be fed whenever he woke up and cried. My mother soon left, and we were undecided about the best method for feeding my baby.

Kasim came home, too. He looked at his little son with admiration, "How beautiful he is," he said. He stayed with us for a few days and was very kind to both of us. We named the baby Nedžad, and we would call him Nedjo, a common nickname for Nedžad.

My little son grew well and was a beautiful baby, with beautiful curly black hair. Everyone said, "He looks like Kasim." Maybe my prayers were granted, I thought, because when I was pregnant I prayed to God for my child to look like his father.

Because it was winter and we would always go visiting in that season, I went to the nearby houses of our relatives and friends with my mother-in-law. Those winter evenings were a delight. We sat by a cozy fire burning in the fireplace. We drank coffee, always with a little milk, from the demitasses that were constantly filled from the Turkish coffee pots that were placed on the polished brazier and leaned on the red, radiating live coals. I listened to the conversations about everyday living and enjoyed watching my baby, who we took with us.

After two months, my baby's growth appeared to slow down, so my mother-in-law insisted that I feed the baby more often, but I stubbornly continued to do what my mother had said—to wait for three hours between feedings, even if my baby cried. It was a mistake, though, because I did not eat well and was so slim, and there was not enough milk in a feeding.

Both my mother-in-law and other people reproached me, but I kept thinking that my mother's suggestions had to be the best. I was ashamed later that I had been so stubborn.

Unexpectedly, something happened and I had to travel to Sarajevo with my son. My mother-in-law insisted that I visit my mother, who was in the hospital because she had just had gallbladder surgery. One of my aunts was in our house helping my father and sisters while my mother was in the hospital. She recovered well, but she still needed to stay in the hospital for some medical treatment. I was happy to see her recovered and joyful, and she showed me the gallstone they took out of her, about the size of a bird's egg, which caused her the pain. I stayed there a few days. My aunt, upon seeing how little my three-month-old baby was, told me I did not have sufficient milk and that I should give him additional food because he obviously was growing very slowly. She made the first meal for me, because I did not dare to, and the baby ate it voraciously.

When I came back to Gračanica, my mother-in-law was glad that I had begun to give my baby additional food. She probably thought it was necessary for me to go to Sarajevo so that my family would be able to convince me to do that. Very soon my little son improved. The days passed, and I was in contact with Kasim only through rare letters. Telephone lines were not yet used for that purpose.

Kasim came back one spring day. He brought many packages with him. He said he could not live alone without me and our baby, so he decided to stop studying and find a job again. Vranica Company in Sarajevo, an army enterprise, was recruiting civil technicians for its construction projects, so he would get a job there, he said. We looked at the packages Kasim brought home in wonder, and when he opened them and showed us many rare things, some of them made of angora wool, some china pieces, and so on, we were surprised. He explained to us that it would be easy to sell them in Gračanica, because things such as these could not be found there and he would get a good price for them. I was sad that he spent the money I gave him, and I did not believe there would be much profit from our selling those things. Yet I was very happy that we would be together in Sarajevo, my home city. So we went to Sarajevo, leaving those things under the sofa in the guestroom, perhaps to sell at another time.

In that year, 1947, many families in Sarajevo were required to accept others in their houses and apartments because the number of people living in the city was much greater than it had been in the pre-war period, when Sarajevo's population was 80,000. Many officers moved in with families in large apartments and houses. There were also many refugees, especially from Eastern Bosnia, who did not have a place to go back to or did not want to go back there. A lot of my mother's relatives, who were from old Sarajevo families and had big houses, got tenants and had to give them half of the house, so these relatives of my mother were losing something very important—their privacy.

In the lower part of our house, my mother took in her cousin and her child. Her husband was killed when he was with the partisans. My mother, my father, and my two sisters moved to the upper floor. My cousin stayed with us only temporarily, while her apartment was being built. She had priority for new housing because she had lost her husband in the war. So she stayed with us, and my mother was able to save us from having some other family in our house.

When Kasim and I came with our little baby, my cousin immediately moved into the large living room, leaving the large kitchen and dining room for us. We shared the bathroom, toilet, large hall, and another small room. In that space, which included the kitchen and the dining room, the independent life of our little family began. The only things we had in our room were a couch, a baby buggy, an oven, a carpet, a table, and a small sofa.

Then my mother got sick again, now from a deep thrombosis of her right leg and she had to stay in bed with lead-water compresses. She no longer had a maid, because my father was retired and did not have enough money for that, so my mother's sister came there to cook meals and my sisters kept the house clean and orderly. My middle sister, Dila, was about to finish her eighth and final year of high school and graduate, and my youngest sister, Suma, was in her sixth year of high school. My mother used to criticize me when I did not go upstairs to her room to clean it and change her compresses, but I simply did not have enough strength to do that.

Kasim was going to work every day in Vogošća or Hadžići, where Vranica Company constructed its facilities, and returning in the evening. I was shopping, cooking, and taking care of our little son. Nobody helped me with him, so he was dependent on me only. He liked to play and go places with me when he was as young as six months. I took him in his baby buggy when I went shopping, and I would often stand in a long line and wait for a kilo of pepper or tomato. In the UNRA (United Nations Relief Agency) packages, we got powdered eggs, peanut spread, and orange marmalade, and it was very helpful, but we had to wait for those things in long lines, too.

While my child was sleeping, I cooked something for dinner and for the next day's lunch for Kasim to take with him in a military dish. As soon as my son woke up, he would raise his little hands toward me so I would pick him up. So I was carrying and carrying him around our yard and house, because I did not have a small bed for him to play in safely alone. Sometimes a little girl, the sister of the cousin with whom I shared my apartment, would take my son to carry him and play with him. But she came rarely. I never forgot that little girl, that short relief she gave me that enabled me to do something at home.

My mother could not understand and later reproached me for not taking care of her when she was sick in bed. When the doctor came to see her, I went up to her, and the doctor gave me her prescription and said, "This young girl can buy it for you in the pharmacy," and my mother replied, "She is not a young girl, she is married and has a son." The tall and handsome doctor looked at me in wonder and said, "Our Czech girls do not get married so early—the only advantage is that children have young parents then." I was a bit ashamed; I also knew it was not normal. I was slim, and I did not have time to eat enough, so I had anemia, which they discovered during a medical examination in the regional outpatient clinic. The doctor prescribed me iron injections, which I had to have every day.

12 Field Work

After a while, Kasim got a more permanent post in Hadžići, where he was to stay for two months. Daily transportation to and from the city was not provided, so he suggested that I and our baby join him there. We would live in a village house—rent a room there and use their kitchen. That idea made me happy, because I wanted to be with him, and I also thought that taking care of our child would be easier in the village. So we found a place in a small house with a creek in its vicinity. We had one room and a kitchen—actually a summer kitchen that was located on the other side of the yard. It was good to see the surrounding gardens and creek beside my house, but taking care of Nedžad was not any easier for me there than it was elsewhere. I could not take him with me to the summer kitchen when I was cooking because there was only an earthen floor, so I left him in the room on the floor to play on a blanket. I would go back and forth from the kitchen to the room the whole time I was cooking so that he could see me or to give him a different toy, and he was always looking for me when I came to check on him. And because he was only eight months old and still crawling, I had to carry him while walking, and he was getting heavier. There was no practical baby carriage or stroller that we could buy then. It was especially hard when I went to Sarajevo to buy tomatoes, red peppers, or fruit—the local villagers did not have them—and I went there by train. The train was always full of tired workers who usually would not give up their seats, so I had to stand up both going there and coming home with my heavy baby and my parcels of produce in my arms.

At work, Kasim met a man who was also a technician. Fiko and his wife also lived temporarily in the same village as we did. They did not have children, so in their free time they often hiked in the surrounding forests. They kept inviting us to join them, but Kasim refused, saying we could not because of Nedžad. Fiko replied cordially, "I will carry the baby," but Kasim did not change his mind. Because I wanted to join them on their hikes, I took Nedžad to stay in Oglavak with my parents and sisters for a short time. My mother's leg was healed by then.

Our house in Oglavak was equipped with only the most important things. There were no more wonderful sofas, pillows, and curtains there. They had all been taken away during the war. My mother's oldest sister, the one who gave the first real food to my baby when I came from Gračanica to visit my mother in the hospital, had come to help my mother, especially with cooking, because she still used her leg cautiously. When I asked her if I could leave my son with them for ten days or so, to rest a little, my mother said, "No way! You did not help me when I had the thrombosis." I asked her again, but she refused. Finally, my aunt interrupted us and said, "Let him stay. I will help with him," so my mother finally agreed to it.

I then took the bus home alone for the first time since giving birth, and I was occupied with my thoughts. I was sorry I left Nedžad there, but I thought it would also be good for him to stay in Oglavak with my sisters. Kasim was not happy that I left our son there, and the next day was empty and bleak for me, too. In two days, my sister came, carrying my son. I ran out to meet her, very surprised by the change I saw in his appearance in only two days. He had lost weight and had very sad eyes. My sister explained that he was crying for me all the time and they had decided to send him back home. He really was used to me, but I thought they would try to amuse him until he got used to them, too. I also thought my staying with him in Oglavak for two days would enable him to acclimatize a bit. So because that didn't happen and he was back home, my hiking in the surrounding forests remained only a desire.

That autumn my middle sister, Dila, was to enroll in a university. My parents were considering whether it was better for her to study medicine at Sarajevo University or to study pharmacy in Zagreb. She wanted to go to Zagreb, and my youngest sister also favored that. Another reason that made Zagreb a good choice was that Dila had been awarded a scholarship for pharmacy, and students who attended that school had to have a scholarship to go there at that time. Students without scholarships could not enroll at all there because the government thoroughly planned the allocation of students to universities. The scholarship was just enough to pay for a room in the dormitory and food in the student dining hall.

So it was finally agreed that Dila would go to Zagreb; when she left, our parents agreed to send her food parcels, because the food in the student dining hall was known to be very inferior. My father was retired, but soon after retirement he had found a part-time job that included translation of old medical books in the library at the Public Health Institute. He went there every day and spent hours translating. His work there made a large contribution to the history of medicine. My mother was happy he was working there, because she now had less worry about their finances. I was very pleased that my sister had enrolled at the university, as pleased as I would have been if I were the one going there. I remembered my father's statements from years ago, when women from our community rarely went to a university. He had thought then that I would surely be one woman who did go to the university, and he did not say that about my sisters.

When Kasim completed his work in Hadžići, we returned to Sarajevo. My cousin had moved out, so we had a complete apartment at our disposal, that is, the whole lower part of the house. Kasim's parents bought us a baby bed, a stove, a kitchen table and chairs, and my parents gave us a sofa and two carpets. The first thing we bought ourselves was a small radio, the first such product of our country's young industry, of the Kozara brand. So we celebrated Nedžad's first birthday and watched him running joyfully around the room. Kasim's father came, but his mother could not come because she had some kidney problems. She always suffered from high blood pressure, too.

Kasim was soon sent to another work site, this time in Vogošća. He went there every day, and then he proposed that I and Nedžad join him. They put up shacks on the construction site where the workers lived, so we got a small shack, too. It was winter when we came there by truck and moved in. We had only necessary things, including a trunk-like stove with an oven, which could be used for cooking and which heated our living space perfectly.

That period of time when we lived in Vogošća was the best since the beginning of my marriage. My son became independent, running around our little place and playing with small pieces of lumber leftovers. His light-colored curly hair drew everybody's attention. In our vicinity there was another shack just like ours in which an army officer and his wife lived. He was also a technician, and they had no children. They were both happy to see our son. I spent most of the day with that woman, who was named Raba. We agreed on what to cook, sewed a bit on her sewing machine, and played with Nedžad. She was from Herzegovina, was a few years older than me, and spoke a Herzegovinian dialect. She was always serene and smiling. I listened to her stories about her husband's experiences when he was with the partisans and to her war experiences. My friendship with her was so enjoyable that I started to feel less emotionally dependent on Kasim. I cheerfully noticed the people around me—such as the German prisoners engaged at the construction site in the work of mixing plaster, transporting wheelbarrows, carrying beams, and other tasks. They would stop their work at noon to have lunch in their military dishes. I remember our shack under the winter sun, with snow shining on the ground in silver crystals. Everything looked idyllic and serene to me, even when in the morning I put my boots on and walked in the snow around our shack in order to light the paper in the chimney opening so as to enable the chimney to tug smoke from our stove. I always got up first in the morning and lit the fire, but a thick smoke came from the stove, so our room was full of smoke in one moment.

If I went to Sarajevo to shop or visit my parents, the only means of transportation was a truck. The bed of the truck had a roof and benches, so I had a place to sit with Nedžad. A lot of people were always standing on the truck, and because the road was uneven and winding, the people who stood swayed back and forth. Because of Nedžad, though, people were especially careful not to fall on top of us. All that could not ruin the good mood I was in as a result of my friendship with Raba. Even today, that woman, always smiling and with her beautiful sparkling eyes, remains in my memory—and shall forever.

We spent the next summer and autumn in Vogošća, and before winter we came back to Sarajevo. During the winter, we agreed to go to the seaside when Kasim got his annual leave, sometime in June, because that summer he was supposed to go repeatedly to a new work site. The Trade Union planned to organize holidays on the seaside for its members, so we were also awarded a fifteen-day stay in the luxurious Excelsior Hotel in Dubrovnik. A few days prior to our departure, Nedžad got sick. He had a high temperature, and because some tiny red spots appeared on his skin, I took him to the doctor, the same one who cured me from unconfirmed typhus and who said that "coward" should be written on my books because (at my mother's direction) I had told her that I was afraid of injections (which was not true). The doctor thought it could be rubella, but she said she was not sure of it. I asked her if I was allowed to travel with him, and she said it was fine to travel. She told me that the rash would go away quickly and gave me some syrup to control his temperature.

During our trip, while we were sitting on the train, Nedžad's temperature decreased and the red spots on his body became bigger, like the ones in measles. There were no other children in our compartment, but near Dubrovnik a lady with a little girl of the same age as Nedžad opened the compartment door. She was looking for her husband, and when she saw our son and when we told her he was ill, she immediately left.

101

The Excelsior Hotel was a luxury hotel and one of the most beautiful or maybe the most beautiful of all the hotels I have ever visited. We had a beautiful, perfectly clean room with a balcony and a sea view. Nedžad went to the balcony immediately, and his spots vanished in a few hours. The next day he was completely recovered. We had to take an elevator to the large stony beach where there were stairs down to the sea and a pebbly, shallow section intended for children and non-swimmers. We often played chess on the beach, as others did. A few times we had group picnics organized by the hotel staff, and we went on trips with other guests to Lokrum Island and Dubrovačka River. The sea was cool, because it was June, but it was heavenly to jump from the stairs into the deep sea and swim. We had already met many of the other guests, so I knew a lot of them.

One morning one of the guests met me in the hall and told me his daughter got sick, so the doctor from Belgrade, also a hotel guest, concluded she had measles. It was the same girl who came with her mother to the door of our train compartment, and although she stood there only a few moments, the little girl caught the measles. After exactly ten days, which is the incubation period, the girl got sick. They were a young couple; he was handsome with a boxer's nose, and she was slim and very pretty. They had to extend their stay because of their daughter's illness. I was very embarrassed and I said something like an apology for his daughter catching the measles from my son, and he waved back with his hand and said, "She would get it one day anyway." I was surprised by such a reaction—he had no anger and said nothing about how we should not have traveled with a child who had a contagious disease. This happened to them at a very bad moment, because they had to extend their hotel stay, which caused an expense they did not anticipate. But still, he was not troubled about it. I felt bad, of course, but there was little I could do to help ease their difficulty.

After we left the seaside, we moved to Hadžići again. We got a little shack, one of several that were built for technicians. There was a large field around our shack with dense, short grass that was good for playing sports, but officers were not much interested in sports, and this was a military enterprise.

MEMORIES FROM BOSNIA

The Zujevina River flowed near the construction site, but we went swimming there only once or twice during the summer. I mostly cooked, cleaned our shack, and took care of our little son. He was almost three years old, so it was easy. He would spend all day playing around our shack and in the neighboring yard with a little boy of the same age named Dodan. I did not have friends, so I visited my neighbor, Dodan's mother, and we had coffee made either by me or by her. She wanted so much to buy better clothes for her children or better furniture for her house, but she could not afford it. Her husband had a low salary as an unskilled worker, and they had only a small garden and several chickens; I do not remember if they had a cow or pig. I was sorry for her, because they had a very hard life. I became aware then of how difficult it is to be poor.

That autumn, my youngest sister was to enroll in a university, too, like Dila. She also wanted to study in Zagreb. To earn some money to go to Zagreb, Kasim found her a job working with his company's administrative offices in Hadžići. So she spent a month with us in our small shack. One day we organized a small one-day company picnic to a beautiful alpine lake, Boračko Lake. We all carried some food with us, both ready-made and for grilling, and we left for the lake in an open truck. Climbing up the serpentine road from Konjic and then going down the road with an unforgettable vista of the lake before us—the lake had a shiny even surface in the middle of all the lush forest greenery—was a magnificent experience for us. And when we got there, it was even better. The lake water was warm, like no other place I had ever been before. We made merry, lay on the blankets or the grass, and had a barbecue. An officer was interested in my sister, and she was really beautiful. She was tall and had light-colored hair and blue eyes. However, she kept silent, and the officer, who had been cheerful, got silent himself at one moment, too. I felt sorry for that, because her conduct toward him seemed belittling.

That summer, Dila got married during her second year at the university. My parents tried to convince her not to do that, but she was in love and wanted to marry. He was a handsome, tall young man who was finishing law school in Zagreb. He was from the Doboj area. My too-proud mother prepared a very rich wedding party with many guests. I also came for a day or

103

two. My sister had a very lovely and very stylish hairstyle—she always had extremely beautiful hair—and she was dressed quite beautifully. People said, "The bride is very beautiful," and she really was.

My youngest sister Suma enrolled in Veterinary School in Zagreb. She wanted to study in Zagreb, and because there was no place for her in medical school, she preferred to enroll in veterinary medicine than to study medicine in Sarajevo. She did not get a scholarship, though, so our parents decided to send her money for her living expenses, although it was difficult for them then. My mother sold an expensive pearl so that they would be able to send her money regularly every month.

13 University Enrollment

At that time, in 1950, it was possible to obtain a scholarship for medical school (a seven-year program of study) in Sarajevo, so it occurred to me to enroll there, for Nedžad was already three and I was able to leave him in a day-care center. I also wanted for Kasim to go back to the architecture school program he started in Ljubljana; he could now also obtain a scholarship for it. He did not agree, though, because he said he could not get dismissed from his duty in the army enterprise, because technicians like him were very much in demand. So I gave up my wish, but I hoped we would be able to implement it when he was dismissed and no longer needed by the Vranica Company.

We spent the next winter in Sarajevo. The construction operations in Vogošća and Hadžići were completed, and Kasim worked on some facilities in the city. At the beginning of the summer, we went to Gračanica and spent our vacation there. It was our second visit to Gračanica since we moved to Sarajevo. My mother-in-law liked Nedžad; she called him Nedjo a lot and wanted me to leave him with her, but I always thought that the parents should discipline their child, because even with all of a grandmother's love and care, the older generation cannot react properly on new requests. Children usually get undisciplined with grandparents because they develop bad habits from too much permissiveness, which grandparents are well known for.

My life with Kasim was the same as always; it was enough for him to have contact with his work colleagues. In the evening he liked me to quickly make him some sweet meal and to stay home. He thought that women should stay at home and said, "How can a woman be bored at home?" Other people disagreed with that view. The times were changing, and women became socially active just like men, especially young women who had their own jobs, just like men. The WAF (Women's Anti-Fascist Front) was a group that organized women's reading groups where we discussed various issues, including food, hygiene, and children. I distributed invitations around to women to come to a reading group, as well as some other leaflets, and I always helped when asked to do that, although it seemed to me that it could be carried out by a less-educated woman. Along those lines, I was increasingly thinking about how to go about doing things so Kasim and I both could begin studying—he would study architecture and I would study at the medical school. We would have to request a scholarship for me, and for him, we would need a dismissal from duty. The Council for Science and Culture awarded scholarships, so I applied for the scholarship. However, it was much more difficult in 1950 to get a scholarship than it had been the previous year, because some two hundred students from Belgrade were supposed to enroll in Sarajevo University. Belgrade University could not accept all those wishing to study medicine there.

My request was considered all summer, and finally, when their reply came, it was negative. I visited Mr. Kreco, the vice president of the Council for Science and Culture, several times and explained to him that I was an excellent student and that it was only in my last year in high school that I did not achieve excellent grades. I was sitting in the small park next to the Council's building and thoughtfully waiting and waiting, and he delayed giving me his answer. Even my father was upset about the matter, so he asked his friend, Dr. Teodor Ilić, to ask the president of the Council, Mr. Butozan, about me. I heard Dr. Ilić saying on the phone to someone, "There are never too many doctors," but it did not help. Kreco offered me the veterinary medicine program that was just created in Sarajevo. After that my father said resignedly, "You really are having bad luck."

Maybe Providence wanted me to meet a neighbor whose son, Alija Firdus, also was unsuccessful in getting a scholarship and wanted to enroll in the medical school. His mother told me that a small number of students could enroll without a scholarship, mainly people who lived in Sarajevo, so her son managed to enroll that way. Those special enrollments had only to be approved by the university rector and nobody else.

I entered the university building wishing to see the rector on the very next day. His secretary received me kindly, and when I told her I came to ask for my enrollment in the university, she left to announce me to the rector. She came back soon and said the rector would see me. I entered through a door covered with a thick green lining and I saw a vast room, with the rector standing next to a table. I walked some distance into the room, and he watched me. I told him that I had been waiting to obtain my scholarship the whole summer and that I was rejected. I asked him kindly to approve me to enroll without a scholarship, explaining to him that I was always an excellent student, and that only my graduation certificate showed less than the most excellent grades, and that was because I was pregnant then. I offered to show him my certificates from all my years of schooling—I had brought them all with me. He wanted to see them, so he saw the constant lines of E^{24} grades in my war-year certificates and A grades in my post-war certificate. He was satisfied and said he would approve my enrollment. I cannot find the words to express how filled with happiness I was at that moment! His secretary was also happy for me, and I will never forget her beautiful figure and smile. I also will never forget the rector himself, who was tall and handsome; I think he was Slovenian.

I enrolled in medical school at the last moment before classes were to start, and Kasim enrolled at the Technical School - Architecture after he was dismissed from his duty at

---

[24] "E" "excellent" during the war was later replaced by "A" as the highest grade.

the Vranica Company. It was not easy to accomplish that. Kasim had persisted in telling me that his dismissal was out of the question and that if he could not study, he would not allow me to study either. I was able to enroll only if both of us could enroll. I decided to go directly to his manager, Mr. Brkić, and to ask him to dismiss Kasim. One afternoon, I knocked on the door of Mr. Brkić's apartment on Kralja Tomislava Street. An old woman with a scarf on her head opened the door, and when I told her I would like to talk to the manager, she kindly invited me in and said he was her son. She opened the door of a room and a handsome man stood up and came to me on crutches. He had lost a leg in the war. The old woman withdrew, and he and I sat and talked for some time. At the beginning, he said technicians like Kasim were in very high demand for their abilities in managing the extremely fast construction processes that the company used. I, in turn, explained to him that Kasim had worked as a technician for many years and now wanted to study architecture. I said that I would also like to study, that I would study medicine, and that we would have our scholarships for living (I would be able to get mine after my first examination, I had learned). He knew there was also a need for highly skilled workers and that an increasing number of universities were now opened, but he still tried to point out that technicians are greatly needed. At one point he asked me, "Why do you care so much about studying?" I explained to him that I was always an excellent student, that for many years my father had told me I would study, and that my father studied in Budapest, too. He replied, "All right, I understand. I will dismiss your husband." I went out very happy, and he kept his word, so Kasim was dismissed from his duty shortly thereafter.

At the beginning, we had only one scholarship, Kasim's scholarship, because I enrolled without it. But mine would be granted soon. However, my father asked my mother to make lunch for all of us, while I made our breakfast and dinner. That autumn, the Department for Oriental Languages was opened at the University of Philosophy and my father was asked to be a professor of Arabic and Persian languages. Accepting that offer and becoming a university professor again meant that my parents' financial status improved significantly. So it was now much easier for them to send money to my sister and to provide us with lunch. Nedžad was in a day-care center; by then he was almost four. The director of the day-care center allowed me to pay only a nominal amount. She was enthusiastic about our studying; she was Jewish and had joined the partisans during the war. She contributed a lot to us by giving us child care for such a low price during those years of study. My mother had told me she could not possibly take constant care of our son, which was understandable to me because of her rather unstable health; something else had to be found. I was lucky to find this woman, and I have a wonderful memory of her and the help she provided to me.

On my first day—actually it was in the evening—at the university, two hundred fifty students filled the lecture hall. We were told that we would meet our professors that night. I found a seat in the third row and felt like a student again. I did not know anybody. When the first professor introduced himself to us, I felt a kind of relief—like I knew for sure that I was in the right place, where I belonged. The professors spoke about how medicine is hard to study and gave us general advice, but I memorized the words of the biology professor and I have repeated them many times during my life, "You are young," he said. "You will enjoy making friends, playing the guitar, and so on. But remember, the one who has fun while solving a mathematical problem knows what real enjoyment is." It was clear that studying medicine would be a great pleasure for us. That evening was soon over, and our classes would begin the next day. I sat next to a student who had her hair braided and decorated with a large ribbon. Her name was Hajdana and she came with other Belgrade students who were not able to enroll in the university there. She was from Montenegro. After our classes, she joined me and was so kind and cheerful that I asked her to go with me to the day-care center to see how my son was doing. It was his first day there.

When we came into the day-care center, Hajdana joined the children and I peered out from behind a glass door, because I did not want my little son to see me. When Hajdana entered the room, he immediately got up as if he was expecting me to come and take him. My heart tore apart upon seeing his sad face, but I did not take him earlier to avoid disobeying their rules and to enable him to get used to being there with the other children. At the beginning, when I took him to the day-care center before my classes, he refused to go, but he slowly got used to it. They had a versatile program: Their teacher told them stories, and they played with toys, ran or played in the day-care center's yard, and slept after lunch. I understood then, as I experienced it later as well, that children did not like day-care centers, although they had the chance to play with a lot of children. Maybe they didn't like day-care because they lost their individualism in a way, and maybe it was due to the sort of discipline necessary in such a place. At any rate, I had to leave him there while I had my classes.

In the evenings, we were all together, and I had to give Nedžad a bath, wash our clothes for the next day, and make dinner for us. There was not enough time to play with Nedžad. Kasim usually worked on his school projects in the evenings. Only on Sunday mornings was I able to tell Nedžad stories while we were in bed. We would have our breakfast slowly afterward, and he especially liked to go to the upper floor to see his grandmother and grandfather. His grandfather made jokes with him, while his grandmother sometimes later in the day made a good meal for him. On Sundays I also took him to a park, most often to the Pioneer Valley, where he would play and I would read my anatomy, biology, or chemistry books. We stayed there in the park for a long time, especially when it was not crowded in the spring and autumn, and he always found several friends to play with. One day I recognized in the *Oslobodjenje*[25] a picture of my son, with two other children playing. A photographer had taken it while I was studying and I didn't even notice. I saved the picture and later gave it to Nedžad.

I was getting into full swing at the university. We were presently studying bones, and we repeated the Latin names—all two hundred fifty of us. The room was large, and the din was terrific. I was lucky to be able to memorize things easily, and I was lucky to have had Latin in all four years in senior high school. Kasim constantly worked on his projects, and his large technical drafting board was always on our table, except during dinner and Sunday lunch. But he was not happy. He did not like my medical studies, and he did not want me to be a

---

[25] Daily newspaper in Sarajevo.

doctor one day because I would have to take care of my patients and have night duties, too. I was learning about osteology, that is, about bones, which was the first major subject in the study of medicine. Students usually learned in pairs, because it was easier for two people to ask questions and explain things to each other. Hajdana worked with a student named Miki, who was from Sarajevo and was the only married man among the students, as I was the only married woman. I did not have a partner to study with, and because I learned osteology rather well on my own, Hajdana suggested that the three of us question each other because our midterm exam was nearing. I agreed and told them to come to my place one afternoon, because Hajdana lived with her grandmother—she called her "nona,"—in a very small apartment.

We arranged for Hajdana and Miki to come to my place one Sunday afternoon. Kasim worked that day on his projects. I cooked, washed our laundry, and cleaned our house. When I told Kasim that my classmates would come to question each other, because our osteology midterm exam was coming up, he got enraged. He screamed at me, "You will bring me now your classmates here?" He stood up, opened the glass china cabinet, and started to throw down the parts of the set I got as a wedding present from my mother's and father's relatives. The wonderful, delicate items were now just a sheet of tiny particles on the floor. Nedžad, who slept in his bed, started to cry in fear and sat up. I took him in my hands and embraced him to remove his fear. I felt worse than in any of my previous stressful situations. After he threw down some more things, he continued on with preparing his project. I put Nedžad back in bed to sleep and picked up and swept the glass particles. Our red carpet was shining due to so many little glass crystals on it. When Hajdana and Miki rang our doorbell, I went out and told them peacefully, "Please forgive me, but my husband does not want any of my classmates to come to our house." They left understanding that, and I knew then that one day I would get divorced from Kasim.

I do not know how I managed to recover from that situation and to learn osteology, but our midterm came very soon afterward and I had to learn it. Finally, the day came and the first students on the list started the exam. The rest of us

111

stood in the anatomy demonstration room to listen to them. The anatomy professor, the famous Hajro, gave a hyoid (tongue) bone to the first student. It was a very little and unimportant bone. The student, whose name was Vukalica, turned it around, looked at it for a bit, and then said, "It is a small mandible," because it looked to him like a lower jawbone, a mandible. Hajro told him, "Enough" and gave him a failing grade. When the first student failed to pass that midterm, the others panicked, because very soon everybody knew that Vukalica did not pass the osteology exam. My turn was in a few days, and although it was my first time facing a professor after the break of several years that I had from academic work, my mental concentration and self-confidence did not let me down. The professor gave me one bone after another and I described them and specified their topographic positions, eloquently showing my knowledge of Latin. I got the best grade—10. My happiness at my success was tempered, however, by the experience I had on that gloomy Sunday that I had to spend with Kasim after his violent outburst.

That year, as well as the next one, I enjoyed studying, and the students got to know each other rather well— chatting between classes, joking, and so on—while my relationship with Kasim was rather dry. Most often he was depressing, asking me to stop studying medicine, because as a doctor I would be engaged too much outside our house. He suggested I go to law school instead. But I did not love him so much anymore that I would sacrifice for him. All things considered, my studying was going well. I passed my other exams without any problems, too. The professor of chemistry, my father's colleague at the University of Philosophy, told him, "She has a brilliant mind." My father was proud of me again, as he was in my high school days and we became closer again, so we often discussed medical terms as he continued to translate old medical books, even in his new job. After the first midterm, I was awarded a scholarship, so our financial situation improved greatly.

I especially remember the test in biochemistry because of one comment from Professor Sabovljev, who we called "Šaco." I carried out some chemical experiments, while he watched and finally said: "You did well, but it is important to use the reagents in their proper order." I had just thrown them in without regard to order. "A person who cannot think out of the box isn't good, isn't good," he said, "But some order is important so that you can successfully find your way." He still gave me the highest grade—10. Many students didn't like him, but he was an extraordinary professor who tried to make us understand the essence of human physiology.

Soon after that, one of the most difficult periods of my life began. I decided to get divorced from Kasim, but I could not think about it very much until after my anatomy exam. At the end of the second year, I passed that exam with a grade of 9. We had a school break after the exam, and I thought that was the best time for our divorce. I was thinking about how to tell my parents about it. They knew Kasim was disturbing me in my studying and wanted me to stop with it, but because they were conservative people, I was afraid to tell them. I told Kasim that I thought it would be best for us to divorce and suggested to him that we separate during that summer—I would go to Oglavak and he would go to Gračanica, and thus we would feel we were separated. When I told my parents about my intention to divorce, my mother said with disapproval, "No way, you cannot discredit us." I told them how difficult it was for me to study medicine in such a relationship. My father understood me to some extent. He thought that a woman should be independent from her husband, and he knew many examples of women who were financially ruined after their husbands' death or divorce. In addition, he did not have much faith in Kasim's emotional stability, a view that he came to hold over time because of various things that had happened. My youngest sister, who was in Oglavak with me at the time, helped me by telling my parents that if they didn't support me in my action now, I would still divorce him when I finished my studies and become independent.

One day Kasim came to Oglavak. I could not believe it when I saw him coming. His behavior was like it always was, the same as my parents'—as if nothing at all had changed— and he said he came from Gračanica to pick up Nedžad and me. He stayed with us one night, and because I said I would stay in Oglavak for some more time and because we slept in separate rooms, he left the next day. It was very hard for me to see him

going down the field and to think about how to explain to
Nedžad why his father was leaving.

When I went back to Sarajevo with Nedžad, we had a
somewhat normal life again. Kasim had begged me to come
back, emphasizing our "idyllic" life, our child, and so my
feelings overwhelmed me and I made up with him in order to
stay together as a family. We were both very involved with our
studies. I took our child to the day-care center, cooked our
dinners, and cleaned our house, while Kasim would working
only on his projects. He was still not satisfied, because I had
my classes and was not tied to him as I had been in earlier
years. He could not stand that I did not make our lunch and that
we had lunch my mother prepared. It was hard for me, too,
because I did not love him anymore. Two months passed. I
then presented him my final plan for our divorce.

I sent Nedžad to Gračanica to be with his grandmother
until we finished with the formalities. I submitted my divorce
request with hard feelings. Kasim did not believe I would go
through with it—that is, not until we were both summoned to
the court for the so-called reconciliation procedure. Judge Peleš
tried to convince us to withdraw our request, but I was decisive
and firmly asked to divorce him. The next time we appeared at
court, Kasim submitted his own report and denied that he
disturbed me in my studying and that he neglected me, adding
that I really did not have any great need for cultural events,
theater, and concerts because, in fact, I really only liked folk
songs. Both of us had our own witnesses: Mine was my
classmate Božana Stuhly, who prepared for exams with me
after Hajdana returned to Belgrade after her first year of study.
Božana was familiar with everything that had occurred with
Kasim's attitude toward my studies and my classmates, and
when she visited me she noticed for herself our disharmony
and the fear I had of even walking with some classmate on my
way to the tram station. If I did so, Kasim would later come to
the station and hide so he could watch me and follow me on my
way home. His witness was Fikret Filipović, the same Fiko
who worked with him as a technician in Hadžići and who
invited us to climb mountains with him and his wife, offering
to carry our child. I was always fond of him after that offer. He
wanted to save our marriage, so he said we had a life before

our studies, and only during our studies, when I was very busy, did my husband feel neglected and express his dissatisfaction.

A lot of our other friends and relatives tried to influence me. Kasim mobilized many of them, and it was very hard for me to stick to my decision while I was listening to the well-intentioned people I respected. Even his mother came and talked to me, and it was painful for me when she was leaving and I did not give her any hope. By nature, I am indulgent and sensitive to others' opinions, but I had to stick to my decision. I was similarly stubborn when my parents tried to convince me not to date Kasim and I was thinking of only one thing—how much I liked him—and now I was sure I could not be his wife anymore because I did not love him and could not have an honest relationship with him.

Judge Peleš listened to us and finally said, "Even one small unpleasant thing, which keeps happening, becomes very difficult to handle." There were many law students listening to our discussion, and I felt very bad about it. On my way home with Božana, Kasim came behind me and said with resignation, "Now you can be good friends."

It was over. But the hard moments continued. When Kasim moved out with the things we divided, I was really shocked. I felt how hard it was to change habits. In the evening, I cried so much that my aunt, my mother's sister, the one who lived in Gračanica and paid a visit to us, brought me water and cube sugar to calm me down. She was so kind and full of understanding for me, although it was painful for her that we divorced.

They brought Nedžad to me after his three-month stay in Gračanica. He was six. I did not tell him anything because he would not have understood, so I told him his father moved out to live near his university. He cried only once while Božana and I were studying and he played in our vicinity, "I want my daddy," he said. I often took Nedžad to see his father, and I felt bad when he looked at me and when we made arrangements about Nedžad in his presence. He had a room in the vicinity of his university, and I behaved as usual before our child so that he would not feel any coldness between Kasim and me.

So I was a divorced woman now with a child and with all of the inconveniences and difficulties of that status. It was not hard for me to take care of my child, since it was mostly my obligation then, the same as earlier, and it did not change much. Because Kasim was a student, he was not obliged to pay anything to me for our child. In addition to my scholarship, I earned some money as a demonstrator for chemistry, and after the third year, for microbiology, too, so it was enough for me and Nedžad to live on. It helped that I still had lunch at my mother's house and paid only a nominal amount for his daycare center. In the spring, a visit to the University of Belgrade was organized, and I signed up to go. I left Nedžad with my mother and went to Belgrade. The students welcomed us, and we visited their medical school and library, and we saw the city. I should have taken more money than I had, so I had to borrow from my classmate Nadja Parčić whenever I needed more money. I was grateful to her and later paid all that money back.

14 Student Life

That third year of medical school was less turbulent than the previous two had been and was without very difficult exams. I still studied with my classmate Božana Stuhly. Because I liked my studies and was always getting the top grades for our exercises and exams, my classmates were fond of me and discussed medicine with me gladly. There were also the people who liked me as a woman. My nature was not like that, though, to find somebody and make love calmly without any emotions, so I eliminated from consideration as a friend those who showed only their sexual desire to me. There were also the ones who really respected me and showed their emotional affection, but they did not attract me. Of course, I could fall in love with somebody, but he was either going to be cautious because I had a child, or at the very least, it would be a very different kind of love than what I had with Kasim. So I was mostly alone, which seemed almost unbelievable to me. A classmate told me once, "You should not belong to a single person—you belong to everybody." That classmate showed real respect for me and fell in love with me, but due to his physical appearance I could not react to that.

At the end of the third year, the Youth Holiday Association organized a trip to the seaside for students. We went to Pula on the Istra Peninsula and swam on the wonderful beaches built while Pula belonged to Italy. Those were the most beautiful beaches I knew. We were lucky, because the opera from Zagreb had its concerts in Pula, so every night we listened to great opera performances in the arena constructed during the ancient Roman period. It was great to listen the wonderful voices of the prima donna and the other operatic singers from Zagreb under the open sky in that huge acoustic amphitheater with its stone walls and benches. I felt lonely as a single woman, but I remembered my professor's words, "The one who has fun while solving a mathematical problem knows what real enjoyment is."

The fourth year of medical school was tough. The pathology lectures and exercises had come to an end already, and we had to pass that exam, which was—as we thought it would be—the most difficult and the most extensive exam. It was the second big obstacle for students; the anatomy exam had been the first great hurdle. The first pathology exercises were painful for me, when we had to dissect the organs of a man who had recently died, unlike the anatomy exercises where the corpses were old and in formalin, a preservative. But during the first months of anatomy exercises, while we were learning about bones, I used to run past the dissection hall, because it made me sick to see corpses on the tables. However, a habit is really something incredible, and I got used to it later and no longer had to run past that room. The same thing happened with the pathology exercises and lectures on clinical subjects, internal medicine, and surgery, which were also in full swing.

Nedžad started to attend the first grade of his elementary school, so my mother brought a young girl from Oglavak to be with him after school. So he did not need to go at all to the day-care center. I was happy about that because I still thought he preferred to stay with his grandmother in our house. This was true even though he got used to the day-care center and had many friends there. My mother somehow became milder with me and started to believe I really would complete my medical studies, something she was not sure about before. Božana and I studied one day at my place and the next day at her place in Višnjik, where they had rented half of a house. Božana's face was slim, and she wore glasses that she always cleaned thoroughly before we began our study sessions so that they were perfectly transparent. Her mother was a modest, hardworking and religious Catholic woman. She liked me and was glad that Božana and I studied together. Božana's sister studied piano at the Music Academy, so we always listened to Bach, Schubert, Schumann, and other composers while we were studying. I became more familiar with classical music at that time.

We were supposed to have our pathology exam either in June or in September. However, usually at the end of the fourth year, students usually would go on a class trip, so our professor of epidemiology, Professor Gaon, planned that for us as well. He obtained necessary funds and agreed to be our guide. We, the students, paid a nominal amount of one thousand dinars. My father was a bit sorry that I would not pass pathology in June; I agreed with Božana to go to on our trip and leave that exam for September. I was never sorry that I did that, because our trip with the ingenious Professor Gaon was unforgettable. I asked the classmates who organized our trip if I could take Nedžad with me and they said I could. I did not even have to pay any money for him. He was about to finish the first grade of his elementary school, and his teacher allowed him to leave classes a bit earlier because his grades were good.

Professor Gaon prepared an ambitious itinerary for us: Belgrade, Zagreb, Ljubljana, Rijeka, Split, and Dubrovnik. We stayed two or three days in each city and had a rich program. Every day the professor got up early and made phone calls to the locations of interest to us, such as public health institutions, pharmaceutical companies, universities, and many other sites unrelated to medicine. In Belgrade we visited what was then the most up-to-date library in the area, which used technology to control room temperature and humidity for optimum maintenance of books. We also visited the Physiology Institute. We went by bus to Avala Mountain to see the magnificent monument of Meštrović[26] there, and I could not imagine that the caryatids were so huge. Kalemegdan Park and the Military Museum were also very interesting to us. In Belgrade we

---

[26] Ivan Mestrovic, the famous Croatian sculptor.

stayed in a student dormitory, and the Belgrade students accepted us warmly. They were especially interested in my son, and female students loved to play with him.

In Zagreb we stayed in a hotel, but cockroaches disturbed us a little. We paid a visit to the Pliva[27] factory, which used interesting methods of drug production. We got a lot of vitamin C on that visit and later went to a very modern and clean city slaughterhouse. We took a boat on Maksimir Lake and in the evening went to the restaurants on Ilica Street. It was really very nice. My sister, who had already graduated from the university and worked as a young pharmacist in the Central Pharmacy on Republic Square, was married and living in Zagreb, so I visited her in her small apartment. My son enjoyed being at his aunt's home, where we spent one afternoon.

Traveling through Slovenia, I enjoyed the hilly landscape that was full of forests and reminded me of Bosnia, and I was impressed by the tidy and clean railroad stations and high transmission-line pylons, which were much higher and straighter than the ones used in Bosnia.

This was my second visit to Ljubljana; the first time I was there was when I was pregnant and enrolled Kasim in the university. Now I was there with my seven-year-old son. We stayed in an empty dormitory in two large rooms, one for men and the other for women, and slept on straw mats on the floor. I slept with my son, next to Božana, and I did not feel uncomfortable. Professor Gaon had obtained permission for us to visit the modern School Polyclinic and the Public Health Institute, which we had visited that day and which provided our spartan accommodations.

The next day we visited Bled Lake and Vindgar. We walked several hours next to a small river that led to Vindgar; I think it was one of the branches of the Sava River. We climbed up the narrow footpaths and crossed wooden bridges. When we reached the top, clouds and fog were everywhere. Our professor pointed to the Austrian border patrol on a plateau in front of us. When we returned to Ljubljana, we also visited the

---

[27] A famous Croatian pharmaceutical company.

wonderful Tivoli Park and the next day continued on with our trip. We stopped near Postojna Cave. When we sat in a small train and entered the cave, I thought we were in some supernatural world. We marveled at all the richness of the stalactite and stalagmite structures, and we were amazed at the acoustic effects of the cave as we listened to the echo of our voices. I was so impressed by this heavenly experience—like no other I had in Postojna or any other famous cave I later visited.

The next day we left neat and clean Slovenia and arrived in Rijeka, which brought to us a new panorama and the beautiful Adriatic Sea. A lot of masts of boats and small craft gave the impression of openness, as if the borders of our country did not exist. Our hosts from Rijeka were gentlemen, and they provided us accommodations in the modern Sušak Hotel, which was as tall as a skyscraper. The next day we visited some public health institutions as the Mediterranean sun invited us to go to the waterfront. Professor Gaon wanted us to visit the famous "Sea Gull" Ship in Rijeka Port, the ship on which President Tito traveled to India and later all over the world. We got permission, so a guide showed us from cabin to cabin and from floor to floor, and we admired the Sea Gull's enormity and equipment, which made it appear to be a castle floating on the water. When we passed through its kitchen, the sailors gave us some navy bread that was black and rather hard, but very tasty.

We sailed by ship at night from Rijeka to Split, so we could not see the wonderful sea and islands we passed by. Professor Gaon realized that we did not have enough time to lose a day, so he decided that we should really travel at night. We sailed all night, and the ship was swaying badly as we passed through a storm. I constantly changed my place, looking for a peaceful corner. I could not find one, but fortunately, my son was sleeping.

It was a wonderful and sunny day in Split, so after a visit to the Public Health Institute according to our formal plan, we spent most of our time in informal sightseeing in the city. We went to Dioclecian's[28] palace, climbed up Marjan Mountain, and swam in the sea. It was great to relax at the seaside, to be exposed to the sun, and even to swim—although the sea was cold. For the first time, I saw that one of my classmates had a lower-leg prosthesis, which I had not noticed before, because he walked with little impediment.

Our trip was coming to an end, and the last city we would visit was Dubrovnik. We again traveled at night by ship, but this time the sea was calm and our sailing was comfortable. We all slept on the luggage, which was scattered on the deck. Sometime after midnight, one of my classmates started to talk with a foreigner in English. I was curious, so I listened to their conversation, but I knew very little English, only what I had absorbed from a short course of several classes given by Professor Bugarski that I attended after the liberation. I admired the classmate for being able to enter into conversation in English.

We did not visit any medical institutions in Dubrovnik, probably because Professor Gaon thought we were so tired already and we had many other things to see anyway. We climbed up the famous city walls and saw the fantastic panorama of the city from that perspective. I would later go many times to Dubrovnik, but I never again climbed up the city walls as we did under the visionary leadership of Professor Gaon. We walked around Stradun Square, visited old churches, saw famous architecture and various monuments, and visited a pharmacy from the twelfth century.

On our last day, we went for a picnic to the neighboring town of Cavtat. We hired two motorboats and left. The sea was not calm, but our guides said we could go. A few hours of waves hitting and jumping over us seemed to last forever. Pale and voiceless, we were waiting for our boats to sink. Professor Gaon was so pale that the spots on his face became even more visible. I was scared for my son. How would I swim with him if we sank? When I told my fears to my classmate Mira Lukić, she replied calmly, "Do not be afraid. I will take your son, because I am strong and swim well, and what is crucial, I will

---

[28] A Roman emperor.

not be afraid since I am calm by my nature. You know I was a champion of Bosnia and Herzegovina in rifle shooting." I was totally relieved by this, and I have always remembered her wonderful words of support and how some people know to show they understand another person in distress.

We disembarked in Cavtat, dazed and determined to go back by bus, not by sea. However, we forgot the storm very quickly and refreshed ourselves in a restaurant. It was great to walk around Cavtat Peninsula, with its forested hills on one side and an ever-changing view of the sea on the other side. Professor Gaon organized a visit to the gallery of Vlaho Bukovac, our famous painter, and the mausoleum of the Račić family that was built by Meštrović. We had to climb a lot to reach the mausoleum, but when we arrived there we were surprised by its beauty and the whiteness of the stone with which it was built. We experienced its acoustic quality when a guard sang us a song. On our way back, nobody mentioned a bus, and so we returned by sea again. This time the sea was a bit calmer. We returned to Sarajevo by a night train; our trip, in a narrow-gauge train, seemed to last a very long time. Part of the reason was that they had to install some special gears while climbing up Ivan Mountain.

When we met again back at our university, we talked about the events from our trip for a long time, and for me it was a permanent, wonderful memory that I often used to speak about.

After the fourth year, students had one-month of obligatory training in some other hospital, city, or even in another republic. Accordingly, I was sent to the clinic for Dermatology and Venereal Diseases in Ljubljana together with three others. One of my new colleagues was Nadja Parčić, the student who so kindly lent me the money when we paid a visit to Belgrade students two years earlier. Two other colleagues were chosen to go to Ljubljana, to the Surgery Department. Božana was able to obtain the assignment at Srebrenica Sanitarium because she could earn some money there.

So I went to Ljubljana for the third time. The Dermatology Clinic was a new, modern building in the hospital complex, and its head, Professor Jakša, was a nice old professor who received us warmly. After explaining to us that we would be present at rounds and what to do in the outpatient area, he gave us his keys to the clinic and said, "The door is locked at nine o'clock, take these keys and you can come back later—just be quiet." I will remember that gesture forever, because it allowed us to go out and then come back later on to meet the chief nurse, Mojca, who showed us our accommodations. We were two in each room, and all was perfectly clean and white. Mojca recommended to us what to see in Ljubljana, and one evening she invited us to visit her in her apartment, because she lived alone. During rounds, the professor showed us patients with different allergic reactions, especially on their hands as results of contact with the primula flower, and he told us as a joke, "If you have an enemy, give him a primula." We also saw a large number of farmers with solar eczema and people with skin infections, which our professor thought were connected with the Ilirija public pool. Although the pool was cleaned regularly, and the people had to have a shower and to pass through disinfected water barefoot prior to entering a pool, the infections were still present because the pool was very crowded.

Something happened to me then that absorbed me for a whole year. Sometime before the end of our stay, our professor organized a dinner at the clinic for all students being trained in Ljubljana. Other than the six of us from Sarajevo, there were four students from Norway and one from Denmark, the ones who had their training in the Surgery Department. It was a gala dinner, and our professor made jokes with us, wanting us to have fun and make friends. He left after dinner and told us to stay and have fun with the music that played on a phonograph Mojca had brought to the gathering. I was sitting on the side and reading something, while the others were already dancing. A bit later, one of the Norwegian students came to ask me to dance with him. He had thick glasses on and golden hair. I got up and danced two or three dances with him, and then we all parted. The Norwegians suggested the next day that we all go to dance in Nebotičnik, the dancing bar located at the top of a skyscraper. We were sitting and talking a lot, I in German and Nadja and Vera in English. We had a good time there, especially because we could dance. So we went there the next two or three nights too. It was strange for me to see how empty the streets of Ljubljana were after nine o'clock, while in Sarajevo it was still very crowded at that time of night. On our last Sunday afternoon, the Norwegians took us in their old car, completely covered by funny sayings and jokes to swim in Zbiljsko Lake. The water in the dark-green lake, which was located in the middle of the forest, was so cold that I thought my muscles would completely stiffen. It was the coldest water I ever swam in at any time in my life.

We had two or three days more and then said goodbye to our Norwegian friends. Kjel, who was the Norwegian fellow who asked me to dance with him, looked at me through his glasses so seriously and was so attracted to me that he provoked my emotions, too. His foreign appearance became attractive to me. But all that occurred was a gentle hug after our walks. On the last day, we parted on a bench within the hospital complex. When I started to cry, he said, "Nicht schön, nicht schön," "It is not nice, it is not nice," and asked for my address. On the way back home through Bosnia, it seemed to me that the poles for the transmission lines were somewhat distorted and positioned from one another at unequal distances, and that the fences were damaged. I was seeing my sadness at leaving Kjel and Slovenia. When I arrived in Oglavak, my son welcomed me joyfully; he came down to the bus station, and I was so happy to have him meet me there.

Both Božana and I passed the pathology exam in September, so we had then finished our pre-clinical subjects. During our fifth year of medical school, we visited different clinics, interviewed the patients there, and felt almost like doctors. The professors and their assistants guided us well. Professor Lušicki made internal medicine very interesting to us by his wittiness and intuitiveness. He taught us to think medically—to think like doctors. Assistant Professor Mikeš taught us the internal propaedeutics[29] so well that I was always self-confident in that respect during my practical work. Assistant Professor Stojšić helped us understand infectious diseases so that we would be able to recognize them more easily. Professor Zec told us at his lecture about medical

---

[29] History and physical exam skills.

psychology, "Always remember that you are here to serve the patients and not vice versa." And so the fifth and even the sixth year passed, and I was always grateful to our professors for making medicine so attractive to us and easy to learn. I began to notice that I had changed while I learned—I became more tolerant and less vain. It was eventually time to part with my classmates. I have always missed the lively discussions we used to have about medicine as well as the witty remarks of my friend Mića Preradović, whose quips we laughed at a lot during our daily breaks.

When I returned home from Ljubljana, I got a letter from Kjel. It was written with deep emotion, saying that he would never forget the days we spent together and that he was very sorry that it lasted so short a time. It was written in perfect German, so I made my best effort to do the same when replying to him. Old Professor Marinković lived across from us. He was a bachelor and lived only with his two pigeons. My father used to tell me that he was a famous scholar who had studied biology in Vienna. I met and greeted him often, and he visited my father usually during Bayram.[30] He was shaky when he walked and had a very dark black mustache. I knocked at his door and asked him to correct the letter to Kjel I wrote in German. He gladly agreed to do it. Each month Kjel wrote me letters and I visited Professor Marinković who corrected my responses. My knowledge of German significantly improved because of his help, and during those visits I acquired much knowledge that enriched me forever. On the wall of the professor's study was a large picture of Buddha. The professor favored Buddhism and Hinduism and gave me the book *Sadhana – The Realization of Life*, written by Tagore, to read in German. Tagore's book about Hindu philosophy touched my heart so much and showed me so much about how to live that I often remembered and retold parts of it to friends and family. Tagore says, "A thirsty sheep will come herself to have water; no need to force her." I also mentioned in appropriate circumstances the wise words of Professor Marinković. When I asked him once why he remained a bachelor, he answered: "Remember, you were born alone, so you will die like that

---

30 The Islamic holiday.

too." He also said, "One should radiate oneself and transfer it to others, and should not require others to radiate at one." His philosophy was, "We should be self-sufficient, but among people and not isolated."

I had feelings toward Kjel for a whole year, supported by the letters he wrote me each month that I faithfully replied to. He sent me two or three photos of some moments we shared in Ljubljana, and I safeguarded them because they reminded me of him. I showed them to Nadja and Vera, who were in the photo too, but I did not give them one of the pictures. Kjel sent photos only to me, and I thought that the others who walked with them should get photos also. Only later I became aware of my egoism—why hadn't I offered a photo to each of them? And then, it was all over, because Kjel wrote me to tell me that he had a girlfriend now. I felt relieved, oddly enough.

In the sixth year of medical school, Božana and I stopped studying for our exams together because she spent a lot of time in Srebrenica Sanitarium and with Professor Ciglar in the Physical Therapy Institute. She wanted to specialize in orthopedics.

My son was a good student in his elementary school and also attended music school and played the violin, beginning in the third grade. He did not like it too much, but I wanted it, because I liked music a lot and was not educated in it, except for my singing in a school choir. Nedžad received lessons from a student whose classes were not expensive. He did not like to practice and often used to say, "When I finish with my music education, I will never take a violin in my hands again." Sometimes I took him to a concert when some famous musician was performing. We were present at the wonderful concert of the famous violinist Igor Ojstrah. I repeated the words Professor Lukač spoke when he had asked us at his lecture if we were at the concert the previous night and we replied, "No, because we had to study surgery." He said, "What makes Sarajevo different from Puračić Village is that you can sometimes be present at a good concert here. And what that means is that you have one more interest in life!" I often mentioned those words later.

I studied eye diseases with my classmate Vaska Janjić. She lived in a small house in Alifakovac that had a beautiful city view, especially at night and in the winter. Her parents were elderly people, and she was the youngest child. Her father usually sat next to the fireplace and added wood periodically, and her chubby and noble-faced mother would bring us potatoes fried in the oven and cheese, while we tried to discover how the eye worked and its various diseases. My life was influenced by Vaska on several occasions later in life, and she helped me to later choose my medical specialty.

As an exercise in public health, Professor Žarković organized us in groups of two and sent us to visit surrounding villages to record the public health status of the population. Vaska and I were assigned to the area of Treskavica Mountain, including the villages around Trnovo. Those visits and our conversations with villagers, especially women, were interesting, and Vaska sympathized with them and their problems. She was taking the blood pressure of many of them with a device she always carried. The roads through the forests and glades were magnificent. We would lie down on the soft grass and look at the sky in a perfect peace that only the birds disturbed. That was when I became acquainted with the real melody of the nightingale and the other songbirds that serenaded us.

When we returned from our work in the field, Professor Žarković analyzed our reports with us and made a plan for the delivery of public health services in villages. He made public health and preventive medicine interesting to us by his informal way of teaching, the discussions we had, and the time he spent with us, which did not include only lectures and exercises. He usually greeted students first and looked a lot like an American. He had spent some time in the United States and had introduced the American system of teaching at the university, such as one-semester courses. Older professors disagreed with the newer teaching methods. They thought knowledge should be gradually acquired prior to exams. I did not think there was a difference—it was important to get knowledge, regardless of how it was acquired. Professor Žarković introduced us to wastewater purification systems, such as the one they already had in Ljubljana. The concept of chemical and biological purification was completely new to us. From a public health standpoint, our professor supported construction of housing complexes that would not be endangered by natural or industrial pollution. We studied his book about preventive medicine, a major textbook in that field.

In my senior year, during a break between two exams, I read one of the best, or maybe the best, book I ever read in my life. My colleague Miga from Nikšić, Montenegro, lent it to me. It was *Jean Christophe* by Romain Rolland (the first four volumes). I will remember that great figure of a musician and composer in my mind always. I often recall his words when as a child he was unjustly punished by his father, the drunkard, and said, "I cried and cried until I cried all my tears out." The injustice was so painful for him. Those words reminded me of the days when it seemed to me as well that I cried out all my tears, in the period when my parents objected to my first love and when I was losing love in the first days of my marriage.

During medical school, most of my reading was about medicine, but I managed to read a few other books: the book by Tagore in German about Hinduism, recommended by Professor Marinković, and *Dr. Arrowsmith*, the book suggested by my professor of biology, Professor Urban. At his first lecture Professor Urban said, "The one who does not read *Dr. Arrowsmith*, by Sinclair Lewis, or *Microbe Hunters, Fighters against Death,* should not study medicine." I found *Dr. Arrowsmith* in the library and read it immediately in spite of its size. I was enthusiastic about the doctor, his loyalty to medicine, and his honesty in his work at discovering ways to fight against diseases. The modest Professor Gottlieb who showed him the way toward research also intrigued me and was very convincing. Many years later, when I read the original version of that book in English, I was pleased to find out that the translation I had read as a freshman in medical school had been completely faithful to the original and that nothing had been missed or left out.

In my senior year, I had to pass several small-scale exams as well as one extensive exam, for gynecology and obstetrics. I left that exam as my very last exam. My parents and I were happy and enthusiastic about the fact that I would soon become a doctor. But just then my parents were hit by a really shocking event. My youngest sister married a Croat from Croatian Zagorje.[31] He was a partisan soldier, even a national hero, some thirteen years older than she was. He was a wise and calm man who was a part-time student of law, a subject he needed in his political career. But it all was irrelevant for our parents, because my sister violated Muslim tradition by marrying a man of another religion. My father had friends married to German women they fell in love with during their studies in Vienna, or Serb or Croat women, and my father respected and liked them. However, women were not allowed to do the same thing. I was exposed to my mother's crying and my father's questioning about whether I had known anything about the marriage. When my sister married, they had asked me to pledge not to do something like that myself. That was the second time I made a pledge to them (the first time I pledged not to see Kasim any more) that I didn't know I could keep. I could not do anything else but make the pledge. So my sister had been secretly married. A few months later she gave birth to a son. My middle sister had a two-year-old daughter then, and my Nedžad had just turned ten.

The time came for me to take my last exam, gynecology. I studied with my colleague Marija Dimitrijević, who had it as her last exam, too. She was from Macedonia; her grandfather was a gynecologist in Skopje, and her grandmother was French, so they spoke French at home. Every day we met, mostly at my place, and studied gynecology and obstetrics. We spent two seven-day blocks in the clinic and were present at childbirths and women's surgeries. On a mannequin, Professor Hübscher was simulating the rotation of a baby at delivery precisely enough that we would be able to do it ourselves. The professor was noble as well, and he told us, "Always think that your sister or your mother is on the table." He was a German who lived in Yugoslavia and was a very charming man.

---

[31] The region behind Zagreb.

15 University Degree

I got the highest grade on my gynecology exam, and so I completed my medical studies. We did not have a final exam per se. When we parted, Marija Dimitrijević invited me to come to her place that evening to a modest celebration of our degrees. When I came home, my parents were waiting for me, and my father said, "You studied for yourself, really." Those words did not mean anything special to me, but later in my life I remembered them many times when I was with medical experts or with grateful patients. That evening my mother's close relatives from our neighborhood came to visit us, and after a short conversation with them, I went to the home of Marija, where we had a modest celebration.

After about four months, our class had a graduation ceremony. There were roughly twenty recent graduates, and Professor Štern was the rector of our graduation ceremony. Present at the ceremony were my father; my mother's cousin (the goldsmith), who lived and had his shop next to our house and who liked me and appreciated medicine; my cousin Muniba, my aunt's daughter with a house next to ours; and my friend Božana, of course. She did not get her degree yet, and was working part-time in Srebrenica Sanitarium. Professor Štern was a dignified person from Zagreb who spoke the

Croatian accent. He had taught us pharmacology, and his lectures were impressive because he spoke slowly and never longer than forty minutes. He always had a large glass full of coffee on his table and used to say, "A cup of coffee per day is a healthy dose for the heart." Speaking about nicotine, he said, "You can smoke as much as you want, but you must not ever say that smoking is not harmful." At our graduation ceremony, he said, "Remember, there is only one step between a doctor and a charlatan," reminding us of the medical oath we take. Later, my father used to mention it often; he liked that remark a lot. So my graduation ceremony was over—I have a photograph as a souvenir, with Professor Štern, my Božana, and my cousin Muniba, too.

Now that I had obtained my medical degree, I could begin immediately with the one-year obligatory internship, but I managed to convince my parents to let me take a two-week trip to Poland as an exchange student. My classmate Vaska Janjić had proposed it to be our reward for graduation. We did not have to take much money with us because our dinar was worth a good deal of money in Poland. We could travel there freely with our Yugoslav passport, so we went by train. It was my first trip to another country. On the way there, we spent several hours in Vienna. We were fascinated by the richness of its shops, and I bought a fountain pen in one of them. We did not have much time for sightseeing in the city, but what we saw was for me quite captivating. We traveled through Czechoslovakia and arrived in Krakow, where Polish students welcomed us. They considered Yugoslav people almost as Americans. We were impressed the most by their open-heartedness and knowledge of history, because they explained every important building to us and told us about their religious practices, such as making the sign of the cross when they passed a church. They were inclined to music, and one student even invited us to her place and played a piano concert for us there. They did not speak English, did not want to speak German due to their war memories, and did not want to speak Russian either. Almost all of them spoke French. I tried to remember as much as I could of my high school French, and I was able to communicate somehow. Our program included a few days on their Baltic seaside in Mjenzizdroe, near Szcecin. We traveled by train through the industrial parts of Poland, a border region that was in the past often seized by the Germans. City by city we saw the endless smoke coming out from factory chimneys. It was a relief for us to finally see the Baltic seaside and the waves on its sandy beaches. Every seventh wave was the biggest one, so the students told us. They said that "siudma fala" (seventh wave) meant something big or challenging, I believe. The sea was not blue as it was in the Adriatic and was colder, but it still looked like a wonderful and huge dark blue wavy surface with sandy and timbered shores. On the shore were large baskets turned sideways to protect the swimmers from wind after coming out of the water.

We stayed in a seaside resort, and our breakfast was very rich, with the obligatory rice pudding. In the evening we danced, and the Polish people danced rock and roll so well that neither of us could follow them. It was a style of dancing that was quite new to me. Dancing always stopped exactly at midnight, when we had to leave. My classmate Vaska sang well, especially Macedonian songs, and our hosts liked her singing a lot and kept asking her to sing more for them.

So we finished with our stay on the seaside, and we were supposed to travel to Warsaw and visit some famous places. Our train was passing through an endlessly flat ground, and it seemed to me we were heading to the North Pole, so I shivered a bit because I felt lost in space. I tried to look at Vaska and other students in our group to be aware of some real place.

Warsaw was a bright city and rather spacious, like any big European metropolis. Their students were proud to show us the fully restored Old City, which had been devastated in the war. For years they put brick by brick back where it had been and restored every single detail, so we were able to experience the original Old City. We also visited a stadium that could accommodate 100,000 spectators, the biggest I had seen until then. In the city center was a tall, newer building that the Russians had built. Our hosts disliked it, and said they found it destroyed the city harmony with its unsightliness.

After Warsaw, we went to the house of Chopin in the place Zelazowa Wola, and after that to Auschwitz, the infamous concentration camp ("Oswiecim" in Polish). The atmosphere was so depressing. Wooden beds, concrete halls, heaps of cut hair and other things, then the gas chambers, all in barbed wire—we could not wait to get out of that truly horrible place! We returned to Krakow again, from where we were supposed to begin our journey home. On our way, we visited a large cave made of stony salt, a very impressive one, named Vjelicka, but it did not surpass my fascinating experience at Postojna Cave.

I bought roller-skates and table tennis equipment for Nedžad and some things for my parents, and for myself I bought a blood pressure manometer and a big lunch service I used for many years. We obtained a lot of Polish zloty for our dinars, so we spent very little during our trip.

I was supposed to begin my internship on September 1. At first, I attended the regional outpatient clinic and got acquainted with the work of a general practitioner. Whenever I met Dr. Ranko Šurbat later, I told him, "You were the first doctor who showed me how to independently work with my patients."

During my training I had to stay in different departments for one, two, three, or four months, depending on how important it was for a general practitioner. In the internal medicine department, I was on call by myself on the days we did not receive new patients. At night, I ordered medications for patients with heart problems and participated in some other urgent situations. I became familiar with the look of patients suffering from congestive heart failure, their pale or dark-red cheeks, blue lips, tumid legs, shortness of breath, and what I was able to alleviate with appropriate medications. Gynecology with obstetrics was the most difficult for me because we had urgent situations constantly, either during deliveries or during surgical interventions. The crying of women in the delivery room was unbearable for me; I thought they were losing their strength by crying. At night, we often had the cases of bleeding due to abortions attempted with old-wive's methods. I vividly remembered one case where I thought that some people really should not have studied medicine. A doctor on call was yelling at the bleeding woman, insulting her with dirty words. If it was up to me, I would have removed him immediately from his position, but I was a young intern without any rights, so I could not do anything like that. Later I sometimes met that colleague at the doctors' meetings and I always had a feeling of loathing for him, although in the meetings he looked like a well-mannered person.

I spent one month of surgical internship in our Surgery Department and the other one in Dubrovnik, which was the idea of my colleague Fikica Mulaomerović, who did the same. We were allowed to carry out our training in any suitable hospital. Our Surgery Department was considered one of the best thanks to Professor Kovačević, who required strict order and discipline throughout. Smoking was forbidden, even in the hallways, and on every restroom door one could read, "Leave this room the same as you would like to find it." The operating rooms were perfectly clean and our surgeons were utterly responsible. Except for his normal working hours, the professor came every night to make rounds with the on-call team. The team would commonly play chess in the call room. The professor liked surgery a lot, and I often remembered his words when he lectured us about antisepsis and asepsis, "We should build a golden monument to Semelweis in his original size." Semelweis was a Hungarian physician who first discovered the association between non-hygienic conditions (students' presence at the delivery) and puerperal fever, and introduced the concept of antisepsis.

I spent my second month of surgical internship in Dubrovnik. Their Surgery Department was not large, and four surgeons were in the operating rooms every day, so my assistance was very helpful to them. The surgeries began at six o'clock in the morning and usually finished before noon, because it was very hot there. Below the hospital was a stony beach, and I went swimming there every day. One doctor, a lady from Zagreb, the anesthesiologist who was the guest of the hospital, also used to come there, so we were the only people on the whole beach. In the evenings I would walk in Stradun, the Old City, and go shopping. I attended the open-air theater performances at the Dubrovnik Summer Festival, Hamlet and Skup, on two occasions. So I had both my training and a bit of a vacation in Dubrovnik, but their Surgery Department was not like ours with regard to discipline. I was shocked to hear an orthopedic surgeon cursing in the operating room because his operation on an upper leg fracture did not go well. I never heard a surgeon cursing in Sarajevo.

    I also remember some other moments during my pediatric rotation. My colleague Boro Ćurčić, whose department I was assigned to, often invited me to go to the Labor Union Club (I do not know why he invited me there) where we read pediatric magazines in French. Boro spoke French well—he was very intelligent, an excellent connoisseur of pediatrics, and a very funny person, too. Every day we laughed at his jokes. I learned a lot from him, especially how to skillfully intervene with babies. Our friendship also had another dimension; it seemed to me he liked me in a romantic way, and I found him a man worthy of my emotions, too. However, Boro had to leave for a scholarship in England, and our relationship afterward was limited to only exchanging letters. He wrote me very nice letters that gave me a good sense of what life was like in London and in all of England. In the meantime, I started working as an independent physician in a small outpatient clinic at the city outskirts. It was good to work with patients, and I felt they liked me. After seven months, I was transferred to the Diagnostic Center within the City Polyclinic. The Center was experimental and patients changed constantly, so my colleague Vera Tadić and I were very busy there. We had to see a large number of patients, collect their laboratory tests and other findings, and establish the diagnoses. That year I also attended my first two English courses.

Sarajevo in 1938

Three sisters (I am in the middle)

Sixteen years old

Graduation ceremony - Taking physician's oath (I am the third from the right)

Part II

16 Surgery

One day I accidentally met my former classmate Vaska Janjić in front of a little park near the Public Health Institute. Because we had not seen each other for a long time, we wanted to talk a bit and so we sat on a bench in the park. The day was sunny, and it was good to recall the days we had spent together as students. Our lives crossed several times, as it happened: As medical students, we learned about eye diseases together, we did our preventive medicine rotation together, and we also traveled to Poland together. She was nice, and I always had a good time with her. But this time, I felt that destiny had arranged for our meeting. She told me that she had started working in the Surgery Department and was to spend an obligatory year in the anesthesiology division, just as I had to spend a year in the City Polyclinic. Those institutions paid our stipend during our internship, and we were now paying it back by our work. "Professor Kovačević," she said, "offered me a residency in pediatric surgery, but I do not want it. I am inclined to faint easily and cannot stand to work in the operating room." "Pediatric surgery?" I asked. "Is there such a specialty?" "Professor Kovačević," she said, "wants to open this new program that has already been introduced in Belgrade, based on the French model, because our babies were commonly dying during surgery." I had always wanted to specialize in pediatrics, but there were some conflicts between two women assistant professors at the Pediatric Department, so Professor Sarvan said angrily he would not accept another woman for the time being. "Maybe I could do pediatric surgery," I said, and she replied merrily, "Let us find Professor Kovačević and tell him you would like to do a pediatric surgery residency instead of me!"

We made an appointment for the next day with the professor's secretary, a woman who spoke several European languages. The professor received us in his large office, which was also a library, and we could see many books arranged in glass cabinets that stretched from the floor to the ceiling. Surrounded by those books, with the professor standing by the table, tall, slim, bowed a little, I felt somehow a bit intimidated. Vaska presented our request and plan, and I confirmed it. I said I could take over her obligation toward the Surgery Department and could work in the anesthesiology division. The professor lifted his head and said with his quiet, rather high voice to me, "Come in as soon as you complete your obligations toward the City Polyclinic and we will arrange for your residency. And you," he said to Vaska, "you stay, too." That was all he said. In two months, I was supposed to come to the Surgery Department, and Vaska would go on with her work in the anesthesiology division.

In two months, when I showed up in the administration office of the Surgery Department, all was settled and I was accepted. I often remembered that situation later, when our administration was becoming increasingly complicated and my young colleagues had to pass many obstacles to get into residency. In those days, only one man made decisions, and yet I found the doctors in the Surgery Department had indeed been very carefully selected.

In his last letter, my former colleague Boro wrote me that he would spend a few days in France on his way back to Yugoslavia. I was sorry that he would extend his stay, but it was even worse when he came back and did not call me for several days. My colleagues told me he bought a car in France and that a French girl came with him. I could not understand why he did not call me, and my feelings were hurt. After some time, he looked for me in the Surgery Department where I had just started working. When we met, he looked as handsome as before, but he was a stranger to me. He said he would explain everything, and it was not like it seemed to be, but his neglecting to call me hurt me so much that I could not forgive him.

The beginning of my surgical residency was good. The professor said, "We will start with anesthesia," and I worked beside an anesthesiologist. During medical school, I had always thought of surgery as a sacred temple, and now I was a member of that big family. In the pediatric surgery division, Assistant Professor Ivan Kafka, the head of the division, had become ill with hepatitis and had to undergo treatment for several months. He was replaced by other doctors who took turns, but they needed young doctors to assist at operations and work on the ward. So I was sent to the pediatric ward. Dr. Milica Lopandić, who came a year before me, also started her residency there. We worked in shifts every day, assisted in surgeries, and worked on the ward. We changed dressings, treated burns, made casts, gave infusions and transfusions, and typed the admission histories and discharge summaries. It was all very dynamic, and we were constantly busy with our patients. The children's ward was located in a hallway that was adapted to be a patients' room. The little beds were lined up in long lines on both sides. Two separate rooms were set aside for more severely ill patients. When a professor saw patients, he was followed by many doctors and, in addition to checking the surgical wounds, he often checked patients' histories and other documentation. Accordingly, we did our best to conduct everything properly. Professor Kovačević often talked to medical students who followed him during rounds. I remember his asking a student who was to have his surgery exam, "Colleague, when will you have your exam?" The student replied he did not have enough time to study, because he also had to work in the Surgery Department to support himself. The professor said, "If you organize your free time well, you will have time for everything." I often repeated that thought later to myself and convinced myself that it was really true.

I remember with nostalgia the beginning of my residency, when I met one of the best friends I would ever have, an unusual woman who I liked a lot. When I came to the pediatric surgery division, Dr. Lopandić introduced to me a young Finnish woman who was married to Branko Bjelogrlić, a young engineer. Her name was Pirkko Hukkanen, or Pirkko Bjelogrlić. She was a senior physical therapist whose work Professor Kovačević respected greatly, because rehabilitation of our surgical patients was very important and at that time we did not have trained physical therapists in our hospital. I immediately felt good in her company, so we often had our coffee breaks together. She spoke our language fluently, using genders and cases properly. Her pronunciation was softer and sounded very pleasant. She spoke German well and sometimes I took the opportunity to practice my German with her. She was slim, a bit above medium height, and her face was a combination of a Mongol with oblique eyes and facial bones, and Nordic, with light hair and blue eyes. Our friendship became more and more close, and we started meeting after work as well. Sometimes we cooked frankfurters in our ward kitchen and bought grapes, and then immediately after work went to Trebević, the mountain close to Sarajevo, by cable car and then on foot to the top. Another time we went to the lake at Željeznica River in Ilidža and swam there.

One day, together with her husband, we had an unforgettable picnic at Oglavak, where my parents were spending the summer. She inspected, with curiosity, the interior of the tekya and burial chamber—she liked their mysticism. My mother liked Pirkko a lot because she showed her exercises for her knees, even though she was pregnant at the time. My father noticed that she was extremely well mannered, and he asked me, "How could she come from Finland and marry a man from our rural environment?" He did not remember the unexplainable ways of love and how charming our people were.

We had so much fun that day that we were late for the bus back. It was a late summer night, and we were hitchhiking on the road waiting for a vehicle to pick us up. There were no private cars then, or only a few existed, so we were waiting a long time until a truck came. The driver took us in the open part of the truck and drove us to Sarajevo. The sky was full of stars, and the three of us were singing and singing on the truck. Pirkko was joyful and sang Finnish songs one after another that reminded me of some German songs from the war period. I sang with her, although I did not know the words. Later my father and mother spoke about her often and always with great warmth.

My father did not like it when I told him I would specialize in pediatric surgery. "Isn't it better for you to take internal medicine?" He asked. "But I would like to work with children, and I have that opportunity here," I said. At that time, surgery was not thought to be a part of medicine, and working with a knife was considered inappropriate for women. Professor Kovačević, however, wanted women for pediatric surgery, and I myself never thought that it was tough or that I could not do it. Many people said, "It is hard to see children suffering, how can you do that?" I did feel for a sick child—but in a way that made me want to help him as soon as possible and to return him to health rather than feeling just impotent empathy. I knew there were many painful procedures, and I always did my best to prevent a child's suffering.

MEMORIES FROM BOSNIA

From that initial period, I remember feeling antipathy toward a nurse who was, in my opinion, heartless with the children. I noticed with regret her rudeness with making dressing changes and giving injections and her behavior with children's bowel movements. I was a young doctor and she was a senior nurse, so I did not dare to reproach her. Later, when her own baby was born with a difficult congenital anomaly that could not be fully removed even after many operations, and when she suffered with her husband, who was an alcoholic, I almost felt those things were necessary for her so that she could change herself and become softer, which she did in fact become.

My work in the Pediatric Division got easier; I was able to follow all patients up until their discharge. I also assisted during less complex operations, while a senior resident had to be present at more complex ones. However, I often had to take part as the second assistant in operations on adults, which I found very uncomfortable and difficult. When the surgeon cut a section and the assistant clamped blood vessels, and when the red blood spots appeared on white compresses, I would immediately begin to feel very faint and need to be helped to sit down. The chief nurse Dulceta had to request another assistant at once, who quickly washed himself and continued with assisting. This happened twice, so one morning as we were washing our hands prior to an operation, Dulceta asked me, "Why do you wash yourself?" Dr. Lopandić answered her, "She is training to be a surgeon." "Yes, the same as I am," the nurse said angrily. "I do not have extra gowns to give to another doctor." At the next operation, I tried very hard not to feel faint, and it was Professor Kovačević who helped me mostly. Whenever the blood left my head and Professor Kovačević came and stood behind us to observe the operation, my mind immediately became clear and I went on with my assisting. Because I was afraid to collapse in front of Professor Kovačević, my blood pressure increased and I felt better. Later, when I got used to it and when it could not happen to me any more, I often remembered this situation.

A few months into my first year of residency, all of us were moved deeply by the passing of Professor Kovačević. He was just coming back from a trip to the Soviet Union when he fell into a coma in Zagreb. I was on call when we heard the news, and all of the employees were shocked, while the main surgeon on call had tears rolling down his cheeks. Assistant Professor Vlado Pšorn, who was the fastest driver among us, rushed by car to Zagreb. He sent us the news every day, but unfortunately the professor died very soon thereafter.

His autopsy showed he had severe cirrhosis of the liver. When his casket came, it was on a display in our amphitheater, and there was nobody who did not cry and join the circle of mourners around it. My Finnish friend Pirkko, all in black, cried a lot, because she respected our Professor Kovačević very much, and he had possessed an extensive understanding of her work. I was also very sad because that noble man died, and somewhere deep inside me I felt fear for the future of the good work Professor Kovačević had been doing. I realized later that my fear was justified, for the Surgery Department, despite its innovations, was never the same as it was during his leadership. Many highly esteemed surgeons were present at his funeral, including some from France, and he was also honored by the university with great respect. The streets from our hospital to the university were crowded with people wishing to pay him their last respects.

After Professor Kovačević's funeral, we went back to work. At first, it looked like it was the same as before. The professor of war surgery, Professor Lukač, became our new head. He was a highly educated man and a good judge of surgery, but he did not have the authority of Professor Kovačević. He could not control the heads of individual divisions, and they became increasingly independent. Professor Kovačevic had managed to control them all, although he encouraged independent subspecialization and sent division heads to the best European centers of education. The orthopedists and trauma surgeons went to Bergen, Norway, the plastic surgeon to London and Edinburgh, the pediatric surgeon to London, the thoracic surgeon to Slovenia, the urologist to Paris and Lyon, and the anesthesiologist to Slovenia. Their independence later often impeded the coordination of the divisions, because they all still belonged to the joint Department of Surgery.

I felt good and had no special worries in that year, 1960. Professor Lukač liked me and praised my work in writing the patient histories, because I highlighted the significant cause of a child's admission to the hospital. Pirkko was a model for me in her method of applying dressings to incisions, and I liked her personal sense of style as well. She wore good-looking clothes—tights and mostly black cardigan sweaters—so I began to wear similar things myself. We went together to the local leatherworking shop to order a big multipurpose bag like she carried. She was an unselfish person and allowed me to do many things the same as she did. During that year we also experienced a rare natural phenomenon together—a complete eclipse of the sun. I had never experienced something so unusual before, nor have I since then. We were in the hospital, waiting to watch the beginning of the phenomenon. We stood next to each other as it was getting darker and darker, as if dusk were coming very quickly. We could not look at the sun, because we did not have the special glasses that would protect our eyes. After a very short time, there was something like a very fast dawn. I felt a bit afraid because the whole experience was very unusual. That year we also witnessed together another natural phenomenon—the earthquake. I had just begun a thoracic surgery rotation. We were in the radiology suite and Assistant Professor Tvrtković was showing us the lungs of the patient who was behind the screen. The x-ray equipment suddenly shook and the walls around us started to crumble around us. I thought the x-ray machine exploded, but fortunately it did not. The shaking and destruction lasted a very short time, and we knew it was an earthquake. Several times later we had less intense earthquakes in Sarajevo connected with more severe ones that occurred in Dalmatia, Montenegro, and Banja Luka. I do not know exactly to which earthquake this one was connected, but it was less intense than the other that occurred that day.

That spring, Assistant Professor Kafka, our division chief, returned from sick leave. I knew him when he had been a resident and taught us various types of surgical bandaging techniques and their Latin names during our surgical rotation at medical school. He spoke the Ekavian dialect and was from Vojvodina.[32] The pediatric division was expanded by the addition of two big rooms that had belonged to the former orthopedic trauma division, which had moved to another building. The new beds were set up in two rows and had red bows tied to the temperature flowsheets. It was all very tidy and neat. Although we now had more beds, they were all full. I had to be pulled back from my external rotations because Dr. Lopandić had received a scholarship in Paris. So I began my work with Assistant Professor Kafka—work that lasted until his death, over 25 years later. Kafka was a calm man with a good nature who smoked a pipe. At that time, after Professor Kovačević died, smoking was allowed in the doctors' personal rooms. He had started to smoke a pipe during his one-year fellowship in England. Professor Kovačević sent him to London to learn new techniques because he was the most subtle and skilled of all the surgeons, as people in the Surgery Department used to say. He was

---

[32] A part of Yugoslavia bordering on Hungary.

very educated and spoke German and English fluently as well as his native Slovakian. His father was Slovak.

After working in the Surgery Department for several months and endless assisting, I was allowed to perform my first operation with the assistance of a specialist. It was the easiest operation in the field of pediatric surgery, a hydrocela repair in the groin. A hernia operation on a child was frequent and more delicate, but the hydrocela operation was much simpler. It was customary to prepare a meal for the doctors whom I worked with at my first operation, so my mother cooked something special for me that I brought to work and they were all pleased. However, in the middle of our relaxed time together, someone called for Assistant Professor Protić, who was the oldest doctor, to come to the operating room for an urgent operation. Getting up, he said, "This is the life of a surgeon, you never know when they will call you." I remembered those words many times later—they were truthful, but that was part of the charm of the work of surgery.

In my first two years of working with Assistant Professor Kafka, I worked hard to learn his surgical technique. I carefully took note of his skill and his often original approach during operations. I also studied his tender touching of tissues, despite his rather thick fingers. I did not know how he managed to do it. And he did not know how to explain it to us. He used to say, "It is all written down in books." To me, that was not the mark of a good teacher. So I had to discover how to emulate his skills on my own. On one occasion later, the chief nurse Dulceta, the one who did not believe I would specialize in surgery because I was fainting easily, said to me, "You have done Professor Kafka's technique better than the others."

My work in pediatric surgery included treating children with burns, and that part of my work was the hardest for me. We often admitted children from Bosnian villages who had burned themselves on outdoor fires. We treated the burns with special dressings, and it was difficult to see the children crying in front of the operating room, anticipating the dressing change. Sometimes we did it with partial anesthesia, in cases of very extensive burns, but often we changed the dressing without any anesthesia at all. Although we carried it out gently, and avoided touching burned areas, the children were still often shaking with fear. After the dressing change, some noble nurse would usually give them something they liked, a chocolate or a drink of juice. We patched their wounds up by putting the skin grafts we took from their arms and legs or from other healthy parts of their bodies. Children went home with visible transplantation scars—but still cured. While placing the skin grafts, I often remembered an old saying of my grandmother, "Patching and suffering hold the world together," and sometimes I used to say that jokingly. Luckily, our treatment of burns became more modern later, and we were able to leave them open under the special protectors, which allowed nothing to be in contact with the wound itself. Anti-infection agents became more efficient, too, so it was much easier for the children in later years.

That summer, my middle sister and her daughter Dina, my mother, and I and my son Nedžad spent fifteen days vacationing on the island of Hvar in the Adriatic Sea. We had a good time, especially because we were all together; my father came later as well. He did not swim—I do not remember whether he ever swam in the river in Oglavak, either. When he took off his clothes, the whiteness of his body was almost blinding. I had a fashionable bikini on, and I was walking around thinking I looked good in it. Only later was I aware that I probably should not have worn it in front of my father, because he was conservative and it may have been shocking for him. But he did not say anything.

17 Chief Editor of *Oslobođenje*

In the second year of my residency, I rotated into abdominal surgery. Sometime before New Year's, we admitted a VIP patient. Professor Protić, the head of the division, walked almost on tiptoe around this man. He told us in a quiet voice, "We have Milorad Gajić, the chief editor of *Oslobođenje*,[33] here." I was ordered to take his admission history. I entered a small room where a middle-aged man was sitting. His smiling face was beaming with joy when we introduced ourselves. He said he came to have a hernia repair, and I carried out a complete medical examination. He covered himself with his hand while I examined the groin. After the examination, he showed me a French magazine he had with him. A bit later, Professor Protić said he would like to discharge him and arrange for him to be operated on after New Year's, because it was not an urgent operation and he didn't need to stay in the hospital during the holiday. At that time, our patients stayed in the hospital for several days after a hernia repair.

I was at Pirkko's place for New Year's. She invited me and Stana Lovšin, the opera singer who lived in the same house with her. We had fun—Pirkko, her husband Branko, Stana, and I—in their small apartment, which Pirkko made comfortable and functional. We all danced and Stana sang some opera songs for us. She was a wonderful

---

[33] The leading daily newspaper in Bosnia and Herzegovina.

lyric soprano and was a famous star at the time, but her career did not last very long—I do not know why. Pirkko prepared a very tasty meal for that night, and I especially liked the vermouth cocktail she served whenever I visited her. It was one of the best New Year's celebrations I had ever had—previous celebrations, including once at the Czech Club with Božana and another time in the Europe Hotel with my cousin and her husband were not as enjoyable, maybe because I liked Pirkko so much. And Pirkko was about to spend several months in Finland—she was pregnant and expecting a child—so that probably affected me as well.

After the New Year's celebration, the VIP patient with the hernia was readmitted to the hospital, and Professor Protić performed the surgery the same day. The surgery went well, and he was soon discharged. After about two weeks, Professor Protić invited me to come to his office. The VIP patient was sitting there, and I thought he came for a follow-up examination. The professor turned to me and said, "Mr. Gajić is inviting us to come to his club in at the *Oslobođenje* one evening." The patient looked very neat, and his face was beaming with joy when he invited me. I thought he wanted to show his gratitude and offer us something, as our patients usually did, to thank us in some way for our help. So one evening I pushed my way among the people who walked along Marshall Tito Street, our main street, to enter the *Oslobođenje* building. I looked for his office, and a young secretary showed me into his room. The room was large and nicely furnished, with various photos on the walls and a large map above the table. He stood up and greeted me cordially, and I asked him where the others were. He replied that they were not able to come for some reason. I felt uncomfortable, but I continued with a normal conversation with him. His secretary brought me a large glass of a tasty juice, and I spent about half an hour there. He told me very interesting stories about the life of a journalist and about his trips, and then he showed me something on the map. When I stood by the map, he came closer to me—in an attempt, I suppose, to charm me—which made me a bit angry. I soon said rather coldly that I had to go, and I went down to the street and mixed with people who were walking there. It was then that I realized that he had wanted to relate to me as a woman. I told myself, "He will not get me!"

The ways of love are full of secrets and you get involved in spite of all your rational thinking. After about ten days, and after I had become fully aware of my anger at having been lured there under false pretenses (I had concluded that the whole thing was staged and that the others never intended to meet me there), I received a telephone call. On the other end of the phone I heard the voice of the editor of *Oslobođenje* inviting me to the cinema to see the very interesting comedy "Joint Apartment," which starred our famous actor, Čkalja. I was surprised. I knew he was married and I could not understand that he wanted to be seen with me in public. Maybe he could do it no other way, because if he had tried to suggest a secret meeting, I would have not have agreed to go. I did not have an opinion about his marriage; it was his private life, but going out in public was not something private. For some reason, I agreed to go and asked no questions. I enjoyed the cinema very much. It was a great comedy, and we laughed a lot. At the end, while it was still dark, he touched me with his warm hand and I relaxed a bit.

That touching of my hand when I was in a good mood, while watching a great comedy, overwhelmed me, and my feelings were awakened. After the cinema, we walked on the riverbank in an idyllic winter atmosphere—everything was covered with snow. We agreed to have another date. And so it started. In few days, he traveled to Germany to procure new up-to-date rotation press equipment for *Oslobođenje*. I was receiving his wonderful letters, and he asked me if I would come to Belgrade, where we would spend two days together on his way back. I made my decision and went. We got acquainted better then. He said that his interests were different than his wife's, that he liked the sea and she did not, and that they never went on vacation together. He also said that she was a good woman, an intellectual, and that she was bringing up their son, who had just enrolled in his first year at the university, perfectly. After that night in the cinema when something in me had responded to him, I was happy when he beamed with joy when we were together, and I became more and more attracted to him—in spite of his sometimes rather unattractive figure, his balding on the back of his head, and the fact that he was thirteen years older than I was. I had somebody to love me now, and I had always thought that a man and a woman make one entity.

As our relationship progressed, it became clear that we would marry. One day when he came to our date he told me, "I decided to divorce, and I moved out and live now in the apartment of my colleague who is in London." I started to cry, "What will I do with my father?" I said. He repeated, "I left and there is no way back." The bazaar in front of which we had our conversation was wildly circling around me, making me dizzy, and for the first time I became aware of

155

the difficult moments to come for my parents and for me, too. Milorad was a Serb. With Kasim, I had jumped into love like an ostrich plunging his head into the sand—without thinking of the consequences. Now I was older and wiser, but I still allowed my heart instead of my head to lead me.

That summer we got to know each other better; we visited the western part of Yugoslavia in his car—Bihać, Plitvice, Zagreb—and then Slovenia, and the maritime coast to Zadar. Then we returned to Sarajevo, through Jajce. What can I say about that trip? It was my first trip with somebody I was in love with and who loved me. Plitvice National Park in Croatia was really fantastic, and later, whenever I enjoyed nature somewhere, I was always reminded of our time in Plitvice. The beautiful green color of the trees and the shadows of the surrounding forest reflected a perfect peace as we glided on the lake in our boat, a sharp contrast to the terrible noise of the cascading waterfalls that fell into the calm Korana River. We later visited Postojna Cave in Slovenia— just as magnificent to me as it was on my first visit there—and our subsequent city-to-city trip was interesting too. In Kopar, we encountered the Festival of Yugoslav Dances, so we joined the audience. They performed the national folk dances from Triglav[34] to Vardar,[35] and we enjoyed their uniqueness and the pastoral folk costumes. After Kopar, we continued along the Adriatic coast to Zadar,[36] where we took the inland route toward Bosnia.

I felt very happy, but there was something that broke through those good feelings and annoyed me. Milorad had a small tent that we set up wherever we stopped. It was poorly equipped, and we slept on some old blankets. He also had a small gas stove, so I was usually crouching and waiting for soup or vegetables to boil. Somebody might like that sort of thing and think of it as an adventure, but for me it was uncomfortable and ruined the picture of a good vacation. It was a relief when we sometimes went to a restaurant and ordered zubatac,[37] or when we stayed in a hotel. There was one funny situation in which we slept in the car. We had traveled until late at night and stopped on the road near Pula, on the Istra peninsula. We parked the car and decided to stay there overnight. Traveling through Slovenia, we had seen large signs saying "auto-moto races" were being held then at a local track.

---

[34] At the top of the Slovenian Alps.

[35] A river in Macedonia.

[36] A medieval city on the Adriatic coast.

[37] Tasty high-quality white fish from the Adriatic Sea.

That night we slept in the car, and cars rumbled by us the entire night. Just before daybreak, I saw he was awake, also. Neither of us had really been able to sleep well, and we both laughed when he said, "We seem to have gone to the races after all!"

Milorad liked the sea a great deal, especially the islands. We spent one day on the little island of St. Catherine, in Rovinj, in the pine forest whose scent permeated the whole island. We continued to travel on the road, taking short breaks in Pula and Opatija, and we stayed ten days in Zadar. In the evenings we went to restaurants and had zubatac, and one evening we attended a concert held in an interesting medieval building called Donat that had wonderful acoustics. The best time of all was our swimming at the islands, Ugljan and Pašman, where we went every day by a local boat. We liked their pebbled beaches, and the sun seemed to be more intense there than on the coast. We enjoyed being alone—there were hardly any tourists, just a group of Austrians who had spent their summer vacations with the same local people for twenty years. We thought it was clever; they had a summer house on the coast without having to take care of it. One of the locals asked Milorad one day, "Is she your daughter?" We laughed, and Milorad said I was his wife. Suntanned and refreshed by the seawater, I looked younger than I was.

We returned through Jajce,[38] where we stayed two days. We were in a hotel, and it was interesting to see the sights in that medieval city. We spent a long time in the Museum of the Anti-Fascist Council for the National Liberation of Yugoslavia, where we saw the documents that created our new state. The most enjoyable places were the numerous water mills on the Pliva River; I already knew about those famous waterfalls from photos. Who knows how old the water mills are that have stood there witnessing the march of history? On our way back home, I was a bit afraid of telling my parents about my intent to marry—I didn't know how to go about dealing with their likely response.

The time immediately after we returned was both good and difficult for me. Milorad loved me, I knew that, and I was happy to have somebody after such a long time of being alone. He mentioned our wedding and wanted to meet my son, who was then almost fifteen. When I said I was unable to leave him with my parents, because they

---

[38] An old town in the middle of Bosnia where in 1943 the representatives of the anti-Nazi resistance movement laid ground for the constitution of the Federal Republic of Yugoslavia.

would surely judge me, and I would not like making Nedžad sad, he said, "I would like him to be with us in any case—the best for him is to be with his mother." That seemed to me quite noble. He told me to bring my son to a picnic with us. Nedžad had just returned from the school resort in Zelenika, where he spent his summer vacation with his school friends every year.

We had a good time at the picnic in the vicinity of Olovo.[39] Nedžad inflated the rubber mattresses for us. Milorad told us about the war and about partisan life, and when we came back home, Nedzad said, "He is really a nice man."

When we got married several weeks later, I was half delirious and only half aware of what I was doing. I hadn't talked to my parents. My maid of honor was Božana. She was always helping me in critical situations in my life—she was my divorce witness and she was with me now again, although she was ill with a fever. Milorad's best man was Branko, Pirkko's husband. Pirkko had just come back from Finland with her little girl Nina. She was happy about my wedding, and she liked Milorad too, but she had told me her opinion—that it was not right for him to leave his wife. Of course, after he fell in love with me, I did not think about that anymore. It was a quiet wedding ceremony, and in the evening we went to a restaurant for a dinner with our marriage witnesses and Pirkko. That afternoon we had picked up Nedžad from school—he just started the first year of senior high school—and we went to a lodge in Stojčevac.[40] Milorad was going to live there with us until the new apartment complex in Koševo,[41] where he was promised an apartment, was built. We stayed in Stojčevac for three months. We had a place to live, so we did not have many worries at the beginning. Every morning a car came to take Milorad to *Oslobođenje*, so all three of us left, the two of us to work and Nedžad to school. We often saw a deer in the morning that came down from Igman Mountain. Milorad had his own car, but was afraid to drive in the winter, because the Stojčevac-Ilidža Road was often icy. When Nedžad had an afternoon class at school, he had to walk to Ilidža and then take a tram and did the same on his way back home.

---

[39] A small town near Sarajevo.
[40] A resort at the head of the Bosna River, near Sarajevo.
[41] The part of Sarajevo where the hospital and sports stadium are located.

In the meantime, my parents were having a hard time. They were visiting my middle sister in Switzerland when Nedžad and I took only the most necessary things—clothes, books, and radio—and moved to Stojčevac. On the night before my wedding, my son and I slept in the same bed, both crying, because we knew our life was about to change. But he followed me without any word, although he had to leave his grandparents and friends who lived on the same street. He trusted me. A year earlier my middle sister had gone to Switzerland with her five-year-old daughter and found a job there as a pharmacist. That was during the period when our borders became more open and many people were going abroad in a search of better jobs. I called her and said I would marry so that she could tell our parents when they visited and try to influence them to accept it as a good thing, but she kept it a secret because she did not wish to expose herself as having conspired with me or to ruin their stay with her. So my parents learned about it when they came back, from my aunt who lived by our house.

In Stojčevac we were often visited by Vilko Vinterhalter, a good friend of Milorad's whom he respected, and Osman Karabegović. Osman was friendly with us and liked me, and I liked him because he supported our relationship. Nijaz Dizdarević and Ilija Materić were also living there temporarily with their families. Sometimes Milorad used to play chess with Vilko and had interesting conversations with Osman. They were all from Krajina[42] and knew each other since their high school days in Banja Luka. But whatever was the view of most people about those men (who I learned were then high officials), they were simple and honest people, without strong national and religious affiliations or a severe liberal ideology. They just wanted progress for our people.

There was no special reaction to my marriage at the hospital. They congratulated me, and some people who liked me showed their joy that I was not alone anymore. Kafka congratulated me simply. However, I felt somehow different, often mentioning "my husband"—I wanted to boast.

I continued with my residency, and I also studied a lot, because I did not have to cook and clean in Stojčevac. Nedžad went to school regularly; he was good and sometimes played chess with the staff. He often walked to the tram station in Ilidža and returned the same way,

---

[42] Border region between Bosnia and Croatia.

and since that was a rather long trip of almost three miles, Milorad would take him by car when he was free.

I met Milorad's parents at his sister Beba's home. She lived in Sarajevo. They were old; his father was tall, rather thin, and diabetic, and his mother was a short, calm, good-natured person. They were very kind to me, although Milorad's divorce occurred at a bad moment, when they came to stay with him. His father had owned real estate, a house and a shop in Klasnice, near Banja Luka, from which they, as Serbs, had to flee from Croatian extremists during World War II, and they went to Belgrade. Milorad's brother, a doctor, lived in Belgrade. After the war, his father wanted to return to Klaš, but his mother rejected the idea because she was afraid to go back. So they stayed in Belgrade and lived with their son in a rather large apartment, and the grandmother helped with the upbringing of their three sons. Just then, they had some misunderstandings with their son and decided to stay with Milorad for a while, whose apartment was also large. Then they stayed with Milorad's sister for a few months and from there went to the other sister's place in Lajkovac, near Belgrade. All these issues burdened Milorad subconsciously. "Love makes the world go around," he used to say. "I would have died if I had not married you." One day, when Nedžad was waiting for him to take him to the tram station by car, he reacted angrily and said, "Get in the car!" which was annoying to me. I later understood how his response had come from his suffering—because of the difficulties with his parents and the pain from the situation with his son, who was then attending the first year of his studies and did not want to have any contact with his father after his parents' divorce.

Each year we attended a "Journalist's Ball." I was the center of attention because I was the wife of the newspaper's chief editor. One of the photographers took a photo of me shaking hands with Đuro Pucar, who was the president of Bosnia and Herzegovina. The president then bowed politely toward me. I had conversations with many high-ranking government officials; Milorad respected some of them a lot, and they were interested in surgery, especially pediatric, and listened to me respectfully. Since they were progressive people, they were enthusiastic about a woman being a surgeon. Milorad liked it too, and he told me he fell in love mostly with how I looked with my hair tied back, and because he admired me as a woman surgeon.

Marshall Tito visited Sarajevo that winter. Milorad was one of the invitees to a dinner, so I had an opportunity to meet Tito myself. Although we were sitting a bit far from Tito, I did notice the moment when Nada Mamula[43] asked minister Ranković,[44] who had an attractive figure, to dance with her. Due to her special voice and good interpretation of folk songs, she was invited to many important gatherings.

At the beginning of February we moved into our just-finished apartment house in Koševo, on the opposite side of the stadium. We had a two-bedroom apartment that was not very spacious. There was a long roofed balcony in front of the entire façade. That building was the first one completed in the whole settlement, so we were walking on clay, sand, and boards, and two or three times our car had a flat tire from a nail on the street. We did not have central heating in our apartment yet, and so we had to use electric heaters. They were insufficient, so we were rather cold. We still had a lot of work to complete, so an upholsterer and an electrician were constantly present. A young assistant upholsterer named Otto took away our blinds, which did not function properly, and came back soon with them repaired. When we showed him something malfunctioning, he said, "I will fix it in a minute." Later we learned somehow that he simply replaced the blinds from the neighboring apartment, because we were the first who moved in. "In a minute, as Otto said," became a slogan I have used ever since whenever I wanted to say I would do something soon.

One day I was coming back home from the hospital and two men passed by me. I heard one of them saying, "Look, he is the chief editor of *Oslobođenje*, and he has his laundry on the front balcony drying." We did not know where to dry our laundry, so we put it on our balcony, and that time I realized it should not be visible on the entire facade of the building.

---

[43] A famous popular singer.
[44] The hard-line interior minister of Yugoslavia.

18 Changes

That spring brought us changes. Milorad had long meetings at work every day and would come home very tired. He was the editor-in-chief of *Oslobođenje* for twelve years. He had many friends, but some people didn't like him, and some even judged him negatively due to our marriage and our use of the official car while we lived in Stojčevac. I did not know about his relations with his colleagues; I knew he was a capable, hardworking, intellectual journalist. However, he was the boss at work, and he thought it would always be like that. But things changed, and some other people came to work there, some of whom didn't like him. So one evening he came home, lay down on the bed, and said, "They removed me from my office." I asked him, "Could you still be a journalist?" And he replied, "Of course." "Then it is not important," I said and gave him a hug.

That summer we decided to travel around the eastern part of Yugoslavia, because we had visited its western part the previous year. We again had an interesting road trip, and some of the pictures we took will remain in my memory forever. I had just got pregnant, but it did not disturb me. Milorad wanted to have a baby, but I did not dare, because I was still in my residency. I said, "We both have our sons and I should not have a baby during my residency." But he insisted, "You have a son, I do not," that was his reply, for his son was angry with him.

I was looking forward to that trip, because I did not know the eastern part of our country at all. Nedžad planned to go to the seaside with his friend who he shared a desk with and who was an excellent student, so I did not have to worry about him.

Belgrade was our first stop. Milorad knew Belgrade well, and I visited it during my student trip, so this time we went to Novi Sad, and Fruška Gora, the mountain, where we stayed one night. In Novi Sad we saw interesting fishermen's huts and small houses lined up on the banks of the Danube. For dinner we had a local favorite, fish-paprikas, but it was too spicy for me. In Belgrade we paid a visit to Milorad's brother, who was a physician interested in microbiology. He was kind to me, although he surely disapproved of Milorad's divorce. He had a long conversation with me, and I think he enjoyed it, perhaps because we both were doctors. His wife was beautiful; Milorad told me she was a real beauty when they married. She worked in a bank. She was a daughter of a general from the Old Yugoslav Army, and she had spent her childhood in Ljubljana.

From Belgrade, our trip continued to the inland part of Serbia. I remember a gentle, rolling country with many farms and forests. We visited Oplenac,[45] the Karađorđević's mausoleum, and it seemed to me there was too much gold in it. Many years later, I had the same experience in the Royal Museum in London; it looked like all the world's gold was there. We continued south to Niš and then Macedonia. Ćele-kula, an Ottoman tower built with human skulls embedded in its walls, was indeed real, and not just a historical imagining as I had previously thought. People often did bizarre things to show power and spread fear.

The next city was Skopje. I liked its location on the Vardar River, and I found it somehow familiar—it reminded me of Sarajevo. For the first time, I had Greek baklava there, which was delicious. We continued toward Ohrid, on Ohrid Lake. We traveled a long way over the Macedonian plateaus, bare and hot, and in vain we were expecting to find some water. We passed the town of Prilep, where we did not take any break and finally arrived in Ohrid. It was an interesting old city. Many houses had oriels,[46] like the houses in the old part of Sarajevo. Their lifestyle reminded me of the old-time living in

---

[45] The court of Serbian kings of the Karadjordjevic dynasty.
[46] Bay windows, common in oriental architecture.

Sarajevo. We spent three days there because of wonderful Ohrid Lake. Its blue color and endless surface gave me an impression of the Adriatic Sea, so I felt like I was on the seaside. I knew the Bled, Plitvice, and Pliva lakes and their green color, but Ohrid Lake was completely different. We took a small boat to St. Naum, but the small church was being restored so we could not see it.

After Ohrid, our adventure continued. Through Tetovo and the monastery of St. Jovan Bigorski, near the road connecting the towns of Debar and Gostivar, which had an interesting carving, we went toward Rugovo Cliff and Čakor Mountain. The road was leading us partly along the Drim River, I do not know which one, maybe it was the White Drim, and then it climbed up to the crags on the border with Albania. When we entered Rugovo Cliff, with a road built between huge rocks, it was terrifying, and we would have preferred to go back, but we continued, maybe for the thrill of it. I was afraid—especially because we were alone on that road. After a long ride, we started to climb up the narrow serpentine macadam road. The only car we met, which was barely able to pass us on the narrow road, was a convertible with its top down. The car had French plates, and two young girls in their swimming suits stood on the seats. After a long ride on the serpentine road, we suddenly came to a plateau and saw a panorama that I had never seen before. It was an endless grassy plateau interrupted by coniferous groves, crisp and bright green in the sunlight. We saw a drinking fountain by the road and a small house nearby, which may have been a border guard house. After Čakor Mountain, we did not see any green surface until we returned to Bosnia. Everything else was brown. Later, when I wanted to relax, I often imagined that green color of Čakor Mountain. Our trip back included climbing up and down the cliffs of Kosovo and Montenegro by a narrow serpentine road, and throughout that segment of the road I was afraid that we would roll right back down the road. We stopped in Prizren, spent the night in Dečani, and visited the famous Dečani Monastery. It was interesting to see many women entering the church dressed in the Albanian national costumes, in the female shalwars. I am not sure if they were Muslims, but I thought that Serb and Montenegro women did not have such costumes. Maybe they were the Orthodox Albanian women, although I thought that Albanians were mostly of Muslims and Catholic religion. We continued up and down the serpentine roads and arrived in Titograd, the largest city in Montenegro. We did not stay long there because it was very hot, but we spent one afternoon in the historical place of Cetinje and we visited the Court of Montenegro's

King Nikola and his Billiards.[47] Then we had a ride down a very steep road to Kotor, and we were impressed by the wonderful panorama of the fiord and the open sea. We wanted to see the Montenegro coast all the way down to Ulcinj,[48] where we spent most of our vacation. On our way to Ulcinj, we stopped to swim on the Miločer's red pebbled beach in front of the former royal residence. I thought about how great it was for the royal family to spend their time in the perfect peace of that place, among cypresses and pines on one side and endless sea on the other side, without any island disturbing the panorama until the coupling of the sky and the sea in the distance.

The small island of St. Stefan was a unique place. This perfectly clean city-island looked as if it wanted to separate from the bridge that connected it to the mainland and just sail away on its own. In a short time, we saw it all and continued on. It was night already, and we traveled in a rather deserted area. We saw on our way some Albanian houses with no windows toward the street but only toward the backyard, probably with the goal having been for their women to be better hidden from view.

Ulcinj was a tourist place with hotels on its coast and an old city from the Ottoman period that looked down on the shore. Especially attractive was a small burial chamber, where the two saintly men were said to be buried. We spent the rest of our holiday in Ulcinj, swimming at the endless sand beaches. One day we drove to the mouth of the Bojana River, on the Albanian border, which had some unusually beautiful beaches, but we did not stay there because they were nudist beaches. We saw a nudist beach for the first time and did not feel comfortable. We stayed in a private house, so every day I cooked a lunch we took to the beach. I did not like that kind of vacation very much, to cook with others, but we had to save money. When Milorad left his position as chief editor of *Oslobođenje*, he was appointed the Assistant Secretary within the Ministry of Information. His earnings were lower, and he began to think more about money. I did not feel or think much about my pregnancy except occasionally, when I felt dizzy while swimming in the sea and connected that to being pregnant.

When we returned home, my pregnancy advanced and I felt good. Sometime near the end of the summer, my middle sister phoned me and

---

[47] Cetinje was the center of old kingdom of Montenegro.
[48] A resort town on the border with Albania.

said she had just come from Switzerland with her little daughter and wanted to visit me and our mother. My happiness was immense, because I had not seen her for two years, and I hadn't seen my mother for about nine months—since my wedding. My sister brought presents for all of us, and she also gave me a golden pendant that I wore for many years afterward. She was always the most generous of us, and I thought then that Switzerland was Eldorado.[49] My mother missed me surely a lot, but she looked somehow emotionally detached, because I was not supposed to marry somebody who was not a Muslim, according to the religious rule. Milorad was a liberal and was the same as his Muslim friends—progressive, broadminded, and very tolerant of different religions—but that meant nothing to my mother. He should have at least had a Muslim name. Milorad's father was also progressive and Milorad used to often say, "I am grateful to my father that he did not burden me with fanaticism." Before World War II, as a young socialist in Belgrade, where he worked for the *Politika* newspaper for many years, he had been beaten by the police during demonstrations.

I continued to work long hours in the hospital. The head of the pediatric surgery division, Assistant Professor Kafka, was angry about my pregnancy. "What will you do now?" he asked me, thinking about my residency. Until then, he used to say, "I need no more associates since I have Dr. Nadja." I managed to do everything; I was in the operating room a lot, ran the outpatient clinic, and worked on the ward. More and more often I performed some not-so-difficult operations by myself with his assistance. I finished the rotations in urology and thoracic surgery, and I passed my quizzes. Kafka recommended the book of pediatric surgery written by Professor Grob to me. He had been one of the world's pioneers in children's surgery and the head of the Children's Surgery Clinic in Zurich. Kafka thought it was the most complete book on pediatric surgery. Fortunately, I knew German and I was able to use that book well.

---

[49] The sixteenth-century South American legend about an extremely rich place with a lake of gold.

19 Childbirth

At the beginning of January 1963, Milorad and I were walking one evening around Sarajevo in search of ski equipment for Nedžad. It was difficult to walk, because the snow was partly melted. The next day I noticed a painful red spot on my lower leg. I knew it was a vein inflammation, especially when the spots began to spread along my upper leg. I gave myself penicillin injections, but still my leg flared up, and when a spot appeared in my groin, the leg became very swollen and painful, and I knew it was a deep vein thrombosis. I asked Assistant Professor Kafka to examine me and he came with the orthopedic surgeon, Assistant Professor Pšorn, and one general surgeon. They were worried about me, because I was in my ninth month of pregnancy. They sent me immediately to be admitted to the Obstetric Department. There was a lot of snow in the street, several feet, and the ambulance could not approach our house, so the attendants had to carry me on a litter down my street to the main road where the ambulance had to stop.

In the hospital, I shared a room with two women waiting to deliver their babies. I had my leg raised on a board. I was receiving a blood thinner, Heparin, by infusion, and I had wet compresses changed on my leg every two hours. Professor Kaufer, who was the head of the Surgery Department in that period, came with a vascular surgeon and examined my leg every day. The swelling persisted up until the delivery, although it became a bit less after application of Credé's ointment, a colloidal silver in an ointment base. Professor Kaufer was a military surgeon who spent the war with the partisans. He was appointed our Head after Professor Lukač retired. I was in the third year of my residency, and there had been many changes. Professor Kaufer wanted to reintroduce the previously used surgical discipline that had been discontinued. He ordered the observance of strict procedures and rules in the operating rooms and in the use of time-cards for employees. He was a very good surgeon and liked the patients, but sometimes he used to lose his patience with his colleagues. When he got angry about some problem, his body would tremble while he was yelling at somebody. He still had a great understanding of surgery, and when we talked about somebody's mistake at the doctors' meetings, he would say, "The one sitting in a glass house should not throw stones on others."

I remained bedridden with my leg on a rod for three weeks, until my delivery. My colleagues visited me often, and my dear Pirkko came to see me on a daily basis. She would stand on a narrow wall under my hospital room window and communicate with me through the window. She bought me baby clothes, because I had not prepared anything yet, and she also made some special diapers like the ones she had brought for her own baby from Finland. She pledged to give me her baby basket because she did not need it anymore.

One afternoon at around four o'clock, I felt rhythmic pains in my stomach. After examining me, Dr. Nadja Hadžidedić said my labor had started. She was supposed to run my delivery and was worried about my thrombosis, so Professor Knežević, the Head of the Gynecology Department, came to examine me and said with a smile that she would be prepared in case a normal delivery was not possible. I do not know how I managed to finish it in four hours, but my baby was with me at eight o'clock. A student kept my swollen leg in her hands, because I was unable to bend it. My baby came out with his posterior first, which was even more difficult than the usual head-first birth, but Providence evidently wanted me to give birth to a healthy baby without any complications—and so all went well. That same evening, Dr. Hadžidedić allowed Milorad to visit me, and when he saw our baby, he said, "How beautiful he is," the same sentence that Kasim had said sixteen years ago when he saw our baby Nedžad. My leg swelling decreased dramatically after the birth, and I began to use my leg in a few days. It was very difficult, though, because I was weak due to both the thrombosis and to having given birth. I felt like I would faint while going to the bathroom. My baby did not want to nurse; he would usually fall asleep on my breast, and they fed him with the milk of some women. In my room was a uneducated woman who constantly pressed her breast and milked it, I supposed with not so clean fingers, and they gave that milk to the babies, including mine. However, he began his life with that milk.

Božana visited me regularly, and one day she even washed my hair while I was in my bed. She was always the one who helped when needed. When we came home, Nedžad looked at the baby and, because he had never seen a newborn baby before, he said with tears in his eyes, "Take care of him—will he survive?" There was no jealousy on his face, and he remained the same with his brother later.

In those days, women had paid maternity leave lasting three months, so I could also recover from the thrombosis. It was hard at the beginning; I was weak and unable to take my baby from his bed. After three months, though, I was ready to continue my surgical residency, but with shorter working hours, which all women were entitled to until a child got to be six or eight months. My shift was from seven to eleven o'clock, and when I was in the operating room, Dr. Lopandić or some other resident came at the end of the shift and replaced me. Kafka was sometimes angry when I had to go home to nurse the baby. Milorad and I hired a young girl from Knin who was helping me at home with the baby and housework. My sister in Switzerland had sent me wonderful cream and powder to soothe the baby's skin, and I used that for a long time. She also sent me a modern dress, which we did not have at that time and which I was proud to wear.

My child was healthy and thriving well, we named him Ognjen (which means "fiery"). I remembered that in my elementary school we learned that the old Slavic god was the god of fire. Later my mother complained because we did not give him some more neutral name like others in mixed marriages do, but those names were superficial for me and I wanted his name to have a meaning. My father told me that my name in Arabic means "saved," and once he said that usually a person's name either matches fully or does not match at all that person. It seemed to me I was often saved from something in my life.

At the beginning of the summer, when my baby was almost five months old, I noticed his right leg was a bit twisted and shorter than the left one. The orthopedic surgeon established he had an inborn dislocation of his right hip, and he recommended that we put straps there immediately to hold the hip joint in place, and we did it. However, my baby cried so much and tried to stretch out his legs that I removed the straps in the middle of the night because my heart was tearing apart. The next day I asked my neighbor to use her sewing machine to sew something similar from a soft cloth that was a bit elastic and did not keep the legs so firmly. But still my baby was waking up and crying—for three nights—so I carried him as much as I could to give him some relief. Luckily, humans can get used to anything, so he was a happy baby afterward, turning himself over and crawling around even with the straps on.

As soon as I got better, I read Professor Grob's textbook on pediatric surgery. I knew German, and I was able to study the book in detail. I could have done it earlier, but I had lent the book to Dr. Lopandić, who was to have her specialty exam before me and asked to borrow it. Kafka already had told me it was the best book on pediatric surgery, and I convinced myself of that while studying the descriptions of diseases. The descriptions were supported by wonderful illustrations, and often the original operating technique by Professor Grob was presented in the illustrations as well. We could not perform some of the more delicate operations covered in the book in our hospital, but the book was very useful for me with respect to diagnostics and the routine operations we frequently performed.

My first maid was not that helpful, except for her taking care of my child while I was working. Some young girls from villages were interested in going to the city and considered it to be a good opportunity to work in the city and go to school at the same time. I spent a long time teaching them about hygiene and about how to perform tasks that needed to be done, but both they and I were dissatisfied because we could not afford to send them to school. We hired several different maids, and two of them stayed with us seven months or longer. We could not find what we wanted, though, a serious girl who was already skilled in housework, since we were not willing to pay double the amount we paid to younger ones.

I spent a lot of my time that summer with Pirkko. She often visited me and brought a box of Turkish delights[50] ("lokum") for me, and we

---

[50] Sweet homemade cookies.

had coffee with them. We went to picnics together; Branko always found good meat, so we had a barbecue on the bank of the Lepenica or Zujevina Rivers. I remember our picnic on Jablanica Lake. We took a boat, and Pirkko suddenly jumped out of the boat in the lake and swam. She told us about the lakes in Finland and could not resist the stunning green color that reminded her of Finland. At the end of our picnic, we were still sitting by the extinguished fire and talking, and her daughter, little Nina, was playing around. Suddenly Pirkko jumped in the water and pulled Nina out. It all happened in a moment, about sixteen feet away from us, when she reacted instantly and saved her daughter's life thanks to her maternal instinct.

At the end of the summer, we wanted to go to the seaside with our little son. Dr. Vera Tadić, with whom I worked as an intern in the Diagnostic Center several years earlier, gave birth to a daughter at the same time I gave birth to my son. She suggested that we go together to a resort in Makarska that was an integral part of the enterprise in which her husband Đoko Tigerman was employed. We were supposed to cook for ourselves there, so we brought pots and pans and took her mother-in-law, who was from Hungary, and my maid Nada to help us with our children. We spent most days under the pines on the beach; we went there usually around nine o'clock, walking in a line, taking rubber mattresses, small bathtubs, and balls with us. We removed the straps from our son only when he was in the water, and we immediately put them back on when he got out, because he had to wear them for a long time. That had been the decision after his follow-up exam. Dr. Vera, who had a good sense of humor, laughed at me because I told Nada not to use too much oil to fry the steaks—she felt that steaks must be fried in lots of oil.

After about ten days of our seaside vacation, there were signs of a terrible storm—heavy clouds and choppy sea—and because it was September, we thought it would last a while. So we decided to go home as soon as possible; we took our things and started over Biokovo Mountain in order to run away from the sea as fast as possible. We climbed up the macadam road, and when we reached the top, the sun was shining and we had a magnificent view of the sea. We were fooled, and unable to go back, so we continued home.

We had another follow-up exam of my son's hips after six months of his wearing the straps. Now he needed to have a harness-type device to keep his legs in the right position—something that worked better than straps—so we put that device on him. It was a bit more of a drastic change in the position of his legs, but he had already gotten used to the straps, and it was not difficult for him this time, either. He used to play a lot in the good-sized playpen that Pirkko had lent me, and we all wondered how he could do all that while wearing that device.

20 Pirkko

After New Year's, the whole Surgery Department experienced a shocking situation—especially me. My friend Pirkko died. We were coming back home from work together and parted at the back hospital gate, at the first stop of the hospital bus. I invited her to have lunch at my place because Milorad was in Belgrade, and she had said she was going to have a potato pie at home made by her young maid Ana, who was from near Oglavak. She showed me that her shoe heel was broken, and said she had to have it repaired. At that moment she also complained to me a little that she would like her daughter Nina to call her "ajdi," which means "mother" in Finnish but that Branko did not support her in that. We said goodbye, and Mrs. Romanić, the wife of the conductor Romanić, who lived in the same apartment house as Pirkko, called me around five o'clock in the afternoon and said, "Mrs. Gajić, Pirkko either died or fell into a coma." I was shocked and told her to call an ambulance immediately, because I could not help; Milorad was in Belgrade and I was still not driving. After I hung up the phone, I was thinking about that stupid expression "fell into a coma," without thinking of death at all. I immediately called Dr. Lopandić and asked her for her husband Sreten to take us to Pirkko's place. When we came to her apartment, Branko was sitting, lost, surrounded by several neighbors, and he said, "The ambulance came and they concluded she died." Our depressed silence lasted some time, and then Branko told us how it all happened.

Pirkko went for a walk with her daughter and took her shoe to be repaired. When she returned, she told Ana to make them coffee and sat down to watch TV with Branko. After a short time, she cried out, "Branko, I cannot see," and fell down with two or three rattles. Branko immediately called the Romanićs and an ambulance, and a doctor who arrived concluded she died. We were sitting there for some time, and most of the people who were present wanted to see Pirkko, even Dr. Lopandić did. But I could not—it seemed to me I would faint if I saw her dead. Her autopsy was carried out in great detail, but the pathologist, Professor Palinkašev, did not find the real cause of her death. Her heart was hypoplastic, as well as her blood vessels, and he assumed that after lunch, her blood was mostly in her abdomen, and with a sudden stimulation when she looked at TV, her heart had stopped for a short time. Only many years later, when Pirkko's sister suddenly died, and her father also died early of a heart attack, did it seem likely that it was an inborn predisposition in all of them. Many people were present at her funeral; she was buried in the Orthodox cemetery because we did not have a Protestant one. She was thirty-two years old.

So Pirkko's sudden death left a sadness and emptiness in my heart. My mother was also mourning, because she knew I lost a girlfriend nobody could ever replace. Božana was also close to me, but she was not so joyful and active like Pirkko. She was single and missing the chance to get married because she disliked any of her potential partners. She later went to Switzerland, where she worked as an orthopedic surgeon. After I married, Pirkko was the only person who attempted to help my father understand me better. She compared it to her case; she had come from Finland to marry a man. She was so cute, my mother told me later, and Pirkko had told me that never before had she met a man like my father—so strongly convinced that his opinion was right.

On the same night that Pirkko died, I took Nina from their neighbor's to my place. My heart was breaking apart when I put her in bed to sleep, she put her little head down calmly, having a sad face, feeling something terrible was going on. She could not stay with me more than two or three days, until the funeral was over, because I was afraid my maid would not be able to manage both my son in his device and Nina, and she might leave me because of that. I always felt sorry for the situation and for Branko, because I would have kept her forever if I could have—I would do that for my friend Pirkko. Nina spent about three months with Branko and Ana, and we sometimes visited them. One day we took them to a picnic with us. She always prepared a pillow for her mother to have when she returns. Finally, though, she understood. When I told her at the picnic that her mother would come, wishing to give her some hope, she replied, "No, she will not come—my mother went to heaven." I was relieved when Branko sent her to her grandmother's in Finland, as they had agreed, because it was the best for the child. They sent me her birthday photos several times, and I could see her growing into a little girl. Each time, I missed anew my dear friend Pirkko.

21 Specialty Board Exam

In the spring we removed the device from Ognjen, because the follow-up x-rays showed his hip was normal after ten months of wearing the straps and the device. Our young maid Nada walked around with him constantly until he was finally able to walk by himself. And then he could not stand still! In the summer, we went to Podgora on the Makarska Riviera, rented a room, and had our vacation there. Zoran, Milorad's son, was not angry with him anymore, and Milorad had proposed that he join us there. I saw him for the first time when we got into our car, the old Peugeot. He was a handsome young man and was very relaxed at our first meeting, and he remained the same during our whole trip. It was like we knew each other for a long time, and he participated in our conversation joyfully. He slept with us in the same room, on a mattress put on the floor, and entered our room slowly if he came back after we had gone to sleep. He always was relaxed and natural, and I maintained the same good opinion of him as a simple, noble man, even when he became a world expert and innovator in the field of electrical and computer engineering. We all went to the seaside with Nedžad a few times during some holidays, such as May 1 and Independence Day. He did not join us during summer vacations, though, because he preferred going with his own friends.

MEMORIES FROM BOSNIA

My specialty board examination was coming closer, and I was supposed to pass it in Belgrade, where there was an established professorship in pediatric surgery. To become familiar with their work and to improve my theoretical knowledge free from my home obligations, I went there two months earlier. Milorad and Nedžad stayed at home and Milorad's mother came to be with Ognjen, who was almost two then. She was always ready to help whenever needed in our family.

Belgrade had the Pediatric Surgery Clinic, which was not very modern but equipped enough for all major operations on children except for heart surgery. There was one professor, two associate professors, one primary physician, and several assistants at the clinic. They received me warmly, as Belgrade people would do in general, and tried to help me learn the maximum amount possible. I assisted with surgeries every day, and we discussed each case at our morning meetings and in the operating room. There were some smaller differences in their surgical technique; they followed the French school, and I followed Professor Grob and Assistant Professor Kafka, who were introducing the London methods. Kafka was enthusiastic about the English and their lifestyle in relation to others, but it was too unfamiliar to me then. However, many years later, I convinced myself he was right. I liked the kind of ease I saw in performing operations in Belgrade, but it was strange to me that they often cancelled already-scheduled operations and instead of seven, as planned, they performed some four or five operations. We in Sarajevo were more accurate in that respect.

After about a month and a half, the examination commission was appointed. I had fifteen days for my recapitulation, and Assistant Professor Rakić, a doctor, questioned me chapter-by-chapter each day as we went through the entire pediatric surgery topic by topic. I never forgot that experience; I became more self-confident about my own knowledge, and he gave me a lot of good advice at the same time. I also did not forget the unpleasant comment made by their primary physician, who did not assume I spoke German and said as a joke, "Gut für Balkan," as they would say for our doctors in Vienna, thinking that I would be anyway "Gut für Bosnia." It seemed to me I had more knowledge, maybe more than him, too.

My examination was good. The commission included a general surgeon, Professor Bukurov, who people considered to be annoying, one orthopedic surgeon, and one pediatric surgeon. They gave me a blind gut to operate on, not complicated, because they usually awarded easier operations for exams, but just hard enough that they could also assess the candidates' operating skill with them. The next day, Milorad came and we spent two days in Belgrade. Celebrating my exam, we met some of his friends, Vilko Vinterhalter and others in the Writers Club; they all congratulated me and I was happy.

When I returned home, my mother came and gave me a diamond brooch on a chain that my father gave her after their wedding. The brooch was manufactured in Vienna and had diamonds in platinum. When I saw it I began to cry and said, "I do not deserve it." I do not know why, but it was my spontaneous reaction. Maybe it was because I knew it was difficult for my mother to accept my marriage and, in general, she was not inclined to me that much. She did not believe I would complete my residency with my new marriage and with a little child, so it was surprising for her.

My youngest sister invited me to visit her in Zagreb, where she lived, to celebrate my specialization together with our middle sister, who lived in Switzerland and who would also join us there. Milorad bought a train ticket for me in a sleeping car, so I went there with Ognjen, who was almost two at that time. We spent three days together, and my middle sister gave me a Swiss watch as her present. Since then I have never bought a watch for myself, because she always gave me one as a present.

At the end of 1964, I became a specialist in pediatric surgery. I could perform independently less difficult and moderately difficult operations, while previously I could do that only with a specialist's assistance. Now we were three pediatric surgery specialists, Assistant Professor Kafka, who became a Professor, Dr. Lopandić, and me. Dr. Lopandić was appointed a teaching assistant, and the assistants' selection ceased just when it was my turn, because there were a sufficient number of them. That year, I got my driver's license and was driving our old Peugeot periodically, but Milorad took over many activities, because he did not trust me. So he always parked our car, drove backward into our garage, and made comments sitting next to me while I was driving. For a long time I was afraid of other drivers, especially truck drivers, and one of Nedžad's sentences helped me to get rid of it. He told me, "You are equal with them in driving and should not feel jeopardized." That sentence really helped me to become a good driver.

22 Belgrade

One day Milorad told me, "I have a surprise for you," and took me to the balcony to show me a new tent. He explained to me that we could stay at a motor camp on the seaside and go wherever we wanted. I was not enthusiastic about it at first, because I remembered our camping in Slovenia and on the Adriatic coast, which was not so comfortable, maybe because our tent was poorly equipped. But this one was more modern. So we spent that summer in a campsite in Kašteli, near Split. Ognjen was two and a half and was running around the campsite. There were a lot of fountains, and I was always washing something. We cooked soup and meals on our gas stove, and we also bought various foods in cans. We met one German family, so I had an opportunity to speak in German, and Milorad always had some Frenchman or Belgian with whom to practice his French. The worst for me was when Ognjen wanted to go to the restroom; I put papers for him to sit down because, although they were rather well maintained, due to the large number of people present there they could not be hygienically clean. Accordingly, we had, as people say, an active vacation.

We made an adventurous decision while camping. Milorad disliked his position as the Assistant Secretary of Information, so he was thinking about looking for some other position. I had passed my exam, and as a surgeon specialist worked more independently, but somehow I was dissatisfied, too. I had to do a lot of routine work because Professor Kafka was not involved in it and Dr. Lopandić, since she became a teaching assistant, trained the students and operated, while all routine activities, discharge of patients, casting and dressing changes, and so on were my obligation. Only the three of us were the pediatric surgeons, and Professor Kafka did not take on any new people to specialize in that field. The residents in general surgery passed through our division during their specialization, but they mostly assisted at operations and could not replace me in my routine work. We published some interesting cases in the local surgical magazine. I often wrote a paper by myself, but Professor Kafka's name was listed first, then the name of Dr. Lopandić, and finally mine. So Milorad and I thought about moving to Belgrade, because he had a chance for a job in the Bibliographic Institute. So I attempted to get a position as a pediatric surgeon in the Children's Orthopedic Clinic in Belgrade and was successful.

When I told Kafka of our plans, he was surprised and immediately began to look for somebody to specialize in pediatric surgery. I explained to him, in order to avoid any possible negative comments, that my husband had to move to Belgrade. I was secretly glad to leave them. We rented a room for me and Ognjen in Belgrade, and Milorad stayed in Sarajevo to wait for his documentation. Nedžad had just passed his entrance exam and enrolled in the University of Electric Engineering. I thought he would join us in Belgrade. He did not want to leave Sarajevo, but I thought he would change his mind later.

Every day in Belgrade I took a trolley and saw the wonderful boulevards on my way to the hospital, which was located in Banjica Square, and at the same time I took Ognjen to his day-care center in Dedinje Square. Although he was not yet three, they accepted him, and that day-care center was very nice and up-to-date. The hospital in Banjica Square was the orthopedic one, so I mainly assisted at orthopedic operations. The general pediatric surgery had only a few operations periodically.

After a month, Milorad's brother Slobodan visited me and told me that he could not allow me and Ognjen to live in one room. He invited us to move into his and his wife Jelka's apartment, which was rather large. It was an attractive offer for me and I accepted it immediately, so we packed our things and went in his Volkswagen to his apartment. The apartment included several large rooms; two rooms were connected by a large opening in the middle, which gave the impression of a huge space. After we moved, Slobodan would often drive us to the hospital and day-care center, and we would come back by trolley. The apartment was on the fourth floor and the elevator was out of order, so I had to climb up the stairs with Ognjen, who could not walk long distances. So I had to carry him up the stairs. That was the hardest part of my stay there. Slobodan often spoke about medicine and brought me various illustrated magazines to read for relaxation. All of us used their kitchen; I cooked for myself and Ognjen, and he and Jelka cooked for their family. They had three sons attending high school and elementary school. Milorad visited us for two or three days, and we went to Lajkovac to pick up his grandmother, who came to look after Ognjen, because he was sick and could not go to his day-care center. Milorad's mother was always ready to help. Slobodan often cleaned the kitchen and hall floor and was not ashamed to do it. I recognized his noble nature, of which Milorad hadn't told me. He always wanted to help, although he was an introverted person and often did not want to communicate.

After about two weeks of living with Slobodan, Milorad informed me he got a negative answer from the Bibliographic Institute. His coming to Belgrade was unsuccessful, and I had no choice other than returning to Sarajevo. However, it was not hard for me to go back to the Surgery Department in Sarajevo; on the one hand, in Belgrade I would not have been working in my specialty, general pediatric surgery, but in pediatric orthopedic surgery, and on the other hand, I had enjoyed a break from my routine work in Sarajevo and the negative things I'd felt about it before no longer seemed so bothersome. I wrote a letter to Professor Kafka and he invited me to come back. Accordingly, after my two months in Belgrade, I returned to Sarajevo and was enthusiastically accepted to work once again in the division of pediatric surgery.

A significant change occurred in the Pediatric Division while I was absent. Dr. Lomas came there, because Professor Kafka needed a resident, and he specialized in general surgery. He decided, however, that he wanted to work with children. My colleague Lomas was an excellent worker, had good manners, and was a very cultured person. He got acquainted quickly with the routine work on the ward, and it became much less burdensome than it was before.

23 Loss

My father passed away in 1966, and that year I experienced many sad and difficult feelings. That summer we had spent the first part of our vacation in the same campground we used to visit near Split, but the second half we spent in the South, in the place named Plat, near Cavtat. It was a natural campground with a small number of guests; we bought milk from the villagers and really had a good time there. During the last week of our stay, there was a weather change, so at night we listened to the noise of the wind and waves, and we could not sleep very well. In my short sleeping intervals, I had unpleasant dreams every night. Our vacation finally ended, and we returned home.

The next day, my mother called me and said my father had been taken to the hospital. I immediately called the doctor on duty, and Dr. Ćerimović told me that my father was discovered to have acute myeloid leukemia. Those three words hit me like lightning—I knew leukemia, and I was paralyzed with fear. My mother and I went hurriedly to the hospital, and my mother had a big pillow for him. I entered his room first. He was lying in a single room, pale, having a small injury on his cheek. I said, "How are you father?" "Not good," he answered. I sat by his bed and he told me, "I was on my trip to Tehran, at the opening ceremony of their biggest library—the Shah had invited me during his visit to us." I also met the Shah on the occasion of his visit to Yugoslavia, when he came to Sarajevo and Milorad was invited to attend a theater performance in his honor. A tall and slim man, he smiled and nodded his head at us after our applause, and he impressed me with his noble attitude. "At the opening of the library," my father continued, "I looked for a seat near the door to leave the place easily because I felt sick and dizzy. The spot on my face appeared on my way back home, I do not know, maybe it is an infection." Since that day, I spent whole days in the hospital with him, and especially the nights when he was uncomfortable. I had to bring him his urinal very often. I informed Professor Kafka and others in my division that my father was very sick, and I that had to take a leave to be with him. I consulted a hematologist in Sarajevo and sent the histology slides to the Belgrade Hematology Institute. Unfortunately, they confirmed the same diagnosis and medical treatment. He received blood transfusions, and because he had the AB blood type and was Rh negative, it was difficult to find the right blood for him. I nearly went berserk trying to find help for him, maybe even abroad, and I informed my sisters about his disease and asked them if there was modern medical treatment for him in Switzerland. They came and brought a hematologist from Zagreb for consultations. Professor Brkić, the head of one of our internal medicine departments, and his deputy, Assistant Professor Rustembegović, were very fair with me and made a detailed analysis of his disease and his treatment schedule together with the hematologist from Zagreb.

During those several days I spent alone with him in his hospital room, we talked about many interesting things, just as we used to. I remembered his comments about German literature in my high school years and when he gave me a book to read. In Oglavak I read the memoirs of the Hungarian president Horti that he had recommended that I read, and he said, "What an interesting and nice life it was!"

One night I went to the nurses' room to get some rest, because I was very tired, and when I came back he told me, "I almost choked." His nose was plugged with dense secretions resulting from the injuries to his mucous membranes. I felt sorry that I had left him alone, but I had really been unable to go on. I was telling him about medicine, which was always interesting to him, and quoted an axiom about the heart told to us by our cardiology professor at his first class, "Primum movens, ultimum moriens," meaning that our heart is born first and dies last. My message for him was that his heart will endure against the disease, but only later, I became aware that maybe I should not have mentioned the word "moriens"—dies. One night a nurse made coffee and I brought a cup for him too, and he said joyfully, "I would like to check to see if I would feel it tastes like coffee." I do not know if it was tasty for him because he said nothing. The time I spent with him for those few days was without any shadow resulting from my marriage, and as if there had not been five years since our last encounter. I was thinking how strong the natural laws were, stronger than the people's.

The treatment failed to induce remission, which would have stopped his disease at least for a short time, and his situation worsened. He was very thirsty all the time, and we were bringing him fresh mineral water. On the eighth day, he became restless and I asked Dr. Ćerimović what to give him to calm him down. He opened the ward pharmacy and said, "Here, give him whatever you want." We agreed on Luminal (a sedative), and I injected it every few hours so he could sleep. On his last night, all three of us daughters were sitting by his bed and our mother had left to rest a little. For a moment, he woke up and said, "Nadja, Dila, Suma, and where is Ašida?" He called us by our names and asked about our mother. Those were his last words. In the morning, Professor Brkić was giving him an infusion, and I held his hand while he was receiving it. He was twitching and withdrawing his hand, sometimes looking at me with his blue eyes. The infusion refreshed him a bit, and at these moments I was thinking how a great brain was falling apart. After he received the infusion, he closed his eyes and the heart, which brought me to this world, stopped beating forever. Both our mother and all three of us were devastated and lay in my mother's beds when our mother's relative, the goldsmith, visited us. He liked and respected my father a lot, and he was very sad. Some other people were coming too, but I do not remember exactly—it is all so vague to me now.

It was a wonderful September day, all in sumac and colorful leaves, when his funeral was held. They took him to Oglavak, to the family cemetery, and a line of cars followed the funeral car. We had to go there partly over the forest trail without cars, but in spite of the steep slope, people were carrying him on their hands to the small burial chamber built by his great-grandfather Sheikh Sirry His students, younger colleagues, and many friends of all religions existing in Bosnia were walking sadly, and many of them, as well as the people from the Oglavak surroundings, wanted to carry him. I received a few very kind condolence letters, from Professor Kafka; Professor Kaufer, the head of the Surgery Department; Dr. Lopandić; and many other people. Jelka, Slobodan's wife, sent me a touching letter, saying, "When we lose our parent, the tiny thread connecting us with the best part of our life, our childhood, is broken." Only after several months, when the memory of his death settled to the bottom, I felt a deep sorrow. Jelka's sentence from her letter seemed to be truthful. Suddenly I was feeling older. Later I would sometimes think about him, not as my father, but a man who, thanks to his modesty, impartiality, dedication, and great intellect, had many of the characteristics of a great man, although he was inflexible and almost brutal, especially when faced with primitivism and human stupidity.

24 Switzerland

I went on with my work as a surgeon and was becoming much better performing the moderately difficult operations. I was periodically also given the opportunity to perform some rare operations under a professor's supervision. Dr. Lomas was my right hand, assisting me and doing all other routine jobs. Ognjen was going to his day-care center, and I was no longer dependent on an uneducated maid. My mother found a young woman who came twice a week to clean our apartment. She was tidy and learned our work method very quickly, so she remained my faithful housekeeper for many years. Her name was Sejda, and I will always be grateful to her for her unselfish work with us, particularly her making our house perfectly clean. My obligation at home was cooking, but Milorad often did that too, and sometimes Nedžad, especially after my night calls. The night calls were difficult for me. I had to do about four to five per month and up to eight or nine during the vacation period. As a second specialist on call (the first one was the general surgeon), I was the busiest. It was particularly hard for me after midnight, but sometimes I enjoyed it. After an urgent operation, we gathered in the nurses' room next to the operating room, had coffee, and often tasted some specialty offered by our nurses. The hospital was the most beautiful at night, my steps echoed in its long white halls, and the ward was peaceful when the nurse and I came to see a patient.

MEMORIES FROM BOSNIA

At about that time, I wanted to go to a European pediatric surgery clinic to become more familiar with the latest European ideas and methods. Professor Kafka had spent a year in London, and during her residency Dr. Lopandić got a scholarship and had spent several months in Paris. I tried to get one for myself but was rejected. I then asked Professor Kafka to allow me to go to Professor Grob's Clinic in Zurich and to spend some time there. He agreed, but we had to find a way to contact Professor Grob. Professor Kafka advised me to try to do it by means of his friend Professor Poljugan, the head of pediatric surgery in Zagreb, who was a very good friend of Professor Grob.

My youngest sister also lived in Switzerland then. Four years after my middle sister Dila went to live there, my youngest sister Suma joined her. Our state borders were more open now, and many experts were leaving for jobs that paid better elsewhere. She graduated in veterinary medicine and earned her doctoral degree at the university in Zagreb; then she went to work at the Veterinary School in Zurich together with her eight-year-old son. Her husband stayed in Zagreb, so for several years they spent summers together on the Adriatic coast, and in the winters he was in Switzerland for a time.

I informed my sister that I would like to come to Switzerland to make an arrangement with Professor Grob, and she instructed me to take a direct train from Zagreb to Zurich. So one day I appeared in the Institute for Protection of Mothers and Children in Zagreb, visiting Professor Poljugan. His younger associates showed me around their pediatric surgery division. It was tidy, and in addition to the well-known procedures in the field, they used some original ones. Professor Poljugan, smiling and with bright eyes behind his glasses, received me kindly. He immediately started to write a recommendation letter for Professor Grob, and very shortly he gave me a stamped envelope.

My trip continued through Austria during the night and part of the next day through the wonderful landscape of the Austrian and Swiss Alps, including a long ride along Zurich Lake to Zurich. My youngest sister was happy to see me, and she called at once our sister living in Basel and we greeted each other by phone. She gave me bus and tram tickets to get to Professor Grob's Clinic. The next day I entered the hall of Kinderspital,[51] a large building in the Swiss style from the beginning of the century, similar to the surrounding buildings. After I introduced

---

[51] The Children's Hospital.

myself at the reception desk, saying that I was a doctor from Yugoslavia and that I had a letter for Professor Grob, a slim, middle-aged woman told me to sit down and wait. I waited for about an hour. Then the woman informed me that the professor had a prolonged operation and could not meet me that day. I came again the next day, and was told the same thing—to wait. I waited that day even longer than the previous day. Then a woman with glasses told me again that the professor was engaged with an urgent operation and could not meet me. "Aller guten Dinge sind drei," as German people say, "All good things come in threes." I went there for the third time on the next day, and they took me in to see Professor Grob.

I entered the room and met Professor Grob for the first time, a man whom I respected a lot because of my experience of learning surgery from his book. His room was small, and there was a tall, slim, Swiss standing by the table with his head a bit inclined who looked at me and greeted me kindly. He read the letter I gave him and then said, in a way that appeared to me to be a sort of subdued pleasure, in German of course, "Yes, I will accept you to be my assistant, but first we have to obtain the agreement of the Fremdenpolizei (the Swiss Immigration Police), but I will do my best to get it as soon as possible." I did not know what Dr. Poljugan wrote him in the letter. He talked to me a little, wanted to know how long I was in surgery. I managed to speak in German and said spontaneously, "Ich freue mich dass ich Sie kennen lerne, weil ich habe viel gelernt aus Ihrem Lehrbuch," which in English means, "I am happy to meet you, because I learned a lot from your book." After those words, I could see a hidden pleasure on his face and it seemed to me that afterward, during my work with him, he looked at me with favor and kindness.

I could not have wished for anything else in my life than to be the assistant of Professor Grob, I told my sister when I returned to her place. I spent two or three days more there, and then I went to my other sister's in Basel. She gave me fifty Swiss francs to buy something for myself, and I bought so many things that she wondered how I managed to buy all of them for only fifty francs. I found inexpensive, high-quality, ready-made clothes, which we did not have yet in Yugoslavia. I was enthusiastic about the richness of their shops. What was most impressive to me was that people waiting for a tram always moved backward to let people get off the tram first—instead of pushing forward as they did on our trams. I did not have time for sightseeing, but I believed I would do that when I stayed there longer.

I came back home happy, and Milorad was happy too—he always supported my professional success and advancement in surgery. However, while I was absent, Ognjen got sick with chicken pox, so Milorad was terrified when he saw him completely covered with small red pustules. Dr. Najdanović, a pediatrician who lived close to us, helped him, and she told him that it was a common childhood disease that would go away quickly.

Two or three months later, I received a notice from the Swiss immigration officials telling me that my stay and work in Switzerland were approved. I took my things and left in May. Milorad and Nedžad said they would be all right alone; Ognjen was over four and attended his day-care center, and Sejda was coming twice a week to help them with cleaning. My Surgery Department colleagues agreed that my work with Professor Grob was a good idea and that it would allow me to become familiar with the operations I had studied in his book.

Upon my arrival at the Kinderspital, Professor Grob and his wife, who was a senior doctor, received me kindly and informed me of certain rules in the clinic. After I finished some short administrative formalities, I immediately began to work. I was surprised when Professor Grob told me on my first day to wash myself and assist him during an operation. It was an operation on a cleft lip and palate that we did not perform in Sarajevo at that time. I had to constantly keep the operating area free of blood so that he could work. I managed to use a tiny suction device without disturbing him, and the operation proceeded just as he had described in his book.

We worked four hours in the morning, had a lunch break of two hours, and worked four more hours in the afternoon. An assistant was on duty at night and would call in a senior doctor or some other assistant when necessary. We worked six days a week, Monday through Saturday, and once a month each assistant had to work Saturday, Sunday, and Monday, including Saturday night and Sunday night. That was our monthly weekend on call, and we stayed at the hospital the entire time. After that busy weekend, we got the next Saturday off and had the whole weekend free, but only once a month.

The oldest of the assistants was Dr. Stauffer, a kind and noble man, a real Swiss, who took me to a real estate agency where I found a room to rent near Kinderspital from a woman named Mrs. Nauer. I had spent a few days with my sister, who had a two-room apartment that was sufficient only for her and her son. She lived far away from Kinderspital, too, so getting there from her place was complicated. Now I had a place to live that was close, and I began to work in the famous Fanconi Clinic with the famous pediatric surgeon Professor Grob. Professor Fanconi, the pediatrician, had already retired, but he came to the clinic periodically, and I was able to meet him. The clinic included the large Pediatric Department and the Pediatric Surgery Department, which were both located in the clinic building.

I used my German well, because the doctors and nurses addressed me in correct German, "Hochdeutsch" as they called it. However, I was unable to understand their Swiss dialect. It was very different from German, and they use it in spoken language, while they did not use it in writing, except for some children's literature and advertisements. Sometimes parents would bring their sick children and were flustered, speaking very quickly in the dialect without allowing me to stop them, so I did not understand a single word. I would ask them finally to say it again in "Hochdeutsch." I can imagine how angry they were, but they didn't show it. They greeted each other with "grüet sie" (be greeted), so many times a day that I was greeting and greeting again and again, because a lot of nurses, doctors, administration staff, and cleaning women were employed with the Pediatric Department and the Pediatric Surgery Department. The Pediatric Surgery Department had, in addition to its head, Professor Grob, two senior doctors—Mrs. Grob, and Dr. Muggiaska from Tessin, the Italian part of Switzerland. He was Italian, and his pronunciation was closest to mine, so I understood him the best. There were five assistants there—one German, one Dutch woman, two Swiss, and me. Dr. Dangel was an anesthesiologist, a handsome Swiss man and Professor Grob's right hand; he was able to find a vein or artery even in the weakest baby, and he was able to run a subtle anesthesia.

I was awarded a permanent position, and in a telephone conversation, Milorad and I agreed that I would resign from my position in the Sarajevo Surgery Department because I did not intend to return there soon. Milorad told me the people in the Surgery Department were surprised and that Professor Besarović, the new deputy head of the Surgery Department and a well-intentional man, begged Milorad for me not to resign and to come back again—because they needed me in pediatric surgery. However, because I had concluded that Professor Besarović would not allow me to have an extended stay in Switzerland—which I definitely wanted—I did not reconsider my decision. And because both Milorad and I were a bit adventurous, we planned for Milorad to soon join me in Zurich.

Almost every day I assisted a senior doctor or Professor Grob at some rather complicated operations, and the remaining time we assistants worked in pairs on less difficult ones, such as groin or umbilical hernia, circumcision, and other less serious operations. Sterile procedures were carried out at the very highest level, and if somebody only gently touched our backs where our surgical gown was tied, we had to change it immediately. We started to work at eight o'clock sharp with washing our hands prior to an operation. Between the surgeries we could refresh ourselves with sandwiches, cakes, and juices in a small room next to the operating room.

Before operations, we had a very rich breakfast in the call room, and I always looked forward to having two cups of coffee with milk. At noon, I would go to a nearby tearoom and eat something there. Then I rested for half an hour in my room at Mrs. Nauer's. In the afternoons, we managed discharges and new admissions. We usually dictated to the secretary, so it was easier than typing it ourselves, like we did in Sarajevo. We worked around the clock when we were on call. We had on-call duty every five days. On on-call duty days, we set fractured bones under the x-rays, treated injuries, and performed casting and dressing changes until late at night. Still, we were most often able to sleep a few hours, unless there was something urgent, or unless a nurse would call us to remove a catheter or change a bandage, for example, on the ward. Usually at two o'clock in the morning, the nurses invited me to have a cup of Ovomaltine (known as Ovaltine in the United States), a chocolate drink with vitamins, because they had a break at that time. The next day we always worked the whole day, and that was the difference from our on-call duty in Sarajevo, when we went home earlier after a night shift.

I got into the swing of things and bought myself the expensive white sandals in which I was able to walk easily in our ward and outpatient clinic, and they were torn apart in just a few months. In the operating room we wore wooden clogs that were ideal physiologically and easy to stand in, although in Switzerland the pediatric surgeons operated while sitting on a high three-legged chair. I liked those chairs, and I wanted them to be introduced later in our pediatric surgery too, but the majority did not want to give up the classic standing method of working. Family visits were allowed in the afternoon of every other day and lasted two hours, but it was never crowded; usually one or two parents came, and we were supposed to talk to them about their child's status and the procedures we carried out. Some of them brought kosher food because we had Jewish children who did not eat pork.

I was most pleased by the absolutely perfect cleanliness there. They constantly washed children, even the heavy sick children, so skillfully rubbing and cleaning them on rubber bases on their beds. Our normal non-operating room working suits—we got three of them per week—were perfectly white. In the clean operating room everyone wore green, while in the infected operating room everyone wore blue. No one was allowed to enter the clean operating room in a blue working gown. The hospital itself was thoroughly cleaned regularly over the course of several days—everything in it was completely cleaned.

After two months, I was approved to take my three-week vacation, because I had planned to go to the seaside with my husband and child. Doctors there usually took seven days of vacation, and only Professor Grob spent fifteen days on his vacation. Milorad and Ognjen received approval to enter and stay for three months in Switzerland. When I submitted my request, Mrs. Grob told me it was easier because I was from Yugoslavia, because it was not included in the Soviet communist countries.

I was so happy when I saw Milorad and Ognjen at Split Airport. Ognjen wanted to run to me, but was not allowed until they cleared customs. I had to open a large suitcase, but when the customs officers saw a big toy truck and a sailboat there, they were disappointed. Afterward we went to Brač Island and stayed at a motor camp in Milna. Nedžad came too; I missed him a lot and he missed me too. We had a great vacation—we went to the far sea rocks, and we barbecued fish and stayed whole days. When our vacation was over, we went to Sarajevo only to pack the things we needed, because Milorad and Ognjen were supposed to join me. We left Nedžad in Split; he remained on the seaside and our parting was sad—he was almost crying. I asked him to join me soon in Switzerland, but he had to attend his university classes because he had already begun to study electrical engineering.

My mother came to visit my sisters in Switzerland. After our father died, she spent three spring months in Switzerland each year. She was depressed after my father's death, and her staying in Switzerland helped her to forget her sadness a bit. Her depression was understandable, because she lost a husband who had such rare qualities; she was loved, respected, and happy for many years of her life. She got used to living alone later, and she made many improvements to our houses in Sarajevo and Oglavak. She was also a strong bond between her children and grandchildren.

Milorad, Ognjen, and I arrived in Switzerland and found an efficiency apartment with pullout beds and a functional kitchen. I immediately started to work in the hospital intensely, and Ognjen started to go to a day-care center. When I took him there for the first time, the head of the center, a lady, kept repeating, "Arme, kein Wort," which meant, "Poor him, he cannot speak even one word," referring to German. However, after fifteen days she told me, "Er versteht," "He can understand," and after the next fifteen days, "Er spricht," "He can speak." They liked him, and he learned a lot of songs in German and in a dialect he remembered for a long time. Sometimes at the beginning, when we took him from his day-care center and spoke in our native language, he would close his ears and said, "Do not speak," I guess he was confused because he had just started to learn German.

The three of us were getting used to Switzerland and went sightseeing not only around Zurich but also in its surroundings. After my one weekend on call, I was free the next one, so we went to Uetliberg, a place for picnics located on the hill above Zurich. We took a boat on Zurich Lake and visited the zoo and other interesting places above Zurich Forest. It all was connected by trams, buses, and local trains that were clean, accurate, and never crowded. One weekend my sisters came and we barbecued in the forest, almost feeling as if we were in Oglavak. The Swiss forests were darker, though, and not as shining as ours, although the paths were great, with benches and barbecue spots.

As a curious journalist, Milorad looked for interesting things in Switzerland. He spoke French and had a lot of material, since German, French, and Italian were the official languages in Switzerland. He retired early because he did not like his position as the Assistant Secretary within the Information Ministry. He allowed Nedžad to take over his pension and spend a part of it for his living. He intended to write something for himself, or something for our newspapers and magazines, because he could not find a job as a journalist in Switzerland.

MEMORIES FROM BOSNIA

We worked hard in the Children's Hospital, and when some of the assistants took a week off, we had more duties to perform. We had two free hours at noon, so I often went to our nearby apartment and had lunch with Milorad. We easily assembled our meal from semi-prepared products. My colleagues mostly had their lunch in the hospital and rested a little in their armchairs, so I did the same when I was unable to go home. I used to talk to a hematologist who was very curious and always interested in our country. I controlled my blood, since at the beginning they discovered I had anemia, and the personal nurse in charge of the employees' health status gave me iron pills that I took for two months. The next follow-up showed my hemoglobin was good, but my leucocytes were too low, so I consulted Dr. Fischer, the hematologist. He performed some tests and said finally, "It is abnormal, but normal for you." I later remembered that strange remark which was proven right.

My job was very interesting. Together with Professor Grob or a senior doctor, I performed almost all of the operations I studied in Professor Grob's book. Operations were performed with one assistant, and very rarely with two, so I had an active role as an assistant. We corrected many inborn anomalies or established almost fully normal positions, and performed operations related to various degenerative diseases. Such diseases were more common and more varied than in our country; perhaps it was related to the overall development of the society or to the fact that most afflicted children with those diseases died at birth in our country—I do not know. Children in Switzerland were frailer than ours, and their muscle fasciae and other structures were thinner and more easily damaged. Professor Grob was a real artist in surgical operations, so it was a pleasure to work with him. It looked like he worked slowly, but effectively, without any unnecessary moves. He always improved his work; once, during an operation on lop-ears, after he finished one ear, he modified the other one, also with good results. Sometimes he made jokes at his own expense if some new operation he did for the first time was unsuccessful, but his next attempt to correct the patient's problem was always successful.

In the 1930s Professor Grob had performed the first heart operations on children, but due to further improvements in surgical techniques, heart surgeons took over doing those operations. He still operated on certain anomalies of the heart and aorta, so once I followed the operation on an aortic coarctation, a narrowed aorta. When the aorta was tightened and its narrowed part was cut, he sutured the wall with meticulous stitches, without a single drop of blood on them when blood started to flow after the clamp was released. We did revision operations on the head where the skull sutures closed too early, so the head was deformed, and we had excellent results. We also did reconstructions of pectus excavatum (funnel chest) and pectus carinatum (pigeon chest). There were also a significant number of operations for congenital anomalies of the urinary and gastrointestinal tracts. Certain cancer surgeries were executed in the best possible way, often resulting in a permanent cure. I was sad to see many severe head injuries, and Mrs. Grob, a senior doctor, said it was due to the sudden proliferation of automobile traffic. Besides the most up-to-date therapy, those children frequently developed more or less severe brain damage.

I can remember two unpleasant incidents from that time. A three-year-old girl came in with an injury to her left cheek. Her dog had bitten off almost all of the cheek, which now hung from her face. Mrs. Grob immediately began the operation, and I assisted her. She sutured it back together with miniature stitches. Luckily, the torn cheek grew back. I remember how the girl's father paced nervously through the hallway repeating: "I always say, 'Don't trust a dog too much.' " Another time, a child only several months old was admitted for a severe burn of the lips caused by electricity. He had put his lips on an electric outlet. I remember the terrible look of the smashed lips on the baby. In several stages, Professor Grob tried to restore the mouth by taking skin flap from the neck and transferring it to the mouth. The cure took a long time, and Professor Grob tried his best to fix the terrible defect. He succeeded to a degree, but the injury was so severe that the child's face remained permanently deformed. Maybe later something more was done by prosthesis, but I don't know.

I particularly liked the way we took care of burns. We applied the silver-based solution and ointment, which was very efficient for the prevention of infections, in addition to other treatment that contributed to better and faster healing. Burned children were bathed daily in a bathtub full of chamomile solution. This treatment cleaned dead burned skin particles from their skin and was less painful than the previous method of removing dead skin using an instrument.

Professor Grob was a gentleman, was open-minded, and had a different approach than the others who strictly followed the prescribed rules. One day I admitted a child with a head injury in the afternoon hours when everyone was on a break and I was on call. I gave him relevant therapy, made an x-ray of his head, and wanted to treat the wound and then consult Mrs. Grob, who was supposed to arrive in an hour. The nurse said, "No, no, we have to call Mrs. Grob immediately." When she came, she was angry and said that if there is even the smallest hint of a skull fracture, she had to be called. We began to operate, and Professor Grob, who was informed about it, watched us. There was only a slight impression on the outside bony layer, which did not have to be operated on anyway, and Professor Grob said to his wife with disapproval, "You made a fuss about nothing."

Professor Grob made rounds on all the wards on certain days. He was accompanied by all of the doctors and the head nurse, in a way that was similar to our old rounds with Professor Kovačević. We presented our patients to him, and he had an insight about every child. A small child was in an isolation room, very weak, suffering from salmonella poisoning and persistent diarrhea that he could not get rid of. Every time we saw him, the main anesthesiologist, Dr. Dangel, Professor Grob's right-hand man, warned us to leave the room quickly so as not to catch salmonella. One day, when he impatiently sent us away, Professor Grob lifted his hands and yelled, "Are they flying in the air?" meaning salmonellas, and we all laughed.

Everything was good until it was time for Milorad and Ognjen to leave Switzerland, because their visas were for only three-months, the maximum allowed period of time for a visit. Milorad could not find a job as a journalist, and he could only get another three-month visitor visa after several months. We thought a lot about that, especially before going to sleep. We finally decided that I would also return to Sarajevo after I spent the three additional months required by my contract. We thought I had already got a lot of practice working with them in Zurich and that I would have three months more to improve. So Milorad and Ognjen left, and I asked for my dismissal, stating I could not be separated from my family. It was a bit strange for them, because they had already started to give me more difficult operations to perform independently. They planned to promote me or Dr. Stauffer to a senior doctor, because Dr. Muggiaska had to go to Tessin. During our phone conversations, my sisters also tried to persuade me not to return home, so I didn't contact my sisters at all during those final three months before my departure for Sarajevo.

In those three months, my only obligation was to the hospital. I moved and rented a room with a bathroom, because the efficiency apartment was too expensive. I spent whole days in the hospital, having my breakfast and lunch there, and I had my dinner in my favorite tearoom. I walked the Zurich streets and went to shops and department stores in the exclusive Bahnhofstrasse shopping area, looking for presents for my mother, Nedžad, Ognjen, Milorad, and my maid Sejda. Sometimes I went to Kunsthaus, the art gallery, where I enjoyed the paintings and sculptures. Only the uniformed watchmen disturbed that atmosphere a little as they appeared from each corner and controlled my moving around. Winter was coming, and when it did, it was nice to walk on the new snow, which reminded me of Sarajevo. I assisted intensely during interesting operations and observed each operation, even if it was not my turn to be there. I took notes in my special notebook, which served as a reference book throughout my career. One day a week, usually on Thursdays, we had case presentations, so I also had an opportunity to present a case to the group—an operation on a chest cancer in a baby. It was well received, and I did my best to learn the proper German pronunciation, because I had to give explanations and comments. Sometimes, when all of us were present, a renowned professor was our guest and gave a lecture. Many of the lecturers came from either Sweden or the United States and not from some other European country. It was as if the Swiss recognized only those two countries to be equal or better than themselves in the medical sciences. At least that is how I perceived it. My colleagues invited me twice to their evening parties, once in a hut where we barbecued and then returned home through a forest—singing the entire way. We cleaned the hut thoroughly before we left it. The second time was when Dr. Gessendorfer, the assistant who was from Germany, invited me to a party at his place and said that other people would come too. I went there and was surprised to see only Dr. Muggiaska (a senior doctor) and Dr. Molkenbuer (the female assistant from Holland) there. Dr. Gessendorfer's wife was absent. It seemed to me the evening was intentionally arranged so that there would be two couples there. It did not take long for me to make it perfectly clear that whatever plan they had would not work. Among other food, we ate raw liver—that was the first time for me.

Sometimes our secretary would invite me to have a cup of coffee with her at noon. People there would be friendly and joyful, so I have great photos I made on those occasions. I also had a photo made in the amphitheater with Professor Grob, the senior doctors, and all of the assistants as a permanent souvenir, since Professor Grob insisted on us having our picture taken together each year during the Christmas season. Through December there was a joyous, celebratory atmosphere in the hospital. Christmas and New Year's songs could be heard in the corridors, patients' rooms, and operating rooms, and on one occasion I noticed tears in Professor Grob's eyes during the Christmas concert for our little patients. We assistants got from Professor Grob a Christmas present, a big basket full of sweets, fruit, juices, and wine that lasted for days, and it was especially good to have them during our night duties. I was on call for Christmas, and also I spent New Year's Eve in the hospital; I did not have to work on either holiday, but I had no plans so I did not care.

25 Return

At the beginning of 1968 I was already thinking of my return home, so I wrote a letter to Professor Kaufer, the head of the Surgery Department in Sarajevo. However, I made a mistake that made him angry. To justify why I stayed in Switzerland, I wrote him that I wanted to learn as much as possible from Professor Grob, whose book I used at preparations for my exam, but I thought that he, Professor Kaufer, would not allow me to stay longer in Switzerland, so I had to resign. He got insulted, as if I thought that he did not support the improvement of young people, and it was reported to me later that he had said angrily, "I will not allow her to come back." Milorad later told me about how it came to pass that I would indeed be able to come back there. Professor Besarović, the deputy head of the Surgery Department, wanted very much for me to return, because he knew how important it was for the Pediatric Surgery Division to have somebody who had trained in the famous Professor Grob's clinic in Switzerland. So because of that argument on my behalf, Professor Kaufer finally gave his consent. Professor Kafka also wanted me to come back. Later, when I came to report to Professor Kaufer, I gave him an apology; he looked at me out of the corner of his eye and was good-natured about it all. When I learned I could go back, I wrote to Nedžad, and Milorad and I agreed that it would be good for Nedžad to come to spend my last two or three days with me in Zurich so that he could see a bit of Switzerland. But later Milorad called, telling me he would come instead of Nedžad—I guess he wanted it that way, so we agreed, although I felt sorry that Nedžad did not visit me in Switzerland at all. Milorad came and we spent three days there until the end of my work in the clinic. One day we visited my sister in Basel and my other sister in Zurich the same evening, because they had invited us. My sisters and I met in a restaurant before Milorad's arrival, and I cried because I had missed having had contact with them for the previous three months. I think they may have been angry at me for going back to Sarajevo. At any rate, Milorad and I bought some things for ourselves and a modern tape recorder and some other things for Nedžad; I was trying to compensate for the fact that he did not come to Switzerland. I earned so much money that we could now return home and buy a new Peugeot, and because we would have to pay a very high tax to import the car, Milorad decided we would sell our old Peugeot. Soon something unexpected happened.

On the eve of the last day of my stay in Switzerland, Milorad and I talked a lot about how we spent those three months separated from each other. I told him about that invitation of Dr. Gessendorfer, which I found to be premeditated, and that in general he had sometimes made comments at my expense. His father had waged war in our country and maybe that was the reason for his attitude. For example, at Christmastime I had a glass of wine from Professor Grob's gift basket, and he said to me, "Muslims drink wine?" The next day was my last day in the Kinderspital, and I had invited my colleagues to a small farewell party after we finished the surgeries. I had asked Milorad to bring from Sarajevo specialties such as Travnik cheese, Gavrilović salami, and halvah prepared with sesame seed syrup. Suddenly, in the corridor, before the party, Dr. Gessendorfer came in front of me and angrily gave me a letter. I began to read it and almost fainted when I recognized Milorad's handwriting—and the text was shocking, "Du bist ein Schwein," "You are a pig, I will complain to your wife." It was written in the German he remembered from school. He mentioned the names of Dr. Molkenbuer and Dr. Muggiaska; I do not know how he could remember them. Dr. Molkenbuer came and was furious, she almost could not look at me. I tried to explain to them that it was only his jealousy. They said they would not come to my farewell party, and two or three times I asked them again to come and take it as only jealousy. I felt terrible and was so confused that I hurt a tiny duct during the hernia surgery I carried out with Dr. Molkenbuer. I immediately attempted to repair it with fine stitches, but it remained as a permanent stain on my career. Dr. Molkenbuer said nothing, and they both came to my party. Other people enjoyed the food specialties, and one Greek doctor who specialized in anesthesia kept talking about the ingredients of halvah, "Sesam Oel, Honig, und Nuss," "Sesame oil, honey, and nut," he repeated to everyone who asked about it. That time I myself learned the ingredients of halvah.

When we were going back home, we traveled by a night train through Austria, and it snowed so hard that it covered the rails. The train could not go on, so we changed for buses and then to another train. When we came home, my apartment looked somehow sad to me, a bit neglected. My mother was with Nedžad and Ognjen; Nedžad missed me a lot, as did my mother, while Ognjen was a bit ashamed, as if he had forgotten me. But as soon as I gave him his toys, he perked up.

When I came back to the pediatric surgery division, Professor Kafka was interested in everything I had seen and learned in Switzerland. We talked a long time, and because he was interested in developments in other countries, he asked me questions and listened with great attention to everything I told him about the clinic, Professor Grob, the Swiss people, and Switzerland. He told me to submit my request for readmission and said that I should wait for the Clinic Employees Council to make its decision. He said that he did not know when the decision would be made. While I was absent, Dr. Gvozdenović, the general surgeon, was employed to work in the Pediatric Division. My leaving was his chance to advance in his career, so he did not like that I returned. At least that was my impression. He was a chairman of the Employees Council and he may have created certain obstructions to my return, because I waited three months to start working again. However, Dr. Gvozdenović became my very good associate later, and with him I dared to perform complex operations of the types in which I assisted in Switzerland, so we brought our pediatric surgery to a higher level. He was also a painter and had his own exhibitions, and we also became very good friends, visiting each other at home, and once we spent a part of our vacation together on a motorboat on the sea.

Milorad applied for a position in the Republic Veterans Union and was hired. He got to study the activities of journalists during the national liberation struggle, a job he did until his retirement. In that period, he published the monographs of the journalists and intellectuals Veselin Masleša and Nikica Pavlić, and his literary work included his previously published travelogue about China, when he was one of a very few journalists who visited Mao Tse-tung. He also published the stories he wrote in his youth.

When after three months I started to work in pediatric surgery again, I could not get my vacation that summer, but I managed somehow to get a week off at the end of September. We bought a new big tent and went to the Montenegro Coast, because we thought that in the southern Adriatic, the sea would be warmer at that time of year. We settled in a motor camp in Bečići, near Budva, and we took my mother with us and found accommodation for her in a private house near the motor camp. The camp was very nice, typical of places designed by Montenegro people—very clean and with excellent sanitary facilities as well as a refreshing creek next to it. In front of it was a big pebbled beach and sea. Our tent was comfortable, so my mother joined us for a barbecue and enjoyed sitting in front of our tent. The sea was warm and the beach was wonderful, pebbled, with a magnificent view of the open sea, which I always liked more than a view of the islands. Every evening we went to Budva for a walk, and one evening Milorad and I attended Miss Cinema, a fashion show of the Italian fashion company "Angelo Litrico." We had a wonderful time that night. At the end of our stay there, the weather changed and it started to rain. One whole day it was raining and even more during the night. Milorad was restless and did not want to go to bed. Instead, he sat in our tent, ready to leave at a moment's notice it if it started to leak. I was sure the tent would withstand the storm, and I was not worried. The roar from the creek became louder and louder, and then suddenly water rushed into our tent. We jumped into our car, which was parked beside the tent. Milorad had already had his keys in his hands, so we were able to leave quickly. Other cars were also leaving, and their headlights crossed each other and brightly lit up the flood that was now racing through the camp. We went to the house where my mother stayed and slept there; I slept with my mother, while Milorad and Ognjen slept on a mattress on the floor.

A sunny day broke, and when we returned to the camp, we saw that it was devastated. None of the tents were upright or even lying on the ground—parts of them were scattered on the beach here and there. The creek had come over its banks. The Austrians, the majority of the guests, made loud protests and complained to the camp management office because they did not warn us in a timely fashion that the creek was dangerous. People were trying to recognize their belongings and take them from the beach. Milorad was constantly bringing our things to us, and I washed them out in the fountain. Ognjen was crying because he lost his Pinocchio, a great doll his Aunt Vera, Milorad's sister, gave him as a birthday present. Each birthday he got a rich package from his grandmother, Milorad's mother, and Aunt Vera, with whom the grandmother stayed. Pinocchio was a wonderful doll with a yellow hat and blue trousers, and Ognjen slept with him. Later, in Belgrade, I bought him another Pinocchio, a little bigger and with a red hat, and he also slept with him, but he never liked that one as much as the first. I washed the dirty water out of the two dresses I bought in Switzerland, but they never looked the same again. A portable radio I bought in Switzerland got waterlogged, so its loudspeaker was damaged. We had it replaced later, but it was not as good as the original one. We found the outside cover of our tent as well as the poles, but its sleeping part was completely torn apart. So our camping experience was brought to an end, and we remembered that creek forever and how dangerous it can be when it rains heavily in the Montenegro mountains.

Upon my return from Switzerland, I had introduced some changes at work to our daily routine. My colleagues supported these changes, but it was a bit more difficult to accomplish than it should have been, because we were also introducing new operations at the same time. Professor Kafka did not like new operations in which the department was inexperienced. So it was going very slowly.

Milorad and I decided to visit Italy the next summer. We went in our new Peugeot, and we took Nedžad and his girlfriend Amra with us. Taking "Del sole" highway was fantastic. Milorad drove faster than ever, our car was comfortable, and at the gas stations we refreshed ourselves with Italian sweets and drinks in big glasses. Our aim was to go to Rome. We stayed there for three days, enjoyed our sightseeing, and had their tasty pasta in the evening. When we visited the Vatican, the painting and sculpture collection was so immense that it seemed to me they were imprisoned there. When I looked through a window and saw some statues in the park, I was glad they were free there. We spent several hours in Florence and even during this short time we saw fantastic art. In Venice we took a gondola, of course. I was thrilled to see first-class accommodations in private houses at acceptable prices, places having marble bathrooms and perfect cleanliness. The private accommodations on our Adriatic coast was not at such a high level of quality at that time. It was interesting to see the lines of cars in traffic in

Rome that almost touched each other but had no scratches or damage—obviously, they were experienced in driving near to one another.

26 Success

Years ago I saw a fortune teller and asked if I would be a part of the student exchange program and go to Norway, because I was told he was able to fortune-tell everything. He said I would not, and it came true, but he also told me something I did not believe in. "You will have a period in your life," he said, "when everything you do will turn into gold." I remembered those words later. All of us have one best period in our lives, usually in childhood, but we live through it unaware of its precious value. People may also have another special period when they are fully aware. It seemed to me I had it in the present. Milorad was happy with his work, researching, writing, and publishing in the field of journalism; he had colleagues he respected, and they respected him. Nedžad studied electrical engineering and passed all the difficult math exams successfully. Ognjen was a good child, and his schoolteacher told me, "When others do not know, Ognjen knows." My mother had stable health, except for her painful knees, so she often underwent physical therapy at the Orthopedic Department. My sisters sent her one hundred Swiss francs each month, so in addition to her pension she had a surplus of money that she spent on various work on the houses in Sarajevo and Oglavak. My maid Sejda came twice a week to clean our house, and Milorad helped in the kitchen frequently. With all this help, I was free to take care of my patients. If I was worried about some patient and wanted to see him at night, Milorad always joined me, took me there by car, and waited for me, saying, "I would be even worse if I were in your shoes," meaning about patients' care. In that period I tried to carry out some new operations, and if they were relatively simple, Professor Kafka approved of my doing them, but he did not allow me to perform more complex operations.

Especially in the field of pediatric urology, there were operations I learned in Zurich that could solve the long-term problems of children and result in their full recovery. The first such operation was a transplantation of a ureter to another place in the urinary bladder and making a new orifice, because the previous one was insufficient and urine leaked back into the kidney. I did that operation together with the urologist Dr. Prica while Professor Kafka was on vacation. Everything went perfectly well and the little girl had no symptoms at follow-ups. When Professor Kafka was absent I continued to perform these operations with Dr. Gvozdenović, who also had an interest in pediatric urology. Later Professor Kafka agreed to perform them also. There were some risky kidney operations, which we also performed with success. Various kinds of congenital anomalies of kidneys could be corrected by these operations.

One other big operation that I dared to do was a reconstruction of a funnel-chest. I remember a little boy who had a severe deformation of the chest, and the older he got, the more his heart and blood vessels suffered. Professor Tvrtković, the head of the thoracic division, admitted that child and asked me if I was able to operate on him. I told him I assisted in many such operations in Zurich, and because he was a thoracic surgeon, we could do it together. He replied, "I know nothing about that operation and I can only assist, and you should do it if you know how." And we did it. We had to cut all the cartilage of the ribs as well as the sternum[52] and to drag a flat metal wedge ("spiess,"[53] as the Swiss called it) through the sternum, which kept it in the correct position. I was given a "spiess" by the head operating room nurse when I left Switzerland, and we procured others from a pharmaceutical company. The child tolerated the operation well and was discharged. We removed the "spiess" six months later. Other children were coming in with the same deformation, one a seventeen-year-old young man who we operated on successfully and who was very happy about the operation. When he came for follow-ups he looked somehow excited,

---

[52] Flat bone in the mid-chest.
[53] A rod.

as if he had fallen in love with me. I am sure he had suffered a lot previously because of that deformity.

We shared our experiences regularly with pediatric surgeons from Belgrade, Zagreb, Ljubljana, and Celje. Pediatric surgery was separated from adult surgery in Ljubljana only later, while pediatric surgery in Belgrade was the most developed and even had certain subspecialties. We presented our achievements and our interesting cases at meetings, mostly in Belgrade, but also in Celje, Zagreb, and once in Ljubljana. One surgeon asked me if it was better to perform the operation on a funnel-chest earlier or later, when a child becomes stronger. The Swiss found it was better and easier to do it earlier, because children's anesthesia had become very safe. I attended those meetings mostly with Dr. Lopandić, my closest associate. We usually arrived in Belgrade by the early morning train and had our breakfast in the Majestic Hotel. I always remembered that great coffee and Belgrade rolls. We talked there in peace about various things. Dr. Lopandić was always like that, and I had never heard her raise her voice. She had warm brown eyes on a very pretty face, but I could see the remains of a scar resulting from a burn she suffered as a young physician. However, with time the scar became less prominent. She was gentle with children, somewhat like a mother; she was always cautious and did not perform risky operations, and she never made any mistake that harmed a child. She obeyed the Latin proverb, "Primum non nocere," or "First, do no harm."

I had good relationships with my other colleagues as well. Professor Kafka was the head of the division, and each of us was in charge of some narrower area, but only formally, because we all did everything. The head nurse was the sister Sergija who had worked there since the period of Professor Kovačević. He kept the sisters who worked in the hospital at the war's end, gave them rooms in the attic part of the Surgery Department, and appointed them as the head nurses of the divisions. He respected their modesty and devotion to their work. Our sister Sergija was rather strict with other nurses, so they complained sometimes about that and because she gave privileges to some of them. She respected doctors a lot, and she never said only "Doctor," but always "Mrs. Doctor." Each morning she brought us a big coffee pot and cups on a tableau, the same as at noon after operations. All those years she never had coffee with us; that is how she showed her respect toward the doctors. We, the colleagues, visited each other at our homes; some of us would periodically organize a dinner party and we would enjoy special food and have fun. Professor

213

Kafka had a good sense of humor, as did Dr. Gvozdenović. Professor Kafka was good at telling jokes, and we all laughed a lot. Usually my mother would make some special recipe from Sarajevo, such as stuffed vine leaves, okra, stewed kebab, stewed apples stuffed with walnut, and so on. One day they all came with their families to Oglavak, so we hiked through the forests, picked up mushrooms, and barbecued in front of the house. There were so many ripe apples in the orchard, so we picked them up and took them home in baskets. They all remembered that picnic, and Professor Kafka said, "Nadja has a ranch." One day we gathered again in Oglavak, but there were no apples that time. Sometimes we used to hike on the surrounding hills together with Dr. Lomas.

The treatment of major burns was very challenging. Repeated skin grafting went slowly, because donating areas, from which we took transplants, had little surface area in children. We did have modern devices for harvesting the grafts, as well as modern antimicrobial preparations. Regrettably, in spite of our best efforts, permanent scars frequently remained that were especially ugly on faces. Children often had burns on their heads, mostly caused by the carelessness of the adults when they spilled hot water or coffee on a child. Particularly difficult were the burns caused by fire or electricity. When the Division of Plastic Surgery was established, which later became the Department of Plastic Surgery, only a plastic surgeon took care of major burns. At that time, our division also became a department—the Pediatric Surgery Department.

We encountered children with intersex anomalies, and we made the reconstruction of the genitals to one or the other sex. We did it once in twin girls; we turned them into females, what they were in fact from the very beginning, but their sex was indeterminate at birth. One child became a boy after our reconstruction, which he was actually from his birth, but was previously considered a girl. We had experience in correcting anomalies of male genitals; we did them well, so the parents were satisfied.

We operated more and more on newborn babies, with life-threatening congenital defects. They had their intestines disconnected, or they did not have their anuses, or their urinary bladders were underdeveloped, or they had their backbones split, or some other defect was present. There were also other abnormalities, and once we had a child with a third leg. We could correct to normal the majority of those defects, but some of them we could not. The most difficult was oesophagus atresia (disconnected gullet), which needed subtle care and special conditions after the surgery. Biliary atresia[54] we couldn't successful operate on, and a child would usually die after few months. We were good at treatment of inborn tumors, often on a kidney, but also in the area of buttocks, neck, and stomach. They were usually benign tumors, but there were also cancers, most often of a kidney, as well as the lymph glands and nerve tissue. In the case of a kidney cancer, after the removal of the tumor and subsequent chemotherapy, a patient would commonly be completely cured. With some tumors, however, we were not successful and it was hard to see a child gradually dying.

We could do all those operations, especially on newborn babies, thanks to our anesthesiologists, who ran excellent and safe anesthesia. My best associates were the anesthesiologists, but the anesthesia technicians were also gentle and skilled. With their gentle fingers, the anesthesiologists, who most often were women, put little tubes down the throats, found the tiniest veins, and gave infusions and transfusions. After the surgery, the anesthesiologists continued to help, coming to our Department because our intensive care block was apart from the adult intensive care unit. Parents were tenderhearted over their newborn babies and very grateful when their child did well. I thought about the great significance of the contribution of the anesthesiologists and about how they did not have contact with the parents, who would no doubt be as grateful to them as they were to the surgeons.

Along with the successful treatment of cancers and difficult congenital anomalies, we had some failures. Fortunately, most could be corrected fairly easily. One day a nurse in the operating room asked me to perform a correction of a genital anomaly of her little cousin. I did it in the usual manner, and while most operations on the same problem went well, in this case the stitches did not last and the wound opened, so the operation was repeated—this time successfully. I did not know the reason, and it can be imagined how I felt when I encountered the nurse who had shown such confidence in me. I also remember another case: One of our nurses asked me to perform a circumcision of her girlfriend's child. We often did circumcisions, because parents wanted for it to be done in the hospital under anesthesia, and not at home as before, when traditionally a barber did it. If done for religious rather

---

[54] Lack of the development of bile ducts.

than medical reasons, the circumcision was paid for separately. The child belonged to a well-known Sarajevan family, and the nurse had selected me to do the operation. I wanted to do it the best possible way, as we did it in Switzerland. There, we did not cut the foreskin too short, but children stayed two or three days in the hospital and we took care to make sure the scar formed properly. This particular child went home immediately, however, and I received flowers and a big baking sheet full of baklava from the parents. There was so much that it lasted for several days. A few weeks later, the nurse who asked me to do that operation came to me and said politely, "Mrs. Doctor, they had to bring a barber to revise the scar." I felt so uncomfortable, and the nurse, experienced in surgery, told me, "Do not worry, Doctor, that is surgery—when you want the best, it can be the worst at the end." I was thinking about that and reproached myself for not following up with the child after the operation. After all, that was why children stayed in the hospital two or three days in Switzerland.

The hardest thing for me to accept was a failure in cases when a sick child came to us too late, because at his or her first medical check up a doctor did not recognize an emergency such as strangulating bowel obstruction, appendicitis, or incarcerated hernia. We often managed to save a child, but sometimes we failed, and it was difficult to tell the parents, who were always full of hope. Still, they understood and were grateful for our efforts, even if a child passed away. I always remembered a two-month-old boy we received too late with a complicated incarcerated hernia. I operated on him at once and thought all would end well, but in a few days his intestines stuck together and I had to operate on him again. Again it seemed it would be all right, and my experienced nurses and I took care of him for several nights, but still the child died. I performed the first operation on a night on which I was on call, and a general surgeon assisted me. That surgeon was used to adult patients and a bit too roughly pushed the edges of the wound to show it better to me. I constantly tried to keep him from coming in contact again with the child's fragile tissues, but perhaps the damage had already been done—the rougher touch of the general surgeon may have caused the adhesions and bowel obstruction that ensued. In spite of the unfortunate outcome, however, after some time I received a present from the child's parents.

I was still rather lucky, as my mother claimed. "God keeps his eye on you," she said when I told her about my operations. One day we had an accident with a child of a fellow surgeon. That colleague had worked for many years as an x-ray technician in the operating room, but he managed to complete medical school and later specialized in surgery. He was intelligent and had a great sense of humor, so we enjoyed his jokes during our night calls. He married a beautiful nurse who worked in the laboratory. They had a boy who developed bleeding from his intestine after few months. We knew it was an intestines anomaly that we had to operate on, and Professor Kafka did it. The operation was done successfully, as was usual when he did it. However, on the fifth day after the operation we were shocked when we discovered the wound had opened up. The child was immediately taken back to the operating room and the professor scrubbed himself to operate on the child. Unfortunately, during anesthesia the child began to vomit profusely in spite of having a tube in his stomach, and he aspirated the stomach content into his lungs. All efforts made by the anesthesiologists, aspirations, artificial respiration, and heart stimulation were unsuccessful, and the child died. It was a tragedy for our department and for our colleague, but his wife held up well. The child's mother was fragile herself, so the child also had extremely delicate tissue structures—yet we had many similar cases that had successful outcomes.

I usually had my vacation in August. We were organized like this: Professor Kafka, Dr. Lopandić, and Dr. Lomas had their vacations in July, and Dr. Gvozdenović and I had ours in August. We were still spending our seaside vacations camping after we bought a new tent, because our old one was torn in the flood near Budva. Milorad enjoyed camping, but I did not enjoy it so much. Camps were usually crowded, cars were coming and leaving, and we constantly heard the noise from car engines starting. Cooking in a small gas stove was slow, and boring as well. Because we had four weeks of vacation, we usually changed camps after two weeks and continued to some other place. We liked to stop in a wild camp with only two or three tents, peace, and the clean sea, but without good sanitary facilities, so we were unable to be there very long. At the end of our vacation, we usually took a room in some inexpensive hotel to rest from the camping for a few days. Although I wouldn't choose camping for my vacation, we still saw many places and beaches along the Croatian and Montenegrin coasts, and we also stayed in the camps on Brač, Hvar, Korčula, and Mljet islands.

For a few years we spent a part of our vacation in Novigrad, near Zadar, where my sisters spent their holidays for many years as well. We were either camping or renting a room in the only hotel there, and once we were in a private house with my sisters and their families, a place they had rented before. They had rented rooms in a house, and a girl from Zagreb they took with them cooked and made excellent dishes for them. My youngest sister's husband liked fishing and usually early in the morning he would take a boat and go fishing with his son Miran, often bringing back several large fish. Before sunset, after we finished swimming, we usually barbecued that fish in the woods on the beach and enjoyed it a lot. One day our mother was with us when we barbecued, tanning her knees in the sun and trying to swim. Several times she spent a few days in Novigrad and returned home with my sisters when they visited Sarajevo. Novigrad Sea was a large and almost completely closed bay with warmer water than in any other place on the Adriatic coast, so we could swim for a very long time. My middle sister's daughter Dina, a teenager, was an excellent swimmer. She looked like a real siren with her beautiful body.

So that we would not be too bored in Novigrad, each year we organized short trips to other places. One of them was the Canyon of the Zrmanja River. We sailed by a boat upstream to Obrovac, for a short trip. The sight of the canyon was magnificent; we could see the sheer, smooth, reddish cliffs towering above, and at their bottom was the emerald green Zrmanja River with its calm stream, a wider bed, and our sailing boat. The canyon looked like it had been carved, as if made by a human hand, but it was a natural phenomenon.

We also visited Pag Island. After we crossed the bridge, we took the highway through the peculiar landscape, which made me a bit afraid. The vast red soil on both sides of the highway looked like the Moon's surface, as I imagined it. We passed through almost all of Pag and stopped in Novalja, because my sisters wanted to meet their friends from Zagreb there. We swam and had fun there, and one of them told us jokes that made us laugh a lot. However, a local woman interjected herself into our group and told us a kind of joke, but an impolite one, and the people laughed, but I always remembered it with disgust. We also bought two or three kinds of the famous cheese from Pag, two of which were new to me, and we returned to Novigrad late.

One of our unforgettable trips was our visit to Kornati Islands National Park. It took us about four hours by a small tourist boat to reach one of several islands that were mainly unpopulated. The sea was deep, and it really had the color of ink, just like the guidebook said, and wonderful dark blue waves were spreading behind our boat. They barbecued fish on the boat and each of us got two fish and a lot of salad, which was very tasty with perfect Dalmatian bread. The guide invited us to climb up to the top of the island in order to have a good view of the other islands and the open sea. When we came there, the view was fantastic—the cliffs swooped down deeply into the sea, the waves made a crashing noise, and we could see far away out into the open sea. That atmosphere became a little less lovely when the guide told us about the tragedy that happened sometime in the 1930s. Tourists visited the island and at that place an English woman enjoying the view lost her footing by not being careful enough where she stood, and she fell into the sea. Her husband jumped immediately after her and the waves took them both. Later, whenever I was in a position to nearly slide off, I remembered the unfortunate English woman and her brave husband.

When we parted in Novigrad until our next meeting in a year or longer, I started to cry, and my middle sister said, "Look at her, she is crying." I was sad because of having to leave them all.

Except for my summer vacation, I had some free days in the winter too, usually collected as the compensation for my night and weekend duties and for working during holidays. We went several times to Jahorina Mountain and spent about ten days in Jahorina or Bistrica hotels. Both Milorad and I liked snow very much, and we tried to walk or ski a little in Paradise Valley. That wonderful snowy valley was crowded with people in red, green, yellow, and black skiing costumes. Ognjen attended a skiing course. One day we accidentally met there Milorad's good friend Savo Golubović, who was teaching his little daughter to ski. When he saw us skiing, as a supporter and connoisseur of skiing, he began to instruct us. Step by step we were losing our fear. He continued to help us later too, during our subsequent visits to Jahorina Mountain. He had a cabin there and sometimes he and his wonderful wife Mira would invite us for a Jahorina lunch, usually a thick bean soup. Thanks to Savo, for many years I enjoyed skiing—even from the top of Jahorina, later a site of the Winter Olympics. Milorad skied a little too, while Ognjen became an excellent skier and proposed becoming a skiing instructor. Both Savo and his wife Mira were very noble people, and once he told me, "Do not be so considerate, you will fail," and in fact he was like that. I remembered his words several times in my life, when things became difficult and I had to sort them out.

MEMORIES FROM BOSNIA

Nedžad skied well, and each year he spent a part of his winter holidays on Jahorina Mountain. While he was at the university, his hobby was underwater fishing. He dived in his diving suit with his friend, usually in Neum,[55] where that friend had a cabin. When we were coming back from Italy, we hid a rifle for underwater fishing that he had bought in Italy deeply in our luggage compartment. A customs officer looked carefully in our luggage compartment and asked, "What is that on the back?" He found the rifle, and we paid customs for it. It looked like he knew what that rifle was for.

In this period of time, Nedžad got married. He graduated from the university and served his military duty in Skopje and then in Zagreb. He had a girlfriend, Amra, who had just graduated in oriental languages at the University of Philosophy. She was beautiful and clever, and Nedžad loved and respected her, and he kept those feelings for good, although some people lose the intensity of their feelings after many years spent together. Her father, Muhamed Šefkić, was a retired lieutenant colonel and her mother Evgenija was a daughter of a Russian immigrant and a Bosnian Croat woman from a famous family from Fojnica. Captain Šefkić was the head of a construction site in Vogošća, where my first husband Kasim worked many years ago. He was handsome, and his uniform fit him perfectly, with his beautiful blue eyes shining. "Captain Šefkić has a beautiful wife," people in the construction site used to say, and I met her once in a truck on my way back to Sarajevo. She was very young and a real beauty with wonderful black hair and eyes. I admired her without knowing, of course, that Nedžad, sitting right there in my lap, would marry her daughter one day.

Muhamed Šefkić, we called him Hamo, bought an old house in a wonderful location on Lopud Island, with a fantastic panorama of Šipan, Mljet, part of the Lopud Islands, and the open sea. He had been restoring the house gradually for many years, mostly by himself, because he was a civil engineer. He was just raising a second big water tank when he invited us to spend a part of our vacation there. Nedžad served his military duty and joined us during his short leave. We put our tent near a big carob tree under which there was a long table with benches, and early in the morning (Hamo got up first and then we, the others, did) we had coffee from Hamo's little demitasses. We had a fantastic panorama of the sea that was usually calm at that hour. When

---

[55] A resort in the small Bosnian part of the Adriatic.

we were sitting there in the evening, the west was magnificent. The sunset reflected a wide red strip that shimmered in the sea. One day, I entered the tank that Hamo was covering with concrete from inside. I asked him if he wanted to have coffee, and he said he had to finish with concreting first. I remembered and brought coffee in the tank. We drank coffee in the deep shadow, and Hamo said the tank was very acoustic. Then I sang a song and it echoed perfectly. I always remembered that moment and the unusual coffee we had in the water tank.

With its smooth cliffs and a deep sandy cove, Šunj, Lopud seemed to be the most beautiful of all the places we saw on the Adriatic coast. Hamo had really good taste to select that place for his retirement. He used to say, "I swam every month except January." He was quite a brave sportsman.

Pediatric surgeons in the Pediatric Surgery Clinic in Zurich (I am in the second row)

Part III

27 Illness

Milorad and I both were in good health. After that hernia operation when I met Milorad, he was later in great shape, without having even the slightest cold. The first two or three years he had annual checkups of his kidneys, because he had a severe inflammation many years earlier. Now, because those checkups had showed good results, he did not need to have them anymore. I had a heavy thrombosis of my right leg prior to giving birth, but I recovered, although it was improving only gradually. For a long time I wore a thick elastic stocking on that leg, because it was the only way for me to stand on my feet during operations. When my colleagues found out I had a thrombosis, they asked themselves if I would be able to go on with surgery, which frequently includes very long periods of standing. That leg was always a bit swollen, so I had an extra pillow under it while sleeping.

In that period, many people were building weekend houses and cabins. Our standard of living was obviously improving, and our Yugoslav communism became more tolerant in terms of private property. Milorad liked the sea a lot, and he began to save money regularly because he intended to buy a boat. He always saved, but now he saved to an exaggerated degree. I told him several times that I did not want to have a boat and that I did not dare to spend our vacation on it without a navigation expert. But he did not give up, and he saved everything he earned in the Veterans Union from his publishing for that purpose. And then he finally bought one. It was well equipped, with four beds, a cooking stove, and a miniature toilet. He passed the captain examination and went sailing with Ognjen for the first time. They sailed three weeks from Lopud, along Korčula to Hvar and then back to Ploče Port. The engine was rather slow, and it took them a long time from island to island. They also had navigation problems; it was hard to get an orientation, and during one storm Ognjen was bailing out water from the boat the whole night. I thought I couldn't be in such a small boat on the open sea, because I was always afraid both of heights and depths. When we were in Ulcinj where the sea is often choppy, I would easily get dizzy while swimming. I was pregnant then and thought that was why I felt that way, but I had similar experiences later, too. During our mountaineering, when we had to cross a log on a river, I usually sat on that log because I was dizzy. Maybe it was because of that I felt very resistant to the idea of the boat.

That autumn the International Pediatric Surgery Conference was held in the German city of Bremen. I wanted to attend it, and I got approval to go, but I would have to bear my expenses myself. Our dinars were not accepted there, but I had Swiss francs that I exchanged with my mother, because both of my sisters sent her one hundred francs each month. That way, I could travel. When I arrived in that northern German city, everything looked unusual to me. The red-brick buildings gave a sense of monotony, and the towers with their peaked tops were also monotonous. I walked in the dark, almost empty streets of the old city awaiting the introduction cocktail party.

At the party, I met my former colleagues, the pediatric surgeons from Belgrade, so I felt better because I knew nobody else there. However, as much as the old part of Bremen was not interesting to me, their Children's Surgery Clinic was contemporary and quite a discovery. The clinic was richly equipped and up-to-date. The Germans received us with gentlemanly manners, and the attendees from Eastern Europe were relieved of all expenses during the conference. Professor Rhebein said we were his guests because he knew it was a large expenditure for us. The conference was fantastic, not only because it had an intensive expert component, but also because of its social activities. The Germans did their best to make them more interesting for us. During the opening ceremony, while we were standing in a big hall, the ballerinas dressed in their national costumes came to the balcony, danced their national dances and gradually went down the surrounding stairs. That scene was really wonderful.

During the conference I met Dr. Gessendorfer, the assistant from Zurich. We greeted each other, and he said he now worked as a surgeon in Germany. Then he asked me, "Is your husband still jealous like before?" I had a bad memory of that terrible letter and I do not know what I replied to him.

One day during a break I saw Professor Grob. I came up to him; he was smiling and greeted me cordially. He introduced me to a middle-aged, good-looking woman who was a nurse in the operating room, as his wife. Then he added, sadly, "Frau Grob ist tot," that is, "Mrs. Grob died; she had a cancer and they only opened and closed her stomach during the operation."

The final part of the conference was very interesting. They took us in several buses for a few hours to some island with a beautiful hunters' house. We had our dinner there, and I tried for the first time various game and other specialties. Professor Grob was close to me and I liked to see him there, and the surgeons from Belgrade and Hungary were sitting at my table.

I had visited Professor Grob's Clinic once again earlier, three years after my leaving Switzerland. I was their guest for one month in the period when Professor Grob was about to retire. They gave me a room in the clinic for a small fee, and I was in the heart of it day and night. They moved to a new clinic next to the old one, both surgical and pediatric, which was built while I was working there, and it was really impressive. There were modern electronic devices that were largely steel and much easier to use and read than others I had seen recently. As their guest, I could only follow their operations, so I constantly moved from one operating room to another, watching operations and making notes in my old notebook. Because certain operating rooms could be entered only if we were dressed in green overcoats, and others only in blue, I changed them several times a day. Maybe I should have been more careful not to waste so many overcoats for washing, but they did not object.

Their work was not much different than it was when I was there, though they had improved some delicate operations and used more plastic materials. The treatment of burns was increasingly modern and faster, and I was impressed by the greater possibilities that now existed for rehabilitation of children after severe head injuries.

MEMORIES FROM BOSNIA

At the end of my stay there, I attended a farewell retirement party for Professor Grob. All the surgeons and pediatricians were present, extending their gratitude to the professor and wishing him good health and success in his future work in a private clinic. Someone presented an interesting and funny poem about his work. We laughed a lot after every strophe. Mrs. Grob was also present there.

The professor left the Surgery Department in charge of Professor Rikham, the former head of the Children's Surgery in Liverpool, and one of the best surgeons for newborn and nursing children in Europe. Professor Rikham was Swiss, born in Zurich, but he worked in Liverpool for many years and Grob chose him to be his successor. I completed my stay there, and I would never have thought that I would meet Professor Grob at the conference with his new wife.

We spent our next summer vacation separated. Milorad and Ognjen bravely sailed all the way to the remote Vis Island. I continued later on with Ognjen and stayed in one of the Solaris hotels in Šibenik. I wanted to be on my own; my relationship with Milorad was disturbed, maybe partly because of the boat and maybe more because my unpleasant memories of that humiliating letter in Switzerland frequently came to mind. I had a good time with Ognjen; we went in for sports often, although I was clumsy. Šibenik was like Dubrovnik, with streets and shops crowded with tourists, and the Cathedral was the first building of that kind I had seen—simple but dignified and without too much decoration.

Ognjen was very upset because his father was not with us; children always have difficulties accepting their parents' misunderstandings, so either that or another event resulted in our not getting along particularly harmoniously. Milorad had an episode of rectal bleeding, and his medical checkup showed he had a polyp on his large intestine. He wanted to be operated on in the Military Hospital, for a reason I do not know but perhaps because of the higher-quality nursing there. The polyp was burned down and removed, so the bleeding was stopped.

We traveled to Lastovo Island the next summer and had a good vacation in a hotel; we swam on the rocky beaches and had lobster specialties. Milorad felt good. But after several months he noticed blood in his stool again, and his radiology checkup showed he had a little bulge in the large intestine. Because he previously had a polyp in that place, his doctor sent him to the Gastroenterology Department within the Military Medical Academy in Belgrade for a comprehensive evaluation. We went there and Professor Elaković, after a short preparation, checked his intestines with an endoscope. I was sitting outside when he came out and told me to come in. He had a note of fear in his voice. In that dark room he gave me a tube to see through and I saw a little bulge. According to its appearance and the professor's reaction, I knew it was not good. He said he would immediately send Milorad to the Surgery Department, where Professor Bervar, then one of the best abdominal surgeons, would operate on him. Milorad accepted it, of course, without knowing it could be cancerous. I returned to my hotel room, lay on the bed, and cried out loudly. It was the biggest shock I'd had since the time I learned my father had leukemia.

Professor Bervar, a short, nice man, told me that the operation went well and that he removed the cancer and reconnected the intestine, so it was not necessary to make an opening in Milorad's abdominal wall. I was happy for that, because I knew it would be more comfortable for him. But I was still worried because they recommended neither x-ray treatment nor chemotherapy. That was because the kind of cancer he had was not treatable with those methods at that time.

28 Recovery

His recovery from the surgery was going very well, and Milorad felt completely healthy. That winter we went skiing in Italy. Our friend Savo Golubović organized a trip of skiers to the Dolomite Alps in Italy. We started from Split, and all of the skiers were from there except us. Savo lived in Split with his family at that time. We took a boat to Rijeka, and then went by buses from the Atlas Tourist Agency through Istra and Italy. Each day at nine o'clock we went by bus to a large number of skiing sites—it was similar to having several Jahorina Mountains together. It all was well organized; the ski lifts and cabins were safe and there were well-maintained slopes for all categories of skiers. Mountain-style restaurants between the ski paths offered different and rather convenient low-cost food. This was my second trip to Italy, and I became convinced that skiing and vacationing in Italy was as good as or better than it was in Switzerland and Austria—and the people in Italy were much friendlier, too.

We went sightseeing and shopping for souvenirs and sports equipment in the evenings, and everywhere we went was brightly lit. We also had fun in our hotel—everybody there was having a good time. We spent most of our time with Savo, his wife Mira, and their daughter Draženka, who was close to Ognjen's age. Savo was always telling us how to ski properly and correcting our mistakes so that we would avoid accidents. He spoke with a Herzegovinian accent, and his face and open green eyes were always smiling a little. His wife Mira had a good figure and was a very good skier. She had a pretty face and especially beautiful blue eyes, whose color seemed to be painted by a master artist who chose the perfect hue and intensity. She laughed with her full heart and was always speaking in a clever and constructive way. She was a perfect homemaker, and when we came to their cabin on Jahorina Mountain, everything was perfect, just like the meals she offered us. I would usually bring a box full of hurmasice[56] made with sugar syrup and marzipans, so each day we had them, and Savo and Mira liked that lot.

That summer I decided to try to go out on our boat with Milorad. We planned to sail just a short distance—from Gradac, where the boat was anchored in a small marina, to Hvar Island and then along the southern coast of Hvar to Zavala, a small bay where we were supposed to meet my sister and her daughter Dina. When we had to leave, the sea was quite rough, and for my sake Milorad asked Valentin, a local fisherman who took care of our boat, to take us to Sućuraj, the closest place on Hvar. I watched him as he guided us to our destination, and he explained the skill that is necessary to apply to successfully go through the waves in order to avoid a stronger swaying or even capsizing of the boat. Early the next morning, while the sea was still calm, we continued to Zavala under Milorad's command. We were waiting for my sister in a small port, and because we waited a while, our boat began to sway back and forth and I felt so sick. I had unstoppable vomiting and diarrhea. Ognjen was so sweet when he helped me to shore to wash myself in a shoal. It seemed to me that the swaying when the boat was in the port was even more difficult for my inner ear than the swaying when the boat was actually moving forward across the sea.

My sister did not come. I watched for her and observed all the cars coming out of the tunnel she was supposed to go through. So in the evening, when the sea was calm, we went to nearby Šćedro Island and spent our vacation there.

Šćedro Island almost fully encircled the big bay, making it an excellent port for boats. There was just one guest house, and its owner, Rato, had a small restaurant, too. He fished every day and had fresh fish on the menu all the time. Tourists, especially Germans, often dropped by to have fish there but stayed a very short time, so we had a

---

[56] Tasty cookies with or without walnut.

really peaceful vacation there. Sometimes we hiked with Rato over the hill to the southern side of the island toward the open sea, but it was not as accessible as the northern side was. That vacation was one of my favorites. We forgot about my sister, and she explained to us later that her daughter liked the town of Hvar so much that they decided to stay there instead. She told me that they had not thought our plan to meet was a firm and final plan that we were committed to—ironic, actually, because I was there, getting so sick with that vomiting and weakness, *only* because they would be coming there too! On our way back, the sea was calm at first, but a strong mistral, a violent warm, dry wind, followed us for several hours until we reached Gradac. We sailed along the island of Hvar. I was lying in my cabin because I could not be on the deck, and I saw Hvar through my cabin's window, sometimes above and sometimes below us, depending on our boat's swaying. It was a very unpleasant boating experience.

I was present that year at one of the largest international courses in the field of pediatric surgery held in London. Every year the British Council organized a special pediatric surgery course, accepting only a limited number of surgeons worldwide. I applied and was lucky to have been admitted. The course was very costly, and I had to look for sponsorship, because our hospital did not have financial resources. The Institution for Scientific and Technical Cooperation agreed to sponsor that course for me, and my colleague Jamila Hadžimustafić, who was the Minister of Health at the time, approved my travel expenses. I practiced my English with Mrs. Šoljan, who was an English teacher and lived in the same apartment house we lived in.

I got my first impression of London during the descent of the plane over a very urbanized and organized city. At the airport, the people working at the passport counter were very kind and cheerful. However, they asked me about Sarajevo, knowing it was the place where Archduke Ferdinand was assassinated in 1914—that long-ago event that was the first in a chain of events leading to World War I. I got on the bus to go to the terminal, which was in another building. When I got off, I saw people getting on another similar bus, and because that place where I now was did not look like a terminal, I thought I had to continue on by another bus and so I got on that bus too. I was surprised when I eventually found myself back where I had started—at the customs building. Because I would have had to wait for another bus, I took a taxi instead. I paid seven pounds to get where I needed to go. When I told my story to our course secretary later, she was surprised by such a high taxi fee. We had our accommodations in a hotel near the Children's Hospital at Great Ormond Street and the course venue. In the evening, we had a reception at the British Council, and some of their members, perfectly dressed and with great formality, came to each of us and talked a bit. One of them asked me about my family, very slowly, so I could understand him well, and I replied. My English was much improved because of all my studying.

We had lectures during the course that were delivered by many professors; each presented his most up-to-date views about pediatric surgery, and we then had a question-and-answer session after the lectures. Sometimes they took us to a hospital's pediatric surgery department and showed us certain cases, and I noticed many black nurses there. In general, in our hotel and elsewhere, I saw a lot of black workers, usually as service workers. We had a break at noon and had a light lunch in the hospital's restaurant. Our professors had their lunch with us, and we were able to ask them questions there, too. They were easygoing, and we addressed them as "Mister," which is the standard form for physicians in the United Kingdom. The food was not tasty at all, and we were happy to be able to have our breakfast and our dinner, which is the main meal in England, in our hotel. One evening, the doctors took us to an Italian restaurant for lasagna. One of our course secretaries explained to me that we would have a special meal, because it was a particularly good restaurant—and it was a delicious meal.

Another time, I met three colleagues from Portugal, Switzerland, and Australia, and we went to Covent Garden for a ballet performance. Their ballerinas looked like they were floating—was it due to their ballet skill or their low body weight? I couldn't tell. One evening we went to an African ballet, which was very interesting, with African rhythm and lively costume colors. I also took a bus tour of the city one day and did some sightseeing, and they showed us the Royal Museum, in which it seemed to me that the whole world's gold was gathered. They took us to Greenwich, the site for the Prime Meridian used in keeping world time zones, and we visited the famous Maritime Museum with its ancient sailing ships.

At the end of our stay, Professor Wilkinson, the host of the course, invited us all, some thirty of us, to have a dinner at his home. We had a two-hour bus ride, and the dinner was most interesting. The old professor and his also-old wife were standing at the table and giving us food in portions according to our preferences. With plates in our hands, we were sitting on the stairs and on the floor, because there were not enough chairs. We could find wine on every table, but their house was modest and modestly furnished. We had a pleasant time there, and we returned to our hotel again by bus. So my course was completed, and later I fully presented its content to my colleagues in Sarajevo.

I was impressed at how easygoing the English people were. On my last day, while getting ready to leave, I accidently got locked out of my room. I went to the reception desk and said, worriedly, what had happened. I explained that I was not yet ready to leave and needed some things that were still in the room. The receptionist smiled kindly at me, took me to my room, and opened the door with his key so I could enter it. When crossing the streets, people crossed them sometimes without strictly waiting for the green signal if there were no cars there. I remembered that when he had come back from London some years ago, Professor Kafka had mentioned Englishmen with great admiration and continued to do so for many years to come.

Nedžad's second son was born that year. His son Dino was born two years earlier, and this one was named Neven. Dino had black eyes and black wavy hair, and Neven had bluish eyes and light hair. It was not only I who loved my grandsons—Milorad also loved them very much and often bought them necessary things, either for the sea or for skiing. Milorad also had two granddaughters from Zoran—Tijana and Bojana—who were a little older than Dino and Neven. They had fair hair and looked like Swedish girls. Milorad loved them deeply, but he showed the same affection to my grandsons Dino and Neven.

That summer we went boating with my colleague Dr. Andrija Gvozdenović and his wife Olivera. Dr. Gvozdenović was fond of Milorad, and he also had a little sailing boat and liked to sail, so we agreed to go together on our boat. We brought canned food and cheese, and baked some meat in advance so we could have it at the beginning of our trip, and I took of course a box of marzipans and a box of hurmasice made with sugar syrup. We started from Gradac, where our boat was anchored. We planned to sail around Pelješac Peninsula to Korčula and to continue to Mljet Island, because we all liked it there. We reached the nearest place on Pelješac without any trouble and then continued along its coast. The sea was mainly calm, except for the strong warm wind of an afternoon mistral that lasted several hours. But that time we put to shore to wait out the mistral, swam, and then continued on our way in the evening when the sea was calm. It was much easier for me on this trip, because Gvozdenović and his wife were with us, and Andrija had some experience in sailing. There was sufficient room for sleeping because we had four beds, so Olivera and I slept in the upper and the two men in the lower beds. Olivera was great company—I liked to listen to her soft, resonant voice and her always clever remarks. She studied biology and was an assistant professor at the Natural Sciences University. When we visited them together with Professor Kafka, Dr. Lopandić, and Dr. Lomas, she usually offered us some rare specialties, and she was an excellent cook. She loved Andrija; they had no children. Their apartment looked like a real art gallery because Andrija, in addition to being a painter himself, owned many wonderful paintings from the most renowned artists of Belgrade and Montenegro as well as some painted by Croatian and Bosnian artists. We looked forward to those visits because of both Olivera's special food and Andrija's wonderful paintings.

We were sailing slowly toward Korčula Island, and the engine was rather slow, so it normally took us several hours to reach the next destination. However, we were not bored, because Andrija told us his funny stories and we laughed at them, and we also had many different subjects to talk about. Besides, the landscape of Pelješac was changing, with cliffs, bays, pine forests, and low greenery, so it was enjoyable to observe it from our boat.

We passed through the port of Korčula and stopped in Lumbarda. There were wonderful beaches there, and in the evening we walked beside a large vineyard and visited a local stonecutter who was particularly interesting to Andrija. He offered us "Greek" wine that was excellent, although a bit strong for me. Early the next morning we went to Mljet, and when we were in the open sea, I was afraid a little of that huge space, where it looked as if we were lost. However, the sea was mostly calm or just a bit choppy, so we luckily arrived in the port of Polače. A local fisherman helped us to find the best place to dock.

We had very good time in Mljet, and we enjoyed being with our friends. We went by our boat to lonely places and beautiful bays to swim, and we usually had our lunch on the boat and then took an afternoon nap in the shadow of a pine tree. Our boat was anchored and a mistral, that familiar strong landward wind, swayed it, so sometimes the anchor got stuck and the rope wound around some underwater cliff. We had to dive and release the anchor, and Andrija did that, because Milorad was not skilled in diving. It was usually Ognjen's obligation when he was with us. Luckily, it happened rarely, and later Milorad also got better at anchoring.

In the evenings, we would sit on the deck until late at night, watching the stars that were always clearer at the seaside. We would also have something to eat and drink, and we talked a lot. Silence was present everywhere, and only in the distance we heard the waves hitting on the cliffs. When I said once, "The sea is raging outside," they said nothing, but later both Andrija and Olivera mentioned that sentence with a laugh, hinting at my fear of the sea.

Before evening sometimes, we hiked around Mljet Lake up to Soline, which faced the open sea, and had fish in a little restaurant. We particularly liked to climb the mountains of Mljet, and we climbed from the place that used to be the Benedictine monastery. It was a hotel now, and we took paths that were partly through a pine forest and partly through low greenery on our way to the seashore. We then climbed down to the coast with its fantastic sea-chiseled cliffs, but we did not swim, because there were many sea urchins there. But from that place, watching the endless sea—its powerful waves hitting the cliffs—was really magnificent.

Before the end of our vacation, a local fisherman invited us for a lunch with him. We had become friends with him, and he always helped us with docking and fixing the boat. We gave him and his wife medical advice and even some medicines. They served us a wonderful roast lamb on a big table on their terrace. I never had lamb before. The soup with tasty Dalmatian bread and the dessert were also delicious. I was surprised and delighted by their warm hospitality and kindness—it was totally unexpected.

It was soon time for us to go home. Early in the morning when we started, the sea was calm, but later, especially in the open sea, about halfway toward Korčula Island, the sea became rougher. Milorad and Andrija fought against waves and made jokes as they tried to drive our attention away from the sea. It was so wonderful to see that Lumbarda was close.

We stayed overnight in Lumbarda, and when we wanted to go swimming, the engine could not be started. As much as Milorad and Andrija tried, they failed. Instead of going swimming, we had to look for some engine craftsman. When they found him, all three of them spent several hours repairing the engine. It was too late for us to continue, so we stayed there, walked to the old city, and had excellent calamari in a restaurant. On the following day we left Korčula and sailed slowly along Pelješac until we arrived in Gradac. There, we said farewell to the Gvozdenovićs and to our sailing, which remained unforgettable in my memory.

Savo again organized our skiing that winter, this time in Austria. President Tito was sick and just had his leg amputated, and we expected his recovery. Milorad did not want to go, maybe because of those expectations and maybe because he did not feel well, so Ognjen and I joined other people from Savo's group. We took a long tunnel toward Schladming, where the skiing centers were very similar to the ones in Italy. Our accommodation was good as well, but the Austrians were not as kind as the Italians had been. A bus driver who took us to the skiing venue showed his dislike toward us. During breakfast, however, some of our people were putting extra rolls in their bags and taking them to the skiing venue, while a waiter was constantly bringing more rolls. I felt bad for that.

That spring, every evening we listened to the radio report on President Tito's health situation, which increasingly worsened until he fell into a coma. At the beginning of May, the President's heart stopped beating. Milorad called me from the Veterans Union, and then on the radio I heard the tragic words of a Belgrade announcer, "Comrade Tito passed away." I was not at work that week; I stayed home, because I had sciatica in my left leg—I could hardly move and had strong pains. Thanks to that, I could follow from my bed the trip of Tito's casket from Ljubljana to Belgrade and his funeral.

The funeral was magnificent. People mourned Tito honestly, some of them confident that his communism was good for us; others who did not support communism mourned him as a person, due to his open-mindedness and his wish for progress both for our peoples and the whole world. My mother, for whom the religion was primary, said, "You should know Tito was a religious person." Of course, some people couldn't wait for Tito to die, because they found themselves subordinate in his Yugoslavia. My sisters told me that Western people asked, "And what will be after Tito?" and I replied, "Nothing, all will be the same." I thought his communism moved gradually toward democracy.

Nothing changed at first, except that many people went to visit Tito's grave. That summer we decided to sail only to Ston on the Peljesac Peninsula and spend our vacation there. It was very peaceful, almost without tourists, so we were alone both on the beach and when we went to a restaurant and had mussels and very delicious date-shells. They grew a large number of mussels in the shallow water there. Milorad always used to like to swim far away, and then he began complaining to me he could not stand a long swim. "I almost drowned," he said after swimming one day. We did not pay attention to it, and I said, "Anyway, you should not swim so far away." Still, that peace and quiet finally became boring to us, and especially to Ognjen, who was with us, so we called Hamo and Nedžad, who were in Lopud and told them we would be very happy to spend the rest of our vacation with them there. Nedžad was very glad to hear this and told us to come immediately, that there was enough room for all of us. We left our boat in Ston rather than going all the way around Pelješac, so we took a bus and boat from Trsteno to Lopud and arrived in Hamo's house on the top of the hill. Everyone was there—my little grandsons Dino and Neven, too, but there was still a room for us.

We enjoyed the days with Nedzad and his family. In the evening Nedžad lit a fire and barbecued Zubatac fish, not fresh but frozen, but it was very tasty. We laughed a lot at Hamo's funny stories about his partisan life, and he also showed us various stars in the sky whose names he knew well. I had an opportunity to tell my grandsons some stories I told Nedžad and Ognjen in their childhoods. They liked to hear several times the story called "Stribor's Forest" from Selma Lagerlef and imagined little dwarfs, including their head Malik Tintilinić. They wondered how the princess in "The Princess and the Pea" could feel a pea under so many mattresses. They laughed at Andersen's story "The Emperor's New Clothes" when the emperor remained naked, because some false tailors fooled him. The most impressive for them was the story "What's Sown is Reaped," in which an uncle left his brother's child in a mountain in order to steal his nephew's inheritance. The uncle finally perished and reaped what he had sown.

29 Loss Again

When we returned from our vacation, we went to see my mother in Oglavak and planned to spend some days with her. However, Milorad began to cough constantly, so we came back home earlier. I asked Professor Tvrtković to x-ray his lungs. He did so and said they were all right, but his liver should be checked. The next day, Professor Lovrinčević made a CT scan of Milorad's liver and we were both shocked to see a tumor in the central part of his liver. Sitting in his office, my legs felt as if they had been cut off, and I was thinking about what to do next. Professor Prcić, the head of the Abdominal Department, gave me his permission to go to Ljubljana to see Professor Kovič, who was an expert liver surgeon. We went to Ljubljana and Professor Kovič said that he would do his best and that he had done a lot of liver resections successfully. Regrettably, after the operation he invited me to his office and said sadly, "I was unable to remove the cancer, because I would have had to make a resection of the whole right lobe of the liver, and since your husband's left part is poorly developed, he would surely go into a coma." To encourage me a little, he told me he injected a new and very efficient Japanese cytostatic agent in the cancer surroundings.

Milorad was still sleeping while I was standing by his bed and crying. A patient, an older gentleman sharing the room with Milorad, watched me and asked me shortly, "Maybe he is not well?" That man called us in Sarajevo after few months to ask about Milorad's health. Regrettably, it was worsening.

Lying in my hotel bed, I was thinking, how come we did not realize his real health situation? It was a metastasis, maybe only one cell came to his liver during his operation or earlier and gradually grew. Unfortunately, he could not take any radiation or chemotherapy because that kind of cancer did not react to those.

I informed Ognjen about it with a heavy heart; he was in his last high school grade, in his happiest period of life, immersed in rock music, and he himself was playing in a band. We both went to Ljubljana to take his father home; he was sad but did not show it before his father. While we were waiting for his discharge from the hospital in a little restaurant, we had pancakes with nuts, chocolate, and cream, like I never had before, and they always reminded me of that sad day later.

Milorad recovered quickly from his operation, and he talked to my colleagues with admiration about the nurses in Ljubljana taking such good care of him—night and day. On his temperature flowsheet he read the diagnosis "meta hepatis" and he asked both me and some of my colleagues about its meaning. He read it wrongly as "meta hepatitis," so he gave us the idea of telling him that it was a kind of hepatitis, and he knew hepatitis can be cured. His Latin diagnosis was "meta hepatis" and meant a metastasis, that is, metastatic liver cancer.

For the Day of the Republic, at the end of November, we went to the Argentina Hotel in Dubrovnik. We listened to the sea waves and walked by the sea and around the Old City, which was always nice, and one day Hamo from Lopud visited us. He talked loudly so waiters looked at him with interest. We had our breakfast, and he took us to the City Caffe, with the best coffee in Dubrovnik, as he said. We agreed he would return home to Sarajevo with us in our car. His jovial spirit filled the atmosphere on our way back. I was driving our Peugeot, and he was talking about everything we could laugh at. Soon we took a break to have roasted lamb, and thanks to Hamo's jokes, it seemed to be our shortest trip home ever.

One day just before New Year's Eve, it was a sunny day, unusual for that time of year. Milorad went to the market, as he often did previously, and when he came back, he came in and said, "I grew well again." His face beamed with joy—maybe he felt his strength was coming back to him. I laughed and hugged him, hiding my real feelings.

At the end of February, we went for a few days to the Koran Hotel in Pale. We walked in the snow, and Milorad was able to walk for a long time, so I thought it was useful for his recovery. When we returned, it was March 8—International Women's Day. I had sciatica in my left leg again, but worse than before. My colleagues forced me to stay in the hospital in the Orthopedic Department, because I was bedridden and could not move at all. Milorad and Ognjen were on their own, but they did not complain. Sejda cleaned the house for them, they cooked, and sometimes my mother and Hamo's wife Evgenija (Ženja, we called her) brought them meals. Dr. Gvozdenović visited them; he liked Milorad and wanted to encourage him with his jokes. I spent a month in the hospital, until I was able to move again, and Milorad and Ognjen came to take me home. Milorad took our car, and when we came home, we had cappuccino he had made for us. I was so happy to be together again. He looked a bit slimmer to me, and his face was somehow paler.

We had a difficult period from April to October, because Milorad was sick, and I watched him deteriorating. Everybody helped us with something. Ženja often made dumplings and brought them for Milorad, because he liked them a lot. Mrs. Đurkin, who lived on the first floor of our apartment house, brought us the afternoon coffee that we had in our bedroom while Milorad was sitting in his bed. His sister Beba brought us beets to make a juice that Milorad took regularly, because we thought it was good for his liver. Dr. Gvozdenović visited him, and sometimes he took us to a restaurant and we walked a little. Milorad got tired very quickly, and Dr. Gvozdenović would look at me with sadness in his eyes.

Several times a day Milorad walked back and forth on our long balcony. His abdomen got bigger, he could not button his trousers, and later he also had a noticeable bulge in the area around his liver. The hernia he had operated on when he met me recurred at that time, also. My colleagues advised him to stay in the hospital to receive plasma and various IV treatments to make him stronger. He agreed, and it helped him a bit. I would sit next to him and we would read some magazines together and talk late into the night, at which point I would go home. Dr. Lopandić visited him one day and wanted to raise his spirits, so she spoke of his charm, and when she said that to him, he commented, "Dear Milica, it is gone with the wind." My heart tore apart, and I could not ever forget that sentence.

When he came home from the hospital, he was well for some time and then suddenly deteriorated. My colleagues agreed he should go back into the hospital again, on our ward in a private room. The nurses helped me, because he could not get up from his bed by himself and was able to lie on his right side only. The head nurse Fatima ordered a nurse to have night duty taking care of Milorad. Fatima came to work at the hospital after sister Sergija retired. She graduated from the Nursing School, was very capable and clean, and treated children like a mother would. It was always very good to see her giving IVs or redressing wounds, because she did it so gently, in such a way that the child could feel as little pain as possible.

Milorad was not in a lot of pain, but he was very weak—he lost his voice, he could not swallow anything but liquid food, and he lost control of his bladder. A nurse, named Marica, helped me a lot. She said, "Mrs. Doctor, please do not do that," and she would put rubber gloves on and clean and redress him. I would take five or six pajamas home for washing and bring back fresh ones. His old colleagues from *Oslobođenje* visited him, as did some people from the Veterans Union and from his family. His mother was alive but weak, and lived in Belgrade with Slobodan's sons. Slobodan and his wife Jelka came to see him from the United States where they had moved several years before. Slobodan was angry, because a more radical operation was not done at his first operation—he was a pathologist and quite familiar with that kind of polyp.

Ognjen was drafted into the Army as he graduated high school that summer. Before leaving for his duty, he sat for a long time by his father's bedside with his head close to his father's. Milorad could hardly speak, but he gave him some advice, "Do not drink in the Army," he said. So Ognjen left, and one evening seven days later Milorad's son Zoran came to visit. We sat by his bed, and Milorad fell asleep. A few hours later, he passed away. His heart stopped beating.

The people from the Veterans Union came to us the next day to extend their condolences and said that the funeral service would be at the Union's expense. We were visited by Milorad's friends, colleagues from *Oslobođenje*, and the Veterans Union. Especially touching were the words of his fellow journalists from *Oslobođenje*. A few articles were written about him in *Oslobođenje*, and there was an especially nice one by Radivoj Papić, who was the editor-in-chief of *Svijet* magazine for many years. Ognjen came, because he got permission from the Army, and although he knew about his father's difficult situation, he was speechless when he lost his father. My cousin Muniba also mourned Milorad, because she and her husband Mašo were our intimate friends. She brought me various meals and gave me her good black jacket for the funeral.

I felt relieved, since it was almost unbearable for me to look at him so sick, and I was especially sorry that he became aware his end was coming. I pretended I was cheerful—he sometimes called me "Nadjenka," so I told him while laughing, "Call me 'My Nadjenka.' " He said it again, but somehow aimlessly. When I was lonely in my emptiness, I remembered our beginning, his breezy spirit and lively intellect.

I went to see my sisters in Switzerland, they invited me to rest there for some time. I had previously visited Ognjen, who served his military service in Postojna, so I entered Postojna Cave again, but I did not experience it like before. I was somehow absent-minded, and that feeling stayed with me for a long time.

I felt good with my sisters. They helped me to buy presents for each nurse who helped me with Milorad, and a special one for Marica. I remained always grateful to them, as well as to my colleagues who had a lot of compassion for us.

I was now a widow, and fifty-four years old. I assumed Milorad thought that when he passed away, I would go on with my life with maybe some other man. But I did not want it, maybe because of him, and because I was tired from my two marriages. My profession filled me enough, and I directed my emotions to my sons and grandsons.

Ognjen was in the Army, and I was by myself and fully devoted to surgery. Our division was made a department and was named the Pediatric Surgery Department. The head of the department was Professor Kafka, and four of us were heads of divisions. I was in charge of the Neonatology Division. However, each of us performed the other operations too, and we usually took turns on difficult ones.

30 Mother

Implementation of a new management system began in enterprises, schools, hospitals, and other institutions. Administration became more complicated, so the doctors spent a lot of time for administration. In that system, the authority of managers decreased, the doctors became independent, and some surgeons performed operations without having the necessary skills. There was less hierarchy in surgery than before. Professor Kaufer retired, and he was replaced by Professor Besarović, who was very capable but without any authority in this new system. Still, each department had competent doctors managing to resist sloppiness and to follow the up-to-date trends in the field of surgery.

Weekends were the most difficult times for me, because I would have spent them with Milorad. He had liked hiking, so we went to many mountains around Sarajevo, like Trebević, Jahorina, Treskavica, and the Vranica slopes near Oglavak. And when we went to the seaside, wherever we were, we also went to the surrounding hills. One day we climbed up Treskavica and it started to rain. We went through a forest for about four hours and got completely drenched. Milorad carried Ognjen on his back, because he was still a little boy. When we reached the top, we saw a fantastic panorama, the untouched greenery with a crystal clear glacier lake in the middle. We often went from Oglavak to the spurs of Vranica Mountain. We climbed up through the forest several hours and then we reached the top of the hill, Zahor, where we rested by the cold-water spring. The road to the spring was a bit complicated, so once, when we were with Dr. Lomas and his wife Dušanka, we wandered around it for a long time and could not find it. Very tired, we stopped at some other place and enjoyed a barbecue, tomatoes, cucumbers, and cakes Dušanka had brought with her.

During the weekends, I often visited my mother, who spent summers in Oglavak. She was there from June to September; she liked Oglavak and did not mind being alone there. She was a communicative person and knew everybody from the neighboring villages—Muslim and Catholic women—and invited them to have coffee with her, giving them health advice she heard from me. I would come in my little Yugo up to the foothills of Oglavak and park in the yard of a girl living with her brother. She was honest and helped my mother by buying food and working around the house. She was talented in many other types of work, too, so she made many repairs around the house.

I climbed up the forest, the same one I had liked since my childhood. The path followed the creek all the way to the top. The smell of forest grass, soil, and light humidity made me nostalgic for my childhood. When I came, my mother said at the door, "Nobody will be so happy to see you like I am." She always had some new juice made of blueberry, raspberry, or blackberry and she would fill a big glass for me. The coffee we had together that time was the best I ever had. It was quiet in the evening and we heard leaking water, although the old fountain was replaced with modern closing faucets. Some relatives had built new cabins there and came often. My mother called them "weekend people." They invited us to join them for coffee and delicious lokum ("Turkish Delights") and we invited them as well. I walked with my mother to my father's grave, taking breaks at several places and sitting on a sheepskin we had with us. We used to sit in our garden, too, and we also picked up sour cherries that were big and not too sour, and we enjoyed the smell of pears, while apples and plums grew ripe later.

I became closer with my mother; I took her to Jahorina Mountain sometimes, and while I was skiing she was walking. She said, "If I was younger, I would also ski." It was interesting for her to see all the skiing costumes in various colors. Earlier, Milorad and I had taken her with us to the Bistrica Hotel, where she was always knitting and talking to women whom she befriended very quickly.

MEMORIES FROM BOSNIA

In the spring, we paid visits to my sisters in Switzerland. They were very happy, and my mother was also happy to have all three of us with her. My visits to my sisters remain as my best memories. They took us to many places, including restaurants on the lakes and rivers, and they gave us money, too, so we bought different things. My mother was crocheting dresses and costumes for them that they appreciated a lot, and I brought them some presents that my thankful patients had given me.

During one of my visits to Switzerland, I visited Professor Grob's clinic again. It was not his clinic anymore, though. Professor Rikham was its head, and Professor Grob had already passed away. It was sad for me to read his dignified obituary, which my sister had sent me earlier. When I visited the clinic, the head nurse in the operating room told me, "Everything is different now." I met Professor Rikham, a short, easygoing man. He came to the break room and had coffee with other doctors between his operations. He spoke kindly to me and was interested in pediatric surgery in Sarajevo and Yugoslavia. I observed their operations and it seemed to me there was no difference from the time Professor Grob was in charge.

Ognjen had already begun to study medicine. He was not too enthusiastic about medicine at first, but his father and I wanted it, so he had passed the admission exam during his father's illness. After he served in the military for a year, he started medical school. He also played flute and saxophone in a rock group called "Zabranjeno Pusenje" ("Smoking Forbidden"). He had attended a music school for six years and acquired a basic music education.

One day he came and told me, "Mother, I found a really nice girl, you will see, she is very nice." And I met her. She really had something attractive inside, and she was well shaped too, because she went in for athletics. She studied law. Ognjen often traveled with his band to different places and Vladana, his girlfriend, often went with him.

31 Conferences

In February of 1984, Sarajevo was ready for the Winter Olympics. For several years the people in charge worked at preparations, including construction and reconstruction of skiing venues, extension and paving of roads leading to them, construction of sports facilities and the Olympic Village, and regulation of city traffic. Many streets were widened, and many of them became one-way streets, which improved the traffic problems in the city considerably. The problems with the water supply and sewerage systems were resolved earlier; citizens had paid a great deal of money over many years to finance the improvements. The water supply system was expanded, and the sewerage system was modernized. Sarajevo was always nice, but now it looked like a big, interesting city.

The people were still worried, though, because there was very little snow. The rivers were low, so we were short on electricity. We had daily reductions lasting several hours. Western newspapers wrote, "Vučko in the Darkness." Vučko was the mascot of our Olympics.

The time had come for the opening of the Olympics. It was a manifestation of perfectly trained young people, with a lot of originality. It started snowing heavily on the first day of competition and snowed throughout the games, resulting in an idyllic picture of Sarajevo. As a token of solidarity, we had many buses from Ljubljana,

Zagreb, Rijeka, Belgrade—and all for free—but they were not crowded. Our people showed their respect for the Olympics. Many new restaurants were opened, offering domestic specialties as well as many other special foods.

As a doctor, every morning I went to Igman Mountain where I worked in an ad hoc outpatient clinic. We watched the events on TV, and some of them we followed live. I was present at the figure skating finals and watched the magnificent dancing of the winning couple, Jane Torwill and Christopher Dean. My sister's son Miran, who had come from Switzerland to watch the Olympics, took me with him. The wonderful violet costumes levitated on the ice, leaving an unforgettable picture in my mind. The Olympics were soon over and engraved in many hearts. It was one of the two magnificent events in my life—the other one was Tito's funeral.

The International Pediatric Surgeons Conference was to be held in Prague the next year. I wanted to be present at that conference, and I got approval to attend. I took Ženja, Nedžad's mother-in-law, with me. She was a housewife, because she married very early and did not finish her education. She was a good person and was always helpful in cooking and doing everything she knew in order to help people, and she was an excellent housewife.

When we arrived in Prague, on our way from the airport, our first impressions included the hills covered with forest and ancient towers. The conference was held at the University of Prague (today, Charles University at Prague), which dates from the fourteenth century and is among the oldest universities in Europe. We sat on highly polished wooden benches with wooden backs, and the smell of the patina and the wood enveloped us. The conference was dedicated to the famous Czech doctor, Dr. Bohdalek, whose grave we visited in the old Czech graveyard. Our hosts took us to Hradczane, the old castle from the Habsburg period, and we looked at the city during our ride. The city ranged over forest-covered hills, and the Vlatava River sparkled in the sun; old bridges, old towers, and churches were dotted here and there, and it struck me as the most dignified city I had ever seen.

During the conference, a pediatric surgeon from the state of Ohio in the United States, approached me. When she learned I was also a pediatric surgeon, she was pleasantly surprised, because there were very few women surgeons at the conference. She wanted to take a photo of me, and I asked her to take it of me and Ženja together, and to send us a copy of the photo. She took a photo with great pleasure and sent a copy to us shortly after the conference. It was a very good picture, and I sent her some of our traditional embroidery and knitted goods. Her husband was a very big man, and he did not like to walk much, so he said, "European people like to see the old things." He was not a doctor but a lawyer.

One evening our hosts took us to a picnic and served us food and a big pint of Czech beer. Ženja said it was great, but I could not make any comment because I disliked beer. Later, when we went shopping, Ženja bought some wonderful Czech china cups for Amra and Nedžad, and I bought some presents too. Their shops at the time were modest and not full of goods like ours were.

We were all shocked the next year by the sudden death of Professor Kafka. He was obese and had diabetes. He stopped smoking and tried to lose weight. He was partly successful in that and was getting in good shape, so I was shocked to hear from Dr. Lomas on the phone, "Professor Kafka passed away." The same day he had operated on a child's spleen and had afternoon rounds. He fell down while leaving the hospital. It was a massive heart attack, and our cardiologists could not help. He was sixty-two years old. At his funeral, I spoke on behalf of our department about his personality, expressing our sadness at losing the wonderful professor who led us for many years with his intellect and surgical capability. He was Bosnia and Herzegovina's first pediatric surgeon.

I was soon appointed the head of the Pediatric Surgery Department. I had been a deputy of Professor Kafka, so my colleagues selected me to be the head. I wanted to perform modern operations, and it was always important for me to leave as few disabilities as possible after difficult operations. My colleagues, the surgeons, helped me; Dr. Lomas was a deputy, and we had several new colleagues as residents, younger and older ones, men and women.

Ognjen was studying medicine and playing in his band at the same time. I was afraid the band could interfere with his studying, but he organized his time somehow and had high grades. His band "Smoking Forbidden" was very popular among the youth. Ognjen had good friends in the band and others whom he knew from the time he was in the military. He and his friends sailed on our boat, which was now anchored in Lopud so that Hamo, Nedžad's father-in-law, could control it during the year. Ognjen and his girlfriend Vladana had a lot of stories about their boating experiences.

In the summer I went to Lopud Island, where Hamo, Nedžad, his wife Amra, and their children spent their vacation. I had a good time with Ženja, and I also have a very nice memory of her mother, who came to Lopud with them. She had beautiful green eyes and spoke only when necessary, and she was a good listener. She was a good person, and Hamo liked her a lot. Unexpectedly, one year in Lopud she had a severe heart attack that she did not survive.

During my stay in Lopud, every day I went by boat with Nedžad, Amra, and their children to Šipan Island, to the opposite side of Lopud, to the cliffs, and always to some other place. It was empty, without tourists, so we had a great time swimming. The children fished, Nedžad often did some necessary chore on the boat, and Amra and I enjoyed being in the sun and talking with each other. Those vacations I had with Nedžad and his family, with whom I always felt at home, made me feeling nostalgic about the irretrievably lost days of my life.

I spent my winter vacation with Nedžad too. He built a small cabin at Jahorina Mountain on the road to the Hotel Šator—he was talented in woodworking and electric wiring, so he did a lot by himself. His cabin was sweet, with a lot of sun in the mornings and with a constant fire in a simple and unique fireplace. We went there usually before New Year's. Ženja made a lot of different cakes, so while carrying a big basket full of cakes, Nedžad said, "Children, look what my mother-in-law made for me." After our breakfast, for which we often had great fritters made by Ženja, we went skiing or sleighing, depending on what each person wanted to do that day, and then we returned—frozen, putting our gloves on the fireplace and enjoying its warmth. In the evenings, we used to tell stories, and Hamo's were especially interesting. Then we'd go out in the snow again and walk around, with the snow squeaking under our feet. The picture was idyllic, everything was under the snow, and only the lights of the little houses were seen.

Sometimes I went there alone and climbed up to the cabin in my small Yugo. I stayed there two or three days and I was not afraid. Ognjen and Vladana also dropped by, usually skiing all day and coming back frozen and eager to refresh themselves. One day I visited Savo in his weekend house, he was by himself because his dear wife

Mira had died. She had a breast cancer operation and felt well for many years, but she had been skiing in Italy and Austria, and her death came suddenly. Savo was like a felled tree.

The Pediatric Surgeons Conference was held in Erevan, in the Soviet Republic of Armenia. I had my paper ready to present at the conference. I took Ženja with me because she always wanted to see Russia. Her father was a Russian loyalist who immigrated into our country after the 1917 revolution. We flew over Moscow, and we visited it on our way back. We spent two days sightseeing in Tbilisi, Georgia. It was a lively, clean, and orderly city, with signage in Russian and in Georgian and rather expensive shops, not too much different from a Western European city. In the city center, on a specially fenced site, was Stalin's monument—he was from Georgia. In the evening our hosts took us to an interesting restaurant with low wooden tables, almost fully in the dark, that had only a central stage illuminated for their folk program.

The Armenian capital, Erevan, our next destination, was peculiar. There were buildings scattered over a large area, all in rose, because they dug stone of that color in the vicinity and used it for all construction. The shops were full of people and goods that were like those in the Near East. The conference was well organized and included a lot of free time, so we enjoyed sightseeing. Our hosts showed us the main office of the head of the Armenian church, Katalikosa, who was their pope, and we also saw their museum. I was fascinated by the unusual artistic creations, many of which were made of gold—much unlike Western museums that did not use so much gold.

We also visited the children's hospital. It was tidy, but it was more modest than in the West. It was interesting to see one-year-old babies swimming in the pool. They swam instinctively, and it was a kind of therapy for them.

One night we went to see an opera written by a famous Armenian composer. In the opera house was a huge room for the audience and an arched stage with three parts, each part used at a different point in the opera. The singers' voices were wonderful. The Erevan people were kind, and the city had a great atmosphere. Silk was very inexpensive, and all of us in the group bought a lot of it.

MEMORIES FROM BOSNIA

We spent two days in Soči, a tourist destination on the Black Sea on our way back. Soči reminded me of our own vacation spots, and we had a great time swimming. We stayed two days in Moscow. We spent half a day waiting in line to see Lenin's mausoleum. I was not all that enthusiastic about it, because, to me, an embalmed body does not represent a person. When I heard that the villagers had carried his body more than thirty miles to Moscow, in gratitude for his ending the unjust feudal system, I realized his importance in their lives. Moscow was a nice city, and the Kremlin and the other buildings in the Eastern architectural style were magnificent, but the whole city was gray and dreary. The people walked about with their heads hanging down, the shops were half-empty of goods to sell, and it was quite a different picture than the one in Tbilisi and Erevan, which was lively. I was not sorry to leave Moscow.

The first Pediatric Surgeons Conference of Yugoslavia was in the preparation phase. We had a surgeons conference every four years that included pediatric surgeons too, but our own association became stronger and we decided to organize a conference with international participation. Everybody agreed for it to be held in Sarajevo.

The conference board, whose members were important surgeons from all the Yugoslavian republics, was very busy. The pharmaceutical companies, drug factories, and a lot of large enterprises made generous donations to our organization. The conference was announced in surgical magazines, and applications to present papers started to arrive. My colleagues also prepared their papers for the conference, and they had a whole year to do that.

Prior to our conference, there was a Pediatric Surgeons Conference in Budapest. I went there with Dr. Mira Potkonjak, one of four women surgeons we had at the time. For me, it was the best conference I had ever attended. Its opening was at Semelweiss University, which was named after the surgeon about whom Professor Kovačević used to say, "Semelweiss should have a life-sized golden monument in his honor erected," because he had been the man who introduced the principles of infection control in operating rooms. When we entered a great hall with high columns, we were welcomed by the students' anthem. The children's flute orchestra opened the conference—some fifty children of ten or so played flutes. The scene was fantastic.

MEMORIES FROM BOSNIA

The presentations were interesting, not only the foreign ones, but also the local ones, and a serious discussion was held. All three days we had a light lunch in a restaurant at noon, a very delicious soup that was a meal. In the evening we enjoyed other delicious dishes.

Budapest, on the Danube, seemed to be a wonderful city. During our drive to Budim, the old part of the city on the other side of the river, our hosts showed us historical sites, some from the Turkish period. In the central part of Budapest, the entire history from—Arpad until today—was visible in the buildings. In Budim, there was an interesting church that had been first a church, then a mosque, and then finally a church once again. Turkish calligraphy was partly visible in that church. During our last night at the Hilton Hotel, we had flambéed pancakes with our dinner that were made in the hall and it was idyllic to see the open flame in the dark room. Together with Dr. Potkonjak, I took the Budapest Metro. It was the liveliest metro I had ever seen—a whole magic underground city. When we parted, I thought about how my father was right when he spoke about Hungarians with admiration, and I thought, "When an Eastern people accepts Western culture, it has a special charm—it is more than one culture."

The preparations for our conference were now in the final phase. Then it was the opening day of the conference, which included an artistic program to welcome our guests. I gave one of the main presentations, and my former colleagues from Zagreb and Belgrade presented their work too. The conference was well organized both in terms of its professional content and in other supporting projects. Ognjen had just received his degree, so he helped a lot during our work; he was cute—behaving like a host, because he also was a doctor. Dr. Kent, the American I met in Prague, came to the conference too, and she had two interesting presentations. As a present, she brought dresses for me and Ženja. She came with her husband, who was still very fat, and one day I invited them to have coffee and my special hurmasice at my place. We were sitting on my sunny balcony, and he said, "Your coffee, Nadja, is the best I have had in Sarajevo."

The participants and their guests visited many places in Sarajevo during the free time periods. We took them to the Spring of Bosna River and Igman Mountain, and my former colleagues, the surgeons from Zagreb and Belgrade, visited our Pediatric Surgery Department as well. The final evening was cheerful, with folk dances and good food. I felt a bit bad when a young man said to me, "Doctor, people don't have enough to eat and you have so rich a reception." It was autumn of 1987, and I was not so sure that our people didn't have enough food. There was, indeed, an economic crisis, but I thought the young man was exaggerating how bad things were. I reminded myself that people made their own decisions about coming to the conference and that our money for the conference had come from donations. That evening I had a TV interview as the head of the Surgery Department with a clear conscience.

32 Retirement

My mother began to behave strangely that summer. She had a tenant and said he stole some things from her room. She would pay a handyman twice, so the man was giving me back the money. She always wanted to have money for her funeral set aside, so she saved a few pieces of gold for that purpose. One day she gave away one of them to the woman who cleaned her house, and on another other occasion she gave away the second gold piece.

When Milorad was alive and for some years afterward, she used to invite all of us, including Nedžad and his family, and Ženja and Hamo, to have lunch at her place two or three times a year. She was no longer able to do that now because she could not safely cook. I asked the parents of the woman who cleaned her house if they would live with her and help her with her meals. They agreed to do that. However, they often went to the village and stayed there as long as they wanted, so I was concerned about my mother's welfare. Whenever I went to see her, I came back home even more worried. At that time I learned that I had high blood pressure, and I had to start taking medication on a regular basis.

My relations with my colleagues in the Surgery Department were harmonious; they respected me, but they began to work on their own whenever they heard about or saw a new method for an operation. They were young surgeons and overly confident in their abilities. At the same time, I had begun to avoid difficult operations that I had previously performed with ease and pleasure. So I decided it was time to retire. I was almost sixty-one and had more than thirty years of service. I planned to spend more time with my mother and to do something other than medicine—maybe to write or to translate.

I had a really wonderful send-off. Many colleagues from all of the surgical departments were there, both those I knew as friends through the years and those whom I did not know had thought of me as their friend. My colleagues presented me with a beautiful painting as a gift. I thanked them and gave a short speech expressing my wish for them: that they would continue to advance pediatric surgery, avoid rivalry, and obey Dr. Lomas, who was supposed to replace me. Ognjen took photos of the farewell party for me, and a lot of people said I looked so young, not like a candidate for retirement. So my surgical career, which gave me many pleasures in my life, was over.

I took my mother that summer to Oglavak; she was still able to be there alone, but only with the help of two girls who lived in the neighborhood. I visited her very often in Oglavak, and when I would leave, she would stand at the door and almost cry like a child, asking me to come again as soon as possible. I dismissed the people who did not actually provide competent help to her and found a woman from the area around Oglavak who had married and now lived in Sarajevo. She already knew my mother and respected her. The people who I fired created problems for me, however, calling me in the middle of the night and cursing me violently. I was frightened. I realized then how people could be terribly cruel when you do something that may not be the best thing for them, even when you have a fully justifiable reason for doing what you have done. I hadn't known their character when I hired them to take care of my mother, so it was a rude awakening to discover their true nature. I soon remembered Anne Frank, who wrote in her diary, "If you want to know somebody, have a quarrel with him."

Even though I was technically retired, I was still involved with pediatric surgery. I had good manuscripts in German I had bought in Switzerland, so each day I translated and dictated to Ognjen, who typed for me. He was about to finish with his internship. He tried to find a job in the Emergency Room but was unsuccessful, although he had volunteered there for a year prior to his internship. One day, Dr. Lomas phoned me and said, "If Ognjen does not have anything else, we will accept him in the Pediatric Surgery Department, because we need young residents. We also feel obligated to you." Ognjen always wanted to do things his own way, without my assistance, but he accepted this offer with pleasure. Very soon he joined the department, taking part in operations and in intensive care, for which he had a special affinity. He was not enthusiastic about medicine when he began studying it, but later he became very fond of it. He said that Professor Fajgelj, who instructed him in internal medicine, was one reason for his change of heart about medicine.

My life as a retired person was quite different from my life as a working person. I missed getting up early in the morning and going to work. On my way there I would exchange morning greetings with doctors, nurses, and other employees going to work also. At 7:00 a.m. I had an hour of short rounds[57] on my patients. Then I had a coffee break with my colleagues and main rounds[58] at 8:00 a.m. My work in the operating room usually started at 8:30 a.m. and lasted until 1:00 p.m., and sometimes later depending on the surgical schedule. After operating, I had the best coffee of the day, or so it seemed to me. Dr. Potkonjak would usually say then, "How about some kava?" She used the Zagrebian name for coffee she learned while a child in Zagreb and I always enjoyed the way that word sounded. I missed it all. Because I was getting up later, the mornings were very short. Nedžad usually made me happy when he came by my place during his break. I always had a piece of spinach pie or some hurmasice for him. Nedžad was very successful in his work—he managed a sector in the successful company Unioninvest, and got his master's degree, too. His wife Amra also received a master's degree and had an interesting thesis: "Printing-Houses in the Austro-Hungarian Period in Bosnia and Herzegovina." She worked in the rare books section in the National and University Library. Nedžad visited his grandmother often, as did Ognjen—they loved her a lot. I was satisfied with the new caregivers; the husband, in particular, was especially kind and compassionate to my mother. She had to be always watched, because she was inclined to wander around and was not able to safely use the stove to cook by herself. In view of this fact, I found a young woman, the husband's sister, who had no other obligations and took care of my mother constantly. I paid her separately, in addition to the payment I made to the other caregivers in

---

[57] Bedside visits to patients within one division of Pediatric Surgery Department.
[58] Bedside visits to patients within the entire Pediatric Surgery Department.

the house, because my sisters sent twice as much money as was needed for our mother's care. The caregivers had the whole house at their disposal, too, rent-free and all expenses paid. So I was peaceful for some time because things seemed to be under control.

One day Ognjen told me, "Mother, I and Vladana would like to get married." I was glad; she was a nice girl, and they had already spent several years together. Ognjen had his job and his salary, and Vladana was at the end of her studies. They planned to marry in March, and it was in that very period that I had an accident with my mother. On Women's Day, March 8, I wanted to take my mother out of the city to the Memorial Vraca, the beautiful park above the city dedicated to the memory of those killed under the Nazi regime.

I wanted to spend that day with her. While thinking about it, I had a phone call from my mother's tenant, who said, "Your mother fell off her bed while getting up and we put her back in bed, but she has strong pains in her left leg and cannot use it." I went there at once and concluded she had fractured her leg in her hip, so we went immediately by ambulance to the hospital emergency room. My colleagues examined her. Except for her Alzheimer's disease, she was well, they said, and she could stand surgery without much risk. Her fracture was a bit below her hip, so it was not necessary to use anything more than the usual steel pins. The operation took place that day.

Fifteen days after her operation, by which time my mother was recovering well, Ognjen and Vladana were married. It was a lovely sunny day and there was a crowd of young people in front of the Municipal Center who came to be present at his wedding. They organized a lunch in a very good restaurant, and then they left the next day to honeymoon in southern Germany, Switzerland, and northern Italy.

I had met Vladana's parents earlier, and my impression of them was that they were intellectuals who were very sociable and pleasant. Her mother taught German in a high school, and her father was a lawyer with a high government position in the Parliament of Bosnia and Herzegovina. They were born in Brčko—one of Vladana's grandfathers was an Orthodox priest in the Brčko area, and the other was the owner of a restaurant in the city. Vladana had a sister four years younger than she. Her parents were, to me, open, up-to-date, and very nice people.

MEMORIES FROM BOSNIA

It was on a stormy day with wind and rain announcing that autumn was coming that Ognjen's first son was born. He was a cute baby; they named him Srdjan, and our relatives and friends came to see him. He grew quickly and when he began to crawl he was so skilled that we all enjoyed watching him. He always tried to grab some soil from a flowerpot, so we always kept a very close eye on him during that stage.

That year, Miran, the son of my youngest sister Suma, asked me to come to his mother's 60th birthday celebration in Zurich. He offered to buy me a plane ticket, because he wanted to surprise his mother. Ognjen was very excited about it and wanted me to go, and I agreed. Miran waited for me in Zurich. We were supposed to celebrate her birthday in Schwarzwald in southern Germany, and we all gathered in a hotel—my middle sister Dila and her daughter Dina too, along with their friends. It was a great surprise for Suma to see me. Her eyes were full of tears and she kept saying, "Thank you, Miran, I will never forget this." We walked in the Black Forest and celebrated Suma's birthday until late at night. I had an opportunity to speak longer with Dina and Miran. Dina graduated from the Actor's Academy in Zurich and was a dramatic actress in Basel, Switzerland, and then in Freiburg, Germany. Miran had studied chemistry in Zurich, had his doctoral degree, and worked as a chemical engineer, mostly on wastewater management projects.

When I returned home, I unpacked and gave Ognjen and Vladana presents I bought for them, Ognjen said, "Mother, we will have another baby." Although I did not think about it earlier, I was not surprised, because I got used to surprises in my life. She was supposed to have her baby born in three months, and I do not know how I did not notice it, but it was my nature—if I am not interested in something I do not see it.

My mother's leg was better and she was able to walk with a cane. Her tenants took care of her, keeping everything clean, and I controlled it all. My sisters sent money for her, came to see her, and noticed she was different than when they saw her after her operation. They had come when she was still in the hospital. Now, my sisters noted that her mental condition was worse. She recognized them, but her speech was not in her usual style. But she was in good shape physically.

Ognjen's second son, Mladen, was a cute baby too. He had light-colored eyes and hair, while Srdjan had dark eyes and hair. He grew well, and unlike Srdjan, he did not crawl before learning to walk. He was very clever, had a very serious gaze, and always seemed quite aware of everything going on around him—including when we changed our plans for something and forgot to tell him! Nedžad and Amra invited me the next spring to go to the new hotel complex, Babin Kuk, in Dubrovnik with them for the May 1 International Labor Day. We had a very good time there, as we always did in hotels during holidays. We spent a lot of time in the swimming pool, and their children enjoyed that especially. However, while watching the TV news in the evening, I was shocked to see that there was an incident in Plitvice Lakes between Croatian and Serbian police forces. We returned home worried, and I then had another shock—the girl who took care of my mother wanted to leave me. My mother no longer had control of her bladder and could not move without great difficulty. Her caregiver did not want to stay with her any longer, although she was helped by the others in the house. Although she was well paid, she insisted she had to leave. I was desperately trying to find somebody for her daily care; I tried to find nuns, too, but nobody wanted to accept my offer due to my mother's advanced Alzheimer's. She could not be accepted in a hospital, so I tried a nursing home. The manager found a place for her in the intensive nursing unit, but after fifteen days she was sent to the hospital. She had developed a prolapse of her large intestine. I consulted my colleague, the abdominal surgeon, who promised to accept her as a patient and try to resolve her problem with an operation. So she went to the hospital, but she never left. Her intestine was no longer a problem that needed attending to because she was hardly moving, and she was not aware of anything. Dr. Sonja Rustempašić, the head of the Anesthesiology Service, told me, "You couldn't take care of her at home. We will keep her in our unit." She spent three long months there, immovable and half-aware. I visited her every day.

I went to the seaside for seven days at the beginning of September, because I was exhausted. When I came back, I had not even unpacked my things when Dr. Durić, the head of the Intensive Care Unit, told me my mother had passed away. Ognjen and Vladana came to be with me. I kept repeating, "She got rid of her miserable life." Nedžad was with her that day, gently touching her hand, and she was not aware of that. So my mother's life was over, and I remained grateful to Dr. Sonja Rustempašić, because my mother had suitable care in her last days.

Her funeral was held in September in Oglavak, like my father's was. I was present at his funeral, but not at my mother's, because I was too upset to go or be seen by people. Mašo Spaho, the husband of my cousin Muniba, described it to me, "I have been to many funerals, but I never saw one like that." He praised my sons, who did their best during the organization of her funeral. There was a prayer for the dead in her house. A lot of her relatives, girlfriends, and neighbors were present. I felt somehow soothed, and some of them told me, "Lucky she, who knows what is ahead of us." I worried about those words, though I could not have known the terrible things that were to happen later.

In a few days, I went to Oglavak by myself. I visited her grave, next to my father's. I took some of her clothes to give to other people, leaving the house gown she liked a lot hanging on the wall to remind me of her. I locked the door behind me. I stood in front of the house and gazed deeply at it, remembering, and then I left.

33 Dissolution

As in the Soviet Union, we also witnessed the fall of communism. The economy went downward, and Yugoslavian republics began to accuse each other of causing that. They each wanted to have greater autonomy, which each had even called for during Tito's rule. In particular, Slovenia wanted to control its assets, because it was the most developed republic of all. The Slovenians were hardworking and thrifty people, and they got sick of financially bailing out the other republics. Croatia always wanted to be a sovereign state. The Albanians from Kosovo had already demanded to have a Republic of Kosovo, and some fighting had started, which disturbed us all.

The Yugoslavian Presidency was a shared power, with members from each republic, and they began to arrange for a future Yugoslavia. They conducted marathon negotiations about the future state in each republic, and we waited for the results with anxiety—but they failed to reach an agreement. When they met to negotiate in Sarajevo, Kiro Gligorov, a representative of Macedonia, which thanks to him experienced the dissolution of Yugoslavia with the least pain, said to them, "Do not allow for this wonderful Sarajevo to be the victim of the conflict." But he knew already what would happen. I remembered his words several times when Sarajevo was burning. Slovenia and Croatia supported a confederation, but the president of Serbia, Slobodan Milošević did not, although it was probably a good solution. Ethnic parties with prominent national symbols were blooming, which also encouraged the dissolution of the country. The Reform Party attempted to keep unity with necessary reforms. In particular, Ante Marković pledged to salvage and improve the economy—but such beacons of hope were a minority. We waited for the election results with great anxiety, and as we feared, the reformists were defeated by the loud nationalists.

With a majority of the votes, Slovenia proclaimed its independence. Slobodan Milošević sent the Yugoslav Army to quash the move, but he withdrew the army after a very brief conflict. Slovenia was a border state with a mostly Slovenian population, so it was not so important for the Yugoslav Army, which was rapidly becoming predominantly Serbian. Immediately afterward, Croatia voted unanimously for its own independence, declaring its historical dream to be a new reality. The war itself started between the newly founded Croatian Army and the Yugoslav Army. The major victims of the bloodshed were the most peaceful and the most tolerant parts of Yugoslavia—the parts that had the most mixed and diverse population—like the wonderful city of Vukovar.

We, the Bosnian people, followed it all and thought it could not happen to us, although the national parties here struggled over which party could defame the other to the greatest degree. The dilemma was whether or not to become an independent state, because many people did not want to stay in the incomplete Yugoslavia without Croatia and Slovenia. Bosnians, in particular, supported independence—the ones who felt like Bosnians, meaning the Muslims, and a lot of Serbs and Croats, too. The elections were held, and the majority voted for independence. Then something unbelievable happened. Bosnian Serbs, persuaded by Belgrade, wanted to unite Bosnia and Serbia, while Bosnian Croats wanted to unite it with Croatia. They were to divide Bosnia, which had its autonomy recognized by Tito when it was established as one of the six Yugoslav republics. Bosnia was a separate entity for many centuries—from the medieval Bosnian state through the Turkish and Austrian era. Muslims had only Bosnia as their state, and tried to defend itself, backed by a lot of well-intentioned Serbs and Croats. It was impossible, however, to resist the Yugoslav Army. The worst thing was that the nationalists were spreading their hatred around, and the heretofore unbreakable Bosnian people began to break apart. The Bosnian population was divided. Everybody wanted to take revenge. Serbs and Croats found they lost their national identity in communism, while Muslims found they lost their Islam. It was partly true, because communism tended to do that, but it passed, and both national identity and religion could have been less painfully revived. I do not know what I was thinking about when I wrote a letter to Izetbegović[59] and to Plavšić and Krajišnik,[60] asking them to be tolerant in their speeches. Maybe they laughed at my letter, maybe they threw it away without even reading it—I do not know.

As soon as Bosnia and Herzegovina was recognized by the United Nations, Sarajevo was attacked. Grenades were sent selectively from Trebević Mountain, and when the wonderful building of the Electric Management Company was bombed, I told my sisters on the phone, "I am sorry they are destroying Sarajevo." I felt terribly sad. A few days later I was with Nedžad when we saw smoke coming from the Unioninvest building. Nedžad gave us his binoculars and we saw that building on fire. My heart broke apart, because it was Nedžad's company—because it was so much a part of his life.

The market was empty, and we could find only large quantities of eggs there. People carried large and small packages of eggs throughout Sarajevo. We thought it all would end with several damaged buildings, but one evening after a strong detonation, the telephone connections were interrupted. The Post Office building was bombed. That wonderful Austro-Hungarian building was on fire. We were disconnected from the world and lived like that for the next several years. Soon the City Hall, the symbol of Sarajevo, was burned and totally destroyed by fire, lit by grenades. The National Library, where my Amra worked, was located in the City Hall, and had been evacuated before the bombing.

---

[59] Muslim leader in Bosnia and Herzegovina.
[60] Serb leaders in Bosnia and Herzegovina.

34 Besieged

The majority of people living in Sarajevo were leaving, especially women and children—by plane, by cars, by all possible means of transportation. Soon the exodus was stopped, because Sarajevo was blocked and besieged from all sides and nobody was allowed to leave. Ilidža, a suburb of Sarajevo, and Grbavica too, were controlled by Serbs, the attackers. When grenades started to fall in and around Sarajevo, and wounded people were coming to the hospital, Ognjen decided to try to find a way to send Vladana and their children to Zagreb to stay with the good friend he met while serving in the military. His friend had suggested that they come and stay in his house in Zagreb. Somehow, Ognjen heard that local Serb and Bosnian commanders were now allowing a large convoy of women and children to leave. The evacuees were to gather at Pioneer Valley. When I arrived to say goodbye, I found Vladana and children there with many others, waiting nervously. The long convoy (probably a few miles long) moved toward Ilidža. It was stopped at Ilidža, and the people were mistreated, closed in a small space at the Sports Center, and many of them were sent back to Sarajevo. Vladana and her little children, together with Vera, the wife of Milorad's son Zoran, and her two little children, had their most difficult days there. They were imprisoned in Ilidža for two days, and afterward they continued on a hard trip over craggy mountainous roads. They couldn't go through Mostar, where there was fighting between the Croatian Army, joined by the newly formed

Bosnian Army, against the Yugoslav Army. Ognjen and I were sitting in our room in Sarajevo—a neighbor, an elderly gentleman, had joined us and had some whiskey and was expecting news from Ilidža—and suddenly we heard a horrible explosion. Zetra, the Olympic Sports Center, which we could easily see about six blocks away down the hill from our house, was in flames.

We had no food; the wonderful supermarkets and shops were wrecked, with broken windows and small pieces of glass scattered around. Everything was looted and empty. We could not find even the smallest green leaf at the market. Instead of lettuce, people picked dandelion leaves; dandelion had a sour taste, but soon it was all used up. There were some private houses with small gardens, and I found a lot of nettle at one place. I asked the owner if I could pick it and she allowed me to do that because she had other vegetables for her needs in her garden. That nettle saved me. I picked lots of it and dried it on my balcony so it could last a long time. Fortunately, new nettle grew quickly, so I had a supply of it all summer. We got some flour in the humanitarian aid, so I made a wonderful pie.

I went one day to see my cousin, who was the daughter of my mother's oldest sister. She had a garden with plants. I talked to her a little about the hardships we suffered, and when I was about to leave I looked wistfully at those plants in her garden, but she did not offer me anything. I never forgot that—maybe she did not remember, I do not know.

We had no electricity, either, so the food in our refrigerators was inedible. People emptied their refrigerators and lost all their supplies, which could have lasted months. Some areas had gas heating, so people managed somehow; they baked meat on gas stoves. I also baked a small quantity of meat I had, with Nedžad, because he had gas heating, dividing it in small portions and keeping it on my balcony. But even with that scarcity, a lot of food was thrown away because there was no electricity for refrigeration. While Sarajevo was ruined and people were killed, we expected that the United Nations would help us. President Mitterrand of France visited Sarajevo, so we thought that would result in a cease-fire. However, only a large number of fruitless negotiations took place. We begged for support from Europe—but in vain—there was no help coming for us. We later guessed that the European Union had been told by the Serbs that the Muslims wanted to have Bosnia as an Islamic state, and for that reason the EU did nothing to help us. But of course that was not true, because Bosnia still belonged to all—to Muslims, Serbs, and Croats. The Serbs called Bosnia the "Dark Province." We then began to have hope in the new American president, Bill Clinton.

Nedžad's birthday was in November, so I invited them, as well as Ženja and Hamo, to celebrate it at my place. I cooked something at my neighbor's, who had a fire stove and offered it to me. We took a photo, and we all looked so bad—we all lost a lot of weight. I lost 37 pounds, and Nedžad and Ognjen almost looked like skeletons wearing their suits.

I had a little battery-operated transistor radio that Nedžad brought me from Iraq, where he had worked as an engineer for some time. It was the one thing I had that I valued very highly. It enabled me to have some contact with the world—I listened to a little encouraging news, too, but also heard about some terrible things done by some wild units from Serbia—rapes and murders. Sometimes I went to the Surgery Department where I used to work, because it had electricity via its generator, and I watched TV there; that's where I heard about what the Serbs were telling the EU. I always had a good time with the nurse Fatima, who gave me coffee. One day I found Dr. Dizdarević, then the head of the Surgery Department who had replaced Dr. Lomas, in the doctors' lounge. Some other doctors came too—the head of the Neurosurgery Department, another neurosurgeon, and an internist. I was open with them about my feelings of sadness about the war, because they were my colleagues for many years and I thought they felt as I did. And then the internist said, "And *you* had to marry a Serb." The neurosurgeon, a son of a university professor, added immediately, "It was a different period then." I answered, "My husband was never a nationalist, but a Yugoslav, like you were." I left with a very unpleasant feeling. I remembered Milorad's words, "Thanks to my father who did not burden me with fanaticism."

At just about that time, Milorad's sister Beba, who lived in Sarajevo, passed away. She had come to the hospital because she had intestinal strangulation and needed an operation. Her health worsened after the operation and she died a few days later. I visited her every day and helped a bit with her nursing. But never before had I experienced such a strange funeral. Her son Nino, Nedžad, some of their friends, and I waited at the graveyard, where her funeral was supposed to be held. We waited and waited there, but the mortuary people did not come. After a long time, we saw some people leaving from a new grave that was a short distance from where we were standing but not close enough that we had even noticed them. We went over to where they had been standing and were astonished to see Beba's name on the wooden marker. The mortuary workers were so afraid of grenades and snipers during funerals and had buried Milorad's sister so quickly and quietly that the whole thing was entirely hidden—both from us and from those who would harm us. There was nothing we could do but pay our last respects to her then.

I slept in the hallway in the middle of my apartment, which I considered the safest place, until one day a grenade hit the central glass part of the neighboring building's roof and destroyed the entrance door of the nearby apartment. Our house was identical and the hallway I slept in was near the entrance door. I was not safe there anymore.

It was wintertime, and we lived in the dark, without water or heat. Only a few public fountains had water, and people stood in long lines waiting to take some water in their canisters. I usually brought water from the hospital, because a cistern was brought there, and I filled small canisters with water. I slept in my skiing outfit with a cap on, covered with a thick blanket, and I always wondered why, even with so much insulation, I still felt cold sometimes. Ognjen was mobilized by the army. He continued to work as a doctor, but he also went to the military bases in Dobrinja and Igman Mountain. One day he came and saw me covered up under the blanket, and said, "Mother, you will freeze, please go to Nedžad's place." Nedžad had already invited me to join them, and I cooked at his place, but I thought I could sleep in my apartment, even it was cold. So I went and we spent three months together. Amra and the children slept on the floor in the living room, and I slept on a couch beside them. I do not know how it was not uncomfortable for me to sleep on that couch. Nedžad slept in the dining room.

Luckily, we had gas most of the time at Nedžad's place, so we cooked on a gas stove, and we also had heat. Amra made a tasty soup with a just a small quantity of ingredients, and I cooked a salty and sweet spread of almost the same ingredients: cacao, sugar, oil, powdered milk, and flour. We waited in long lines to get limited quantities of bread; we cut it in slices and dried it so that we had bread even when none was distributed for some reason. We would not have been able to survive from humanitarian aid if my sisters had not managed to send us some German marks, because daily supplies like sugar, oil, powdered milk, batteries, wood, candles, and coffee could be bought in that currency only. We made coffee from roasted wheat, adding a very small quantity of coffee. Sometimes my sisters were able to send packages for us delivered by ADRA, a humanitarian organization. Ognjen and I got packages from Vladana's mother several times. Vladana's parents were refugees, staying in Belgrade with the parents of Vladana's father.

Nedžad went to work every day—I do not know if he was busy, but he still went to the place his company had been able to set up a temporary office. Other people went to their jobs, too. I looked at him from the window; he was slim, wore a tie, and was always a target for a grenade or sniper attack. Amra accompanied Dino to his music school—she could not let him go by himself there. Both Dino and Neven had to stop going to their high school, which was closed, empty, looted, and had broken windows.

One day, Dino escaped from a grenade by a hair's breadth. He went to bring some water from a public fountain near their apartment. As he was on his way home, carrying a full canister of water, a grenade fell near the public fountain. The fountains were always the targets of grenades. Dino was struck by a small piece of shrapnel on his leg, without any real injury. The places where people gathered were the targets of grenades several times, such as near the Main Bank, where scores of people were standing in a line for bread. When the grenade fell, many of them were killed and twice as many were wounded. Children were injured and killed one day while sledding on the snow in the vicinity of Skenderija. Many people were paralyzed by sniper shots in the back. Accordingly, every moment spent in the streets was dangerous—but people still had to move around.

Ognjen used to visit us sometimes, bringing something for Dino and Neven, and once he brought two apples for them, which made them very happy. Ognjen told us how he washed himself in snow on Igman Mountain, because he had no other place to do that. "It was sunny, so it was easier for me to do it," he said. He took me once to an amateur-radio operator to talk to Vladana. He kept in contact with her over the radio that way and through letters brought by foreign journalists. She remained in Zagreb with Ognjen's good friend and his wife, who warmly received them. He and his wife had no children. The man's father lived with them too, and was especially kind. He said to Vladana at the very beginning, "You will never see on my face that you are a burden to me." Their behavior was the same during the three years that she and the children stayed there. I cannot say what was sadder for me—hearing the forlorn sound of Vladana's voice or seeing the bleakness we passed through to get to the place with the radio. Not a single tree was left where there once had been the beautiful lane near the hospital. People cut trees because they were short on power. Our neighborhood looked terrible; there was nothing left of a previously wonderful park with a lot of trees. There was one single poplar remaining, and it was wounded too, with a branch broken by a grenade. People dug out even the remains of cut trees, so I used to meet a neighbor, the university professor, digging. He always smiled when we greeted each other. Balconies looked bad as well—instead of colorful flowers, there were dark cardboard boxes and jumbled piles of wood.

At the beginning of that winter, while I was in bed one day, I did not feel well, so I took my stethoscope to check my heart. I was shocked to hear a clear murmur in my heart that I had never heard before. Because I did not believe my ears, I repeatedly checked it, but the murmur was constant. As a young doctor, I had heard such murmurs in people with heart disease. The next day I went to the Cardiology Department, and the doctor did an ultrasound examination of my heart. He concluded that I had a serious prolapse of my left heart valve and a minor prolapse of the right one. I asked him if it could be the result of my sudden weight loss, but he did not offer an opinion. He increased the dose of my high-blood pressure medication and told me I had to use the medication permanently. I had his diagnosis in writing, and his therapy remained the same later, when I was examined by more renowned cardiologists. Even in that horrible period in our country, many experts did their jobs seriously in spite of surrounding dangerous living—like Archimedes, who said when the army came, "Do not disturb my circles."

Spring came, the wonderful Sarajevo spring, although without tree blossoms, and spring gave us a certain power and feeling of joy. I came back to my house, because it was not as cold there now. The hospital tinsmiths made a little stove from a can for me that I used for cooking on my balcony. I wondered if I could ever make bread with only papers, cards, and thin wood as fuel. One day Ognjen brought children's toys for me to burn—the smoke was so dark that everything around it became black. People burned everything possible—shoes, clothes, anything that could be burned.

MEMORIES FROM BOSNIA

    I went downtown for only the second time since the beginning of the war because I wanted to pay the rent for my apartment. My retirement allowance was one million six hundred thousand dinars. One German mark was worth two hundred thousand dinars, and the price of one pencil lead was ninety thousand dinars. Many important articles—candles, transistor batteries, and wood—could be bought only with German marks. Sarajevo was a ghost-like city. No window was intact; glass was broken, and plastic sheeting was used instead of glass to keep rain and snow out of buildings. Tram traffic was stopped, and streets were empty and covered with heaps of glass, plaster, and bricks. I felt a searing mental anguish and yet had to hurry to avoid snipers or grenades.

    It occurred to us that we should sow some vegetables in my mother's yard. Upon my mother's death, I rented her house to a girl who was employed with Energoinvest. The war began and she was jobless, so she did not pay her rent, but it was important for me to have somebody in the house. A bursting grenade hit our roof one day and broke a wooden beam and several roofing tiles. Nedžad fixed it, somehow tightening the beam with a thick steel wire and replacing the roofing tiles with new ones my mother had kept in reserve. The roofing tiles were old-fashioned and could no longer be bought anywhere.

    So Amra, Nedžad, and I took the seeds we were able to obtain and some tools Amra had—a little hoe, a little shovel, a spade—and we dug up several garden beds. We allowed my relatives living in the vicinity to dig beds for themselves, too. It made us very happy. We took secondary roads to get to the house, because they were safer, and we dug and weeded the vegetables that grew a bit, even without any special care and without watering. We had small quantities of onions, carrots, lettuce, and spinach. I usually took coffee in a thermos bottle and some cake I made with a little oil and a tiny bit of sugar, so we used to sit in the garden forgetting about the war for a while. One day while we were sitting there, my cousin called us from her window to tell us she heard on the radio that Radovan Karadžić, the Serbian leader, had signed a cease-fire agreement in Greece. I will never forget that happiness! I jumped up like a child, embracing Amra and Nedžad. But my happiness did not last long. When we returned home, we learned that he did not sign that agreement after all.

    One day Amra told me, "I dreamed that Oglavak was completely covered by fog." A few days later, we heard that Oglavak was burned down by Croats. In that period, there was fierce fighting between Bosnian Muslims and Croats, also. Everything was burned down in Oglavak—the tekya, the burial chamber, and the other burial chamber in front of which my father was buried. I also had a dream that a huge fire was burned in Oglavak, thinking it was something good, because my grandmother told me it was a good thing to see fire in your dreams. Many young people died because they were drafted and got weapons without being properly trained to use them. Some Muslim units from the city of Zenica, called Mujahedins (I do not know if they really were Mujahedins), ravaged Croat villages. Two priests were killed in Fojnica Monastery when that occurred. So Oglavak, the most wonderful memory from my childhood, vanished.

There was no more gas in the areas of Sarajevo that used to have it, or in Nedžad's place, so they cooked on a small gasoline stove. People excavated and installed gas pipes everywhere on an ad hoc basis, so maybe that caused the gas pressure reduction, and its supply was disturbed due to the war anyway. People used mostly wood for fuel, which could fortunately be found in the market for German marks. The tinsmiths from my hospital made a trunk-like stove with an oven for me, and for Nedžad too. We installed gas in our house, too. We paid for it with German marks. A doctor who moved into an empty apartment in our house did not want to pay the full amount for installation of her portion of the gas line; she said the price was incorrectly calculated, which was untrue—the price was not high at all. I felt sorry for the young man who broke the concrete surface, dug, and installed the gas pipes. It was her debt to him—and he had a little child. I spent the money that my sisters sent me mostly on various repairs. The main water supply pipe in our house broke, and Ognjen's boiler broke due to ice. A grenade also hit a part of our roof. The neighbor tenants paid me for fixing the water supply pipe; some of them gave me German marks, some gave me oil, and some of them never paid for it.

Ženja, Amra's mother, often invited me to visit her neighbor, Mrs. Popić, to see her paintings. I always hesitated to go, but I finally went. Her apartment was wonderful—perfectly arranged, with carpets, stylish furniture, paintings, everything all perfectly polished and clean— reminding me of a Habsburg's castle in Vienna. She had a lot of paintings by famous artists, including Ljubo Lah, Ismet Mujezinović, Mehmed Zaimović, Nedeljko Gvozdenović, Mario Mikulić, Ibrahim Ljubović, and Mica Todorović. She offered us one dry and sweet crescent roll each, but did not have a place to make coffee. She started to cry after showing us a photo of herself and her husband; he looked noble, and she had lived fifty-three years with him. When we went out, I looked at that rather worn out building and thought how nobody would believe the treasures to be found in it.

Even in that difficult period, there were many cultural events. Generous musicians, writers, and filmmakers came to Sarajevo—although it was dangerous. Together with members of the local arts community, they raised our spirits. The famous conductor Zubin Mehta also paid a visit to Sarajevo. At one event in New York dedicated to Sarajevo, the author Salman Rushdie said, "There is the 'Sarajevo of the mind,' an imagined Sarajevo whose present ruination and torment exiles us all. That Sarajevo represented something like an ideal, a city in which the values of pluralism, tolerance, and coexistence have created a unique and resilient culture. In that Sarajevo, there actually exists that secularist Islam for which so many people are fighting for elsewhere in the world. The people of that Sarajevo do not define themselves by faith or tribe, but simply and honorably, as citizens. If that city is lost, then we are all its refugees. If the culture of Sarajevo dies, then we are all its orphans. The writers and artists of Sarajevo are therefore fighting for us as well as for themselves." Those were the words of Salman Rushdie.

One day I went to a little theater to see a modern play. Another time Ognjen, when he was on a short leave from the military, took me to see a performance—I do not know if it was "Audition" or "Surrealists' Top List."[61] The stage was located outdoors in a hidden place, and the young actors were excellent, so we laughed a lot. After a few years, when I watched the tape with "Surrealists' Top List," I admired the masterpiece they had made while living under the conditions we all experienced. After that show, on my way back home with Ognjen, I felt terribly empty when we passed by the damaged façades of buildings that had distress notices and obituaries posted on them. We went by the medical school and the hospital, too. Both were damaged by bombing—yet both managed to operate.

Sometimes I visited my cousin Muniba. She lived on Kranjčevića Street, far from my home, but I went there because I always felt very good with her and her husband Mašo. I always had a good lunch with them, and they had a rather stable living situation; Mašo brought water,

---

[61] The comedies famous in the pre-war period.

and Muniba cooked and cleaned. I liked to talk to Mašo because he spoke realistically and constructively. I liked him. Muniba invited me to go to an art exhibition in a small gallery near Skenderija. We were looking at the exhibits when suddenly Muniba greeted a couple and wanted to introduce me. I recognized Šeka, the girl who tormented me in the second grade of elementary school, immediately. She smiled at me and I wanted to get out of there as fast as I could, to escape. That moment is another dark and painful memory of the war.

Somehow we managed to celebrate our birthdays during those sad days. Amra usually made a cake without a single egg—from flour, oil, sugar, cacao, and marmalade—and it was a real cake! It was very delicious and later I called it "Amra's cake." Women had to improvise and cook many salty and sweet meals from the limited array of ingredients they had at their disposal. A war cookbook was even published. One day Ognjen and I were on our way back from Amra's mother's place, where we had a little party. We went through the hospital and passed by the new diagnostics building, when suddenly there was an explosion in front of us. Ognjen felt a little piece of a grenade scratching his face, and we quickly took what cover we could find. After less than a minute, we continued on and saw a wounded man being carried away far ahead of us; when we got to that spot we saw his blood beneath our feet. A few seconds later, we were almost hit ourselves by a grenade.

The winter came again. I did not go to Nedžad's place that year, though, because I had gas and a little stove in which to burn a fire. The gas pressure was bad, so I warmed up the baking sheets in the kitchen and brought them to my living room to heat it. I used gas throughout the night, because its flame was so poor. We were out of gas very often, so I made a fire then. I had to save fuel, so I put only two pieces of wood and several splinters in the fire at a time, so it took a while for the fire to be lit. I remembered an anecdote my father had told us. A Gipsy said, "It is strange, people have full stoves burned in fire, and I have only one piece of wood, which does not want to light up." I laughed, as I had a situation in which two pieces of wood did not want to burn.

We had water sometimes, so I took those opportunities to wash my bedsheets with the soap we got in our humanitarian aid using the boiler water, which was not too cold. Ognjen also brought his military bedsheets to me, because they did not have a place to wash them. My hands became swollen and red, so I put on rubber gloves to feel less cold when washing. On those special occasions, I would wash myself with boiler water, too, and in general I rubbed myself with soaped gauze and dried myself afterward.

At night, while lying in my living room and looking at a poor flame in my little stove, I listened to my transistor. The Studio 99 radio station was a bright spot in that horrible period. I always remained grateful to Adil Kulenović, who had the courage to broadcast his open-minded and hopeful views. I listened to the program about the establishment of the Yugoslavian Republic of Bosnia and Herzegovina after World War II. Miro Lazović, the Parliament President, spoke nicely about it. They also broadcast a play of Mak Dizdar and Mozart's "A Little Night Music."

I listened once to an interview with the French ambassador in Sarajevo. People asked him questions and accused Mitterrand of willfully preventing a military intervention by visiting Sarajevo. They also said that the French people were Crusaders, and that they still wanted enmity with Muslims. The Ambassador said something like, "If we go that far, we can go back to the seventh century, when Arabs assaulted France." The announcer stopped a listener who wanted to insult the ambassador. The ambassador explained that French UN soldiers had actually helped us a lot, fixing problems with electricity, water, and gas, which was true. When I used to wake up at night and look through the window, my eyes always set on the devastated and burned roof of the Zetra Olympic Center, once a wonderful building.

In the evenings I went downstairs to visit Mrs. Djurkin, my neighbor on the first floor of my building. She was a former chemist and university professor. We sat covered in blankets looking at some weak light we could see in the hospital that sometimes vanished. We heard on the radio that only three megawatts of electrical power entered Sarajevo. On the day following such an announcement we were usually without bread because the bakers were unable to produce it due to the power shortage. Doctors performed operations using lights similar to those used by miners. My conversations with Mrs. Djurkin were very nice, and I have kept them safe in my memory.

I often visited Nedžad in the evenings and stayed until late at night. We sat by an oil lamp made of a glass of water, a little oil on the top, and a burned string. Even a candle was a luxury—the price was four German marks, and candles could not always be found on the market. We often had a poorly burning fire in a little stove in front of a big stove. I watched the huge and ghostly shadows of our heads on the walls. Those nights were still idyllic, somehow; we had conversations full of hope—because Nedžad was an optimist. I came back home late in terrible darkness and often in fog. I counted the stairs between houses, and I descended them—there was no more fence, because people burned it down as firewood. I was fearless—sometimes I felt a silhouette passing next to me, but there were no attackers because nobody had money or anything that was worth money. I reached my home in ten minutes. For dinner I had a glass of cacao made of a small spoonful of cacao, powdered milk, wheat seeds previously watered, a little sugar, and bottled water I had previously chlorinated. Then I had two little dried slices of bread softened by water with a tiny bit of a chicken spread we had received from humanitarian aid. I looked through the window; in the distance, I could see only a few lighted spots. Although it was dark, I could see many houses nearby with their weak lights, because there were no trees. The sound of the stirring plastic sheeting on the windows was audible even in the lightest wind. I wanted at least to dream about something, but in the morning when I woke up I could not remember my dream—I only knew I had to blow into my little stove to start a fire.

Sometimes I went to my old Surgery Department and watched TV when they had power. One day I sat next to the TV and several children were in front of it. Suddenly I noticed a two-year-old boy who reminded me of Ognjen's Mladen a lot. He had lively moves, blue eyes, a face like Mladen's. I got up to hug him, and my heart was full of a terrible sadness.

Spring came and Ognjen was moved to another military post, Olovo, about thirty miles from Sarajevo. He could not visit us any more, and he sent his letters through a journalist from Olovo. Every day I had coffee with Mrs. Djurkin, one day at my place, another day at her place. She always had a little cake for me, and I offered her my cake with a little oil and a tiny bit of sugar. One day I walked further into our neighborhood without knowing why, but some invisible hand led me to see Jarmila, Božana's sister, who was always playing piano while we were studying medicine. We were pleasantly surprised to see each other after so many years. She came to my place and told me that Božana had retired in Switzerland and wanted to return to Sarajevo; she had even bought an apartment near their house, but the war chased her back to Switzerland. Her mother was alive, and when I saw Jarmila she was on her way to the Red Cross to get some food for her. She was a teacher in the Music School. While talking to her, it occurred to me she could help Dino, my grandson, to prepare for his final exam in the Music School. She agreed, and after that, they came to my place every day and practiced. They sat on the floor for hours and studied counterpoint and played piano. Dino was very disciplined. Amra often said that he only had to be introduced to a new thing in order to begin working on it "in perpetual motion." I usually offered Jarmila coffee and some cake, and her lessons were not expensive. One day she took me to visit her mother, who was happy to see me—she had always liked me. She looked the same to me, slim and agile, although now very old. She gave me a kohlrabi[62] from her garden, the most delicious food I had during the war. Jarmila was satisfied with Dino's progress and she proved to be correct in her judgment, because Dino completed Music School with high grades and passed the admission exam for the Music Academy. That enabled him to get a scholarship awarded by the Austrian Government for young musicians to continue their education in the Vienna Music Academy. Because of the war, Dino was able to start a career that he liked a great deal. Dino was able to leave Sarajevo and go to Vienna, and Amra accompanied him and stayed in Zagreb with Ženja's aunt until the war ended.

Ognjen longed for his wife and children, who remained with his good friend in Zagreb. They had been separated for almost two and a half years. One day he called me from Olovo and said he might be able to obtain permission to visit his wife and children. He told me to look for him working in the Military Hospital, but when I went there the news was discouraging. He called me again in a few days, saying his leave was cancelled because soldiers who had been on leave themselves hadn't returned yet. When they finally came back and it was his turn to leave, all of the official leave permissions were suspended. He soon sent me a sad letter, saying he could not live anymore without his family, so he would either bring them back where he was or leave in order to join them here. He explained that he intended to leave the army, and he asked me to send him his passport and to obtain a Croatian visa for him. So I went to the Croatian Embassy, where I spoke with an embassy employee whose child I operated on a long time ago. He helped me to get a visa for Ognjen. After two or three days, I was riding the partially restored tram, heading toward the TV building. I gave a letter to the journalist from

---

[62] "German turnip" (in the cabbage family).

Olovo and asked him to give it to Ognjen, and he said, "I will do everything for my Olja." My conscience stung me a bit when he said that, because his words were full of confidence and I thought he must have had no idea Ognjen would be leaving the army.

Ognjen called me from Zagreb in a few days. Everything went well with the Croatian visa, and a truck driver, whose child he operated on for a hernia earlier, took him in his truck to the Croatian border. The army officer called me after Ognjen left and said that Ognjen could come back to the army without any repercussions. But I think it was predestined that just then in Zagreb Ognjen got a letter from his uncle Slobodan, Milorad's brother, who was now living in the United States. Slobodan told Ognjen that he would sponsor his trip to the United States. Ognjen had written to him at the beginning of the war, but there had been no reply. So Ognjen and Vladana decided to make a request for entrance into the United States, because they did not want to return to Sarajevo—nobody could predict when the war would end. Ognjen's life suddenly was taking another direction, and I felt empty. I did not know if I should be sorry for feeling that way or not.

After two months I learned that Ognjen and Vladana had been advised that they were accepted as refugees by the United States. They were supposed to leave in few months. I felt really sad, because I thought I wouldn't see them again. I decided to go to Zagreb to see them off and to visit my sisters in Switzerland too. There was a bus leaving from Hrasnica, a suburb of Sarajevo outside the siege area, that went through Herzegovina and Dalmatia, north to Zagreb. I had learned about the bus from the man who helped me to obtain the Croatian visa. Nedžad's son Neven joined me, because he wanted to see Amra, his mother, in Zagreb.

It was a cloudy autumn evening when Neven and I gathered with all the other people who wanted to leave Sarajevo in front of the entrance to the tunnel, which was the only way out of Sarajevo. It was close to half a mile long and had been dug underneath the airport to the free territory. There was no other way to leave the besieged city. It looked like the end of the world, as my grandmother would say, with many people moving nervously back and forth, worried, some of them crying. The man who called our names in alphabetic order kept repeating, "Be calm and patient—this is not a tourist trip." Neven and I were separated according to alphabetic order, and he was far behind me. Some children offered to take our bags for money, and I gave them two suitcases, mine and Neven's, and one other bag. Nedžad came to see us off. When we began to move into the tunnel, I looked back at him, so slim and so worried. I would not see him again for two and a half years.

The tunnel was so narrow that we had to go single-file, and the ceiling was so low (about five feet) that a taller man could not stand up. There were curves in some places and occasional light bulbs. We walked and walked, and at the exit there was no light, because there was no electricity. I left the tunnel and entered complete darkness. I waited for Neven. Nobody else came out; they waited for the electricity to come back. In a few minutes, the light at the exit came on and people began to come out. Neven showed up carrying his guitar. He told me of the wait he'd just had, "You could not, Nana, stand to be in the dark tunnel—I sat on the ground and it was horrible." We went to the only light we could see in the total darkness after being told to gather ourselves there. I did not know where I was going; I walked in the mud and through some creek, until we finally reached a deserted house and set a fire in a big space. We dried ourselves there, because we were wet and muddy. The bus that was about to take us to our destination stood in front of the house. The children came with our suitcases too, bringing them into the bus. I paid them with German marks and was so grateful to them, because the help they gave me was worth more than I could pay. I gave Neven some chocolate and tangerines that Nedžad had prepared for us, and we had a few sandwiches. The bus driver asked us, "Do you want to climb up Igman Mountain on foot, which is safer, or do you want to go by bus and to be the target of grenades or snipers?" We all agreed to take the risk and go by bus.

The bus started on the familiar old road up Igman Mountain that Milorad and I had traveled on many times, enjoying the beautiful scenery along the way. I sat next to the window in order to protect Neven from possible snipers and covered my head with a jacket to protect myself. Of course, there was no light in the bus, and the driver drove without lights, I think. When we had climbed up to the top and started to Hadžići village, the driver said we were safe. We stopped before the Ivan Tunnel, and we washed ourselves at a cold fountain at two o'clock in the morning. We got into a different bus and then continued on. At some point soon afterward, we had to show our passports, and several hours later we arrived in Split, where it was a sunny morning. After walking a little and washing ourselves again in a public fountain, we continued traveling for a long time. I watched the beautiful Adriatic Sea, but in the vicinity of Zadar we saw the traces of war again. A bridge had been destroyed, so we crossed on a pontoon bridge that had been put up there and went on. We had two breaks during which we had something to drink, and Neven even paid for drinks for some boys. It was evening when we reached Zagreb.

I do not know if passengers like us had ever come to Zagreb before. We were so tired and so muddy—our suitcases were just covered with mud. Vladana, Ognjen, Amra, and her cousin were waiting for us. I hadn't seen Vladana for a long time, and she was smiling and happy to see me again. Amra was happy that Neven was also able to leave the city. I went to the home of Ivo, my youngest sister's husband, who lived part of the year in Jelačić Square, and I promised Vladana to visit her the next day.

Ivo was glad to see me and was not bothered by my dirty suitcases and clothes. I washed myself and my stuff for several days, and he was always in a good mood and happy that I was able to come. Ognjen took me to the day-care center to see his children the next day. They were bigger—I had not seen them for two and a half years—and they were a bit bashful because they forgot me. In the days that followed, I played with them and told them stories that they liked a lot. I usually lay on the bed to tell them stories, with one child laying beside me on each side, and they both listened carefully. Srdjan listened to me quite seriously, indeed.

My sisters sent me money to go to Switzerland immediately, and I obtained a three-month visa in two days. I said goodbye to my little grandchildren with a heavy heart. Vladana recorded me singing a few children's songs, like "Little butterfly, Little colorful" and "Swan is swimming," which was my gift to my grandchildren so that they could remember their country. She always did thoughtful things like that.

Ognjen accompanied me to the bus terminal the next evening, because they lived in the western part of Zagreb, Podsused, which was near the terminal. While I waited for the bus, I gave him a golden bracelet and a diamond ring to give Vladana. Milorad had given them to me, and I wanted her to have them now. It was like Milorad's gift to her. So my ten days in Zagreb were over, and I was on my way to Switzerland.

My sisters were very glad to see me—it had been more than four years since we'd seen each other. I spent about two weeks with each of them. I often had long walks in the wonderful Swiss landscape with my middle sister Dila and her friend Edo, the Swiss who lived in her apartment building. He was a retired pharmacist and a well-educated person, so it was interesting to talk to him. We usually went by car outside Basel and then would decide where to hike. When we returned home, we always had dinner prepared by my sister. Occasionally I would make something such as pie or stewed apples stuffed with walnuts.

I had a great morning coffee with my youngest sister, and the whole apartment smelled great while it was filtering. She made an excellent hurmasice and I made baklava sometimes. We walked every day in the nearby forest, always having a good time together.

Nedžad phoned me one day. He had come to Zagreb and was supposed to travel to Kuwait for his company, Unioninvest. He was now waiting for the visa. Ognjen and Vladana were still waiting to get their permission to travel to the United States. Dino was already in Vienna, and I did not see him for the next seven years.

Three months passed very quickly, and I was just about to come back home. It was midwinter, and my youngest sister Suma asked the Zurich authorities to extend my visa for two more months. She explained to them that if I had to return, I would be returning to the war in Sarajevo. Somehow, she managed to convince them. I stayed there two months more, until the beginning of April. She did her best for me to have a good time with her; once we went to the opera, and one sunny spring day we visited the Botanical Garden in Zurich. My sisters bought me the things I needed, like a good suitcase and high-quality clothes. We were visited by my niece Dina, who was an actress in Freibourg, still single and very unhappy due to the situation in Bosnia. She took part in a theatrical play performed for Sarajevo. My nephew Miran also visited us; he was very upset and felt sympathies for our hardships.

It was time for me to go home, and my sisters were sad and worried because I had to return to the hell in Sarajevo. Ognjen and Vladana had already gone to the United States, and Nedžad had gone to Kuwait. Amra and Neven had been waiting for their Kuwait visas. My cousin Diba, sister of my cousin Muniba, helped me in our embassy to travel to Sarajevo by a UN military plane. When I got on the plane, I saw that it was full of some bags and military equipment, and a few of us sat on some benches. A nun got on the plane too, and I recognized Sister Vilma, with whom I had worked in the Surgery Department for many years. "Sister Vilma, you bring me luck, and I am happy to see you," I told her. She reminded me of many great moments we had after our operations when she offered us her wonderful homemade cakes in her little room. She was a very hardworking person, especially with seriously ill patients. We were both concerned and distracted about our situation. We had a long trip, we flew over the sea partly and finally reached a UN-protected part of Sarajevo Airport. We ran to a military vehicle, which took us to the city, and I took a taxi near the central park and came home. I would not see Sister Vilma ever again.

Mrs. Djurkin and Ognjen's best man Mladen, who now lived in Ognjen's apartment, were happy to see me again, so we had coffee together at Mladen's place. I felt a pang when I saw a photo of Vladana and the children that they had sent to Ognjen. At the same time, my sister Dila phoned me from Switzerland because she worried about my return, and I told her cheerfully how it was. We were lucky our telephone lines were repaired and functioning again.

I enjoyed the Swiss chocolates and coffee, and the next day I went to see Nedzad's in-laws, Ženja and Hamo. They were very happy to see me again, because they were alone too. I saw a lot of them after that. Every day I had my morning coffee with them, and I visited them often in the afternoon, often staying overnight. I always had a good time with them, and I will never forget those war days. Even then, Hamo made us laugh with his amusing stories. He often went to the outskirts, Sedrenik, to bring us some wood. Ženja was always cheerful and close to me, spreading her optimistic view of life around. She used to bring home heavy canisters full of water when the cistern used to come to the neighborhood.

Sarajevo was again a target for heavy grenades that summer, and grenades fell on our neighborhood more and more often. One day a grenade hit a boy in front of our house, and another time one badly injured a young girl, a student. It was dangerous to go to the public fountains, so the trucks with water tanks came to the neighborhoods. It was very crowded then. Many people came there with canisters, making long lines to get some water. A lot of water would be wasted in such situations. When it rained, we took water from the gutters, running down the stairs and collecting the water at night. Sometimes, early on cold mornings, I used to stand in my nightgown and collect water from the gutters.

In that fourth year of the war, the situation was a bit more normal in that we had electricity and gas. We were often out of gas, and it would suddenly come on again, causing fires and tragic accidents due to people forgetting to disconnect it when it went off. Amra's colleague, a librarian, was burned in such an incident, and one of my relatives suffered massive burns. We could buy fruit, vegetables, and various things in the market, but a heavy grenade attack at the market killed and wounded a lot of people there one day, so it was still very dangerous for us to go anywhere people gathered.

I had periodic phone contact with Ognjen and Vladana, and for my birthday they sent me a tape with the children's voices recorded, with their congratulations and a song they sang for me. I had coffee with Mrs. Djurkin regularly, alternating between her place and my place, and I also went to nurse Fatima's to study English with her. She was ambitious and wanted to learn English, so we studied from my old introductory and advanced course books. We began our study of English in the third year of the war. I went to her place and her husband Iso lit a fire in a small stove on the terrace and made coffee for us. Her place was perfectly clean, and I enjoyed those moments I spent with them. In the beginning, when I did not have a place to cook, I went to the Surgery Department sometimes, and she used to leave some good soup for me.

I had a lot of time, so I read some of Louis Bromfield's books that Mrs. Djurkin lent me. I particularly liked *Mrs. Parkington*, whose character was very impressive to me. Amra gave me Kerubin Šegvić's *Fall of the Medieval Bosnian State*, which I read with great interest, because we were not taught much about medieval Bosnia. A lot of Patarens[63] tombstones were left as traces of that period. Earlier in the war, I wrote several pages in my diary, and when I read them a bit later, I decided it would be good if I continued to write, but in those dangerous and poor living conditions it was difficult to stay concentrated enough to sit and type. We now were a bit less burdened

---

[63] A Christian sect in medieval Bosnia (called Bogumils in Bosnia) that was persecuted by Catholics and Orthodox Christians and by the Crusaders. It is thought that many Patarens accepted Islam during the Ottoman Empire and became today's Bosnian Muslims.

and had more of the necessary things we had lacked for so long, so I was able to work on my writing. When I was satisfied with a story I had written in English, I sent it to the British Embassy, which had announced a contest for the best short story. In "The Woman in the Fog," I described my experience on foggy nights when I went to Nedžad's place and came back home late. Anja Tomić, the daughter of one of my colleagues at the Surgery Department, corrected it. Mrs. Djurkin said my story was very good, but I did not win the prize. Certainly there were better stories, and mine was too long—that, I found out, was its deficiency. So what would become the last summer of the war was passing.

And then, as the summer wore on, one night we experienced something we had wanted to happen for a long time. In the middle of the night we heard terrible explosions and detonations, and we saw great flashes of light across the sky. We knew the Americans were bombing Serb positions around Sarajevo. This was the second time in my life I had experienced being liberated. The first time was after World War II, when I was a young girl sharing my fear with my fiancé as we listened to bombs and explosions. In the morning we were liberated by Tito's partisans. This time, too, it was in the morning that we heard on the radio that the war was over because the Serbs could not resist the Americans.

In about three months, Ognjen passed the first part of his nostrification exam, which would enable him to transfer his medical degree to the United States, and he passed the second and third parts soon afterward. He could apply for a residency position only after January 1, so he worked temporarily as a nurse's aide in a nursing home. Vladana attended computer classes and worked with a lawyer. Ognjen invited me to apply in Zagreb to come to the United States as a refugee. He was sorry that I was alone since Nedžad also left. "Mother, please go to the American Immigration Center in Zagreb and apply, and I will be your sponsor. If you do not do that now, who knows when you will be able to visit us; you have no chance to obtain a tourist visa," he wrote me. I missed them very much, so I decided to try. I informed only Ženja, Hamo, and Mrs. Djurkin about my intention. I took some paintings and documents to Ženja's place for safekeeping, packed only my most necessary clothes, and bought a bus ticket for Zagreb. On the evening before I left, Mrs. Djurkin and I sat sadly in my room, where we had spent many war days together. It was dark when Ognjen's best man Mladen took me to Ženja's place, and early in the morning we went by taxi to the bus station. There I parted from Ženja. I looked sadly through the window glass at my friend with whom I shared a lot of moments.

When the bus passed through Ilidža[64] people watched us with curiosity from their windows and doors. I guess they wanted to see "Mujahedins" from Sarajevo, because the power of war propaganda had poisoned them. Near Ivan Mountain the road was partly destroyed, so we circled around a sheer rock that made me afraid we would go over the edge of the road. We passed by Mostar, and I saw there was nothing left of that beautiful city. Later we had our passports checked, and we reached Split in the evening. People left the bus to refresh themselves a bit, and I felt like vomiting, but had nothing to vomit. A woman sitting in front of me was just getting up to go outside, and when she saw me like that she said, "My goodness, human beings are so weak." I guess she wanted to say that we were all exhausted after the war. I also went out of the bus; it was a bit windy, and my head was beginning to clear, so I slowly recovered. We traveled all night; I slept a little, and we were in Zagreb in the morning. Our ride lasted twenty-four hours.

I stayed at Ivo's place again, and he was very happy to see me. We took a walk in the evening. Zagreb was nicely decorated, because it was Christmas Eve. In a few days I went to submit a request for refugee status, as Ognjen instructed me. Soon I had an interview with a young man who could barely speak Croatian. I was successful at the interview, and I had to wait for the American major who came every fifteen days to have my second interview. It all went well, I think, because I was not interviewed again, I had my son's sponsorship letter, and I was in a mixed marriage. They found there was no place for people in mixed marriages in an ethnically divided country.

While waiting for my departure, I had a good time with Ivo; he liked the baklava I made sometimes, and our morning and afternoon coffee was a real ritual. Sometimes his friends came to play chess, and it was always interesting for me to listen to their conversations. Ivo liked a coffee bar in Jelačić Square, and we often went there and talked. Periodically, we walked a little too. But I had long walks with Mr. Čusak, the father of Ognjen's friend who took Vladana and her children in, sheltering them for three years. Mr. Čusak was the man who told

---

[64] Sarajevo suburb that was under the control of Serbs forces during the war.

them at the very beginning, "You will never see on my face that you are a burden to me." He was a great man who lived with his son and daughter-in-law, and every Sunday he invited me for a lunch he cooked himself. We walked a long way—he was in good shape and I somehow followed him, so I got familiar with Zagreb's outskirts too. I am grateful both to him and Ivo, because they made my three-month stay in Zagreb comfortable.

35 Exile

We gathered at the place where the bus was about to come. There were many people waiting, all from Bosnia. I knew none of them. Many others came to see them off. We got on the bus in the dark and went to the airport. We sat on or beside our suitcases and flew to Rome late at night. After several hours of waiting at the Rome airport, we flew to the United States—a place I had never thought I would ever see.

It was a day flight, and due to the time difference we landed at the New York airport in the afternoon. As we were coming closer, I looked at the islands and bays of the Canadian and American coasts—it was a wonderful picture, with orderly settlements intersected by forests. We had a short customs procedure at the airport, and then a small plane was to take me to Providence, Rhode Island, where Ognjen lived. Its departure was in the evening, and the flight lasted only half an hour. I saw Vladana and the children at the airport; Vladana took some pictures, and I embraced the children. Ognjen waited for us in his car because parking was not allowed there.

Their apartment was nice and comfortable, and they had just moved in fifteen days earlier. They spent one year with Ognjen's uncle Slobodan, who had a big house. Each child played a song on the synthesizer for me, and Ognjen showed me my room—the bed, a table, a place for a TV they bought me several days later, a tape recorder, and a wardrobe. There was a lovely painting of white sailboats on a blue sea with a blue sky on the wall, which I kept and always had above my bed.

I had brought twenty five pieces of "kinder eggs"[65] with me and gave them to the children. I should have brought them even more, Ognjen thought, since his children really liked them a lot. I bought them some vests in Zagreb, but they did not like them very much. I was always sorry I did not bring any clothes to Vladana and Ognjen, because I was wrong when I thought that everything was better in America. I gave them money to buy something for themselves. I am sure they would have been very happy to receive a dress or a shirt from me.

When I was accepted as a refugee in Zagreb, we had a short course in the culture of the American people and in the English language so that we could fit more easily into the society. For me, it was easier because Ognjen and Vladana already had a year of experience, and my first impression was about how well-organized a country and how open the people were. The houses were unique yet similar to each other, but still they had different colors and details, with clean and neat grass around them. On the opposite side of our house was a big soccer and basketball playground, so I went there with the children, watching and supporting them while they were playing. I tried to tell them the stories I used to tell in Zagreb, but they were not interested in them anymore, because they already spoke English quite well. Srdjan attended the first grade of elementary school, and Mladen went to the kindergarten.

Ognjen wanted to show me as much of America as possible, so we drove around Providence whenever they were free. I was fascinated by the long bridges connecting islands, the huge parks with forests, and the rivers and lakes. Each park had a memorial tablet describing the life of the person who

---

[65] Chocolate egg with a little toy in it that is very popular in Europe.

gave land or money for the park. They bought new bicycles for the children, and they instantly learned to ride them around the park. On the first weekend after my arrival, there was a traditional St. Patrick's Day parade on the occasion of the big Catholic holiday, with a brass band and people processing down the street in their brightly colored Irish costumes. Ognjen told me Americans liked parades—something that I convinced myself later was very true, indeed.

Ognjen wanted me to learn the language as soon as possible and the country's history, so he brought me from the library audio and video tapes for learning English and many movies as well. I watched my favorite actress, Vivien Leigh, in "Gone with the Wind," the movie I watched once back home in our cinema on New Year's Eve. I knew English from the classes I attended in Sarajevo, but the pronunciation I was hearing in America was very different from what I had learned, so it was hard for me to understand. They had one car, which they both used, so I did not even attempt to renew my driver's license at first, although Ognjen brought me a handbook, because I would have to take a test. The distances were long between places I might want to go, but they had a bus, and for senior citizens, people over sixty-five, it was free.

My little grandsons did not have much contact with me, probably because of the language. I sometimes took them for ice cream and bought them some little things while their parents worked all day, and Ognjen often all night. I felt like a member of a forgotten generation that was no longer interesting for young people. I was told in Zagreb that as a refugee over sixty-five years old, I would have a guaranteed allowance, medical care, and a little apartment. When I arrived in America, this was confirmed. But I had declined the apartment because Ognjen and Vladana said that I could stay with them, and I thought they needed me to be with the children.

In spite of the great distance, I often walked to the library, always finding something interesting there and reading. I learned about Americans everywhere I went: They were open and cheerful people. One day I went to a department store with Ognjen and he accidentally broke a marmalade jar. When we reported it to the cashier, she only smiled at us without asking for any money, while a man came and cleaned up after us.

I soon had an obligatory medical checkup; I was seen by a cardiologist who performed an ultrasound examination and acknowledged the diagnosis of my cardiologist from Sarajevo. My therapy was a bit changed; each doctor wanted to add something. Everything was well organized in the medical field as well as in the city administration so that people would not be mistreated.

I learned a lot, both the language and American achievements. The country was much more than I thought it would be, and I remembered one wise sentence I had heard along the way, "One never finds what he looks for, but he finds many other things."

It was summer, and we swam at the large sandy beaches on the Atlantic Ocean. Ognjen was about to leave because he was accepted in a residency in internal medicine in Brooklyn, New York. He knew the pediatric surgeons at Brown University in Providence. Dr. Kent, the pediatric surgeon I met in Prague and who was in Sarajevo, introduced him to them. He worked with them as an observer for some time, but specialization in pediatric surgery could not be obtained directly. He had to do a general surgery one-year internship first. He would have a long way ahead toward pediatric surgery. So he tried at some other places and got a residency in internal medicine in New York. I learned at that time that Dr. Kent's husband had passed away and that she had moved to Argentina.

Ognjen visited us in Providence almost every weekend, and we went swimming and visited interesting places. One day we went to a natural aquarium with fascinating fish and amphibians, and the dolphins put on an amusing show. Vladana took us to see the fireworks on the Fourth of July, the biggest American holiday (Independence Day), which were spectacular.

After my six-month stay in Providence, we moved to New York, because Ognjen moved to an apartment subsidized by his hospital. For their farewell party with their colleagues in the nursing home, I made stewed apples stuffed with walnuts, which Americans found very tasty.

It was late afternoon when we drove toward New York. Ognjen drove a rented van with all our belongings, and Vladana drove our car behind him. As we went southwest, it was wonderful to see the sunset, which I kept in my memory, along with the highway passing through unbroken forest on both sides. The same highway led to the north too, and when we sometimes went to Boston, we passed through thick hardwood and coniferous forests. We came to New York City late, and we had to go through a large portion of the city to reach our apartment, which was near Ognjen's hospital in central Brooklyn. Ognjen had a map, so we managed to find the four-story building in the British style, like all the others on that street. Our friends from Sarajevo who were now living in New York came at midnight to help us carry our things into our new apartment, and I offered them a meat pie and hurmasice.

We stayed in Brooklyn for three years, until Ognjen finished with his residency. Living in New York City enriched us a lot, especially with Ognjen, who was very curious and made everything accessible to us. He sent me to see the cardiologist who worked in the hospital, but he had a private office too. I went there, but when I showed my insurance card to the nurse, she said, "The doctor does not accept that kind of insurance." When I told her he arranged it all with my son, she replied, "Come in if you want to see him, and if he tells me to, I will accept you." I returned home, but went there again the next day as Ognjen told me to do. The nurse accepted me, made my ECG and left me on the table. A tall young doctor entered and said loudly, "I apologize for not telling the nurse about you," and I replied spontaneously, "She was right, she was right, I don't belong here." I thought that perhaps my insurance would not pay for the doctor's services. He looked at me in wonder and protested, "You do, you do belong here." He took an ultrasound of my heart, saying I had moderately prolapsed valves, and he increased my therapy to lower my blood pressure. He also asked me about my profession as a pediatric surgeon and was very interested in it. I was his patient for three years and got his services in spite of my insurance, which paid only a fraction of his price.

New York, people said, was a crowded and mad city, but it is not. After five o'clock in the afternoon when Ognjen finished his work, it took us some twenty minutes by car to reach the first Atlantic beach, with many huge sandy beaches lined up to the north. It was all free, and most of the beaches had lifeguards to take care of swimmers. It was always good weather there, never too hot, since a breeze came from the Atlantic.

If we went to the other side, we crossed the magnificent, for me, and always fascinating bridges and entered Manhattan, the heart of New York. We had to circle around to find a parking place, but we always managed to find one and avoid paying the expensive parking garage. We climbed up the Empire State Building and the Twin Towers, or found some other attractive place, and we walked around Manhattan avenues while the children rode their bicycles or roller skated on the sidewalk—and nobody got angry about that. If we apologized, the American would always say "OK" and smile.

We could never neglect going to Central Park, which covered a huge part of Manhattan. The children would immediately go to the open skating rink—including Ognjen and Vladana, too— and it was very simple and inexpensive to rent skates. At the entrance to the park stood a large, gilded-bronze sculpture of General William Tecumseh Sherman on a shining horse. I liked that general, because with his last, even if brutal attack, he finished the Civil War, and the enslavement of black people was ended. I wanted to have a photo beside that monument, so Ognjen took a very good one. We used to sit in the Central Park meadows just as we sat in the meadows in Oglavak. The people were allowed to light a fire in certain places, and the only difference was that we saw the Manhattan skyline there!

We often went down to Pier 17 and Battery Park, places on the East River and the Hudson River, always finding some delicious, inexpensive meal and watching the ships there. We often took a free ferryboat to nearby Staten Island, which had a great view of Manhattan, especially after sunset when it was illuminated. We looked at the Statue of Liberty, a gift from the French people. We could stay everywhere for hours without any problem, because each and every place—such as a department store, restaurant, museum, mall, park—had clean and neat restrooms. They had sinks with liquid soap and lots of toilet paper. During my whole stay in America, I never smelled urine in restrooms. The rinsing technology was such that it was impossible for even a little bit of excretions to be left there. They resolved that problem in the 1930s, after polio epidemics had occurred in the United States. President Franklin D. Roosevelt had contracted polio in 1921, when he was thirty-nine, and he stayed in a wheelchair the rest of his life. I watched a TV show that explained that all Americans had contributed one dime to clean America. They built modern toilets and even gave them a name—restrooms. Most American bathrooms had a shower fixture, so people could wash their hair and clean their body at the same time.

Although dozens of people waited in front of each attraction, everything was in perfect order, with many people engaged in operating the attraction, so we never waited too long. The tickets for senior citizens were always less expensive, so that was good for me. In my mind, I associated the efficiency I saw with an anthill, where busy ants moved in lines, never crushing each other. In America I became especially aware of the meaning and importance of good organization and discipline.

Vladana's parents visited us after five long years of not seeing Vladana and the children. They were happy with the children. In the vicinity was Brooklyn's big Prospect Park, with its meadows, groves, and a lot of sports fields. We often went to watch children's sports, because they were always registered for something, like soccer, baseball, or basketball. Ognjen used to say, "America looks like ex-communist countries where everything was organized, including sports." The grandfather, especially, spent his time with the children in the park, often playing soccer with them, and Vladana's mother made food for them and helped in the house. Many homes had laundry rooms, but we did not have one in our house, so Vladana with her big handcart and I with my little handcart took our laundry to a laundromat. Vladana's mother helped her, because she always had lots of laundry to wash. We used our handcarts for shopping too. Vladana purchased huge quantities of food and brought it home in her handcart, while I brought my supplies in my little handcart. I could always take a short rest on the way there and back, sitting on the clean steps of some house and enjoying looking at the trees and buildings around me.

Vladana's sister, Biljana, visited us with her little daughter. Because of the war, she had moved first to Africa and then to New Zealand with her husband and daughter. She gave me a book, the memoirs of an Australian lady, and as I read that book, I got the idea to write my memoir.

We often went to a party or a gathering with our countrymen; some of them were from Sarajevo, and they also visited us. We had an especially nice celebration of my seventieth birthday, when we had a big party. Ognjen wanted to show us all as much of America as possible, so whenever he was free we went out of New York to places such as the historic city of Philadelphia, where American independence was proclaimed, and to the gambling casino in Atlantic City. We also swam at the wonderful beaches and visited Manhattan very often. One day he took us to see the United Nations building. I always had a good time with Vladana's parents, because they were nice, measured, and well-intentioned people.

That year I also visited Nedžad in Kuwait. I hadn't see him for two and a half years, since our parting in front of the tunnel on that cloudy day. I traveled there by way of Athens, where I had to wait a long time, so I arrived in Kuwait very tired and sorry to look as I looked. I was fascinated by the Kuwait airport, with its red, yellow, green, and violet lamps illuminating the runway, which was a spectacular sight at night. Nedžad welcomed me in the big modern airport building. He was not so slim anymore. Amra and Neven were also happy to see me again, and I spent a very good time with them that month.

We went out in the evening, for it was hot, although not yet too hot—it was May. We rode in their big car along the bay that was lined with beautiful private houses made of white stone. Young trees stood between the houses. Climbing up a big water tower, we could see the wonderful panorama of the bay and the city. We went to high-quality shops and big galleries with first-class goods, often rather inexpensive, and always had a break someplace to have coffee, cake, or ice cream. We visited our countrymen there; they were mainly dentists, and they treated us to their food specialties and also paid visits to us—I like to recall those nights spent in friendly conversation. I had pleasant mornings with Amra, too, over coffee and breakfast, and several times we went together to see the doctor, Amra because of some inflammation on her finger and I because of my heart. The health service was well organized, with clean and richly equipped outpatient departments.

I liked the architecture of the white stone buildings, and the different Shiite and Sunni mosques. The Shiite mosques were more decorated, often with some tiles and green lights. In their attempts to make their city green, there were the young tree-lined walks that had to be specially cared for.

I was present at a spectacular event in Kuwait, Neven's graduation. He attended American High School and some thirty pupils were graduating. The ceremony was held in the wonderful building of Regent Palace. It was all very formal; the graduates wore blue togas and hats with long fringes, and after congratulations, we began to eat and have fun. A large selection of food was placed along one side of the hall, and I had never seen such hygienic protection—and many meals were made directly on the spot and served. Many exotic meals were also served there. Kuwaiti men wore long white robes and white scarves on their heads, and looked tall and attractive, but there were few women, and they were mainly without scarves. I did meet Kuwaiti women in the department stores, though, walking briskly in their long black dresses and black scarves—only their faces could be seen.

Then came the time for me to leave Nedžad, Amra, and Neven again; they sat with me at the Kuwait airport, and we had juices and spoke a little. During the flight, in my sad thoughts I observed the lights of Damascus and other cities we flew over. I brought many presents from Kuwait from me and from Nedžad who wanted to send something for Ognjen and the children, and especially for Vladana.

Wishing to get familiar with America as much as possible, I studied a lot, watched TV, and read. I paid particular attention to the TV interviews that an American journalist had with famous people—American and foreign actors, politicians, artists, and other prominent individuals. I noticed that Americans laughed a lot and were relaxed—they laughed a good deal even during the most serious conversations. If I sometimes accidentally looked at some passer-by and he noticed it, he would immediately smile at me. My sister told me once I smiled too much to foreigners, which was not usual in Switzerland, so I thought that she should only see Americans! Watching those TV shows, I noticed American openness, because they spoke of everything—sex, criminals, without any topic being forbidden, and I thought of the Latin proverb, "Homo sum humane nihil a me alienum puto." That is, "I am a human being, and nothing human is strange to me." This concept seemed to be just a part of normal life in America.

I constantly attended the English conversation course to understand Americans better, since their pronunciation was difficult and not understandable for me. It was much easier for me to read English than to understand spoken English. I came back home partly by bus or metro in the evening, and partly on foot, and although it was already dark at nine o'clock in wintertime, I never experienced any accident or attack. I observed people in the metro, black, white, Hispanic, and I never saw dirty jeans or shoes. The New York metro fascinated me in general; as I learned from a TV show I watched, it was built over the course of many years, and scores of people died during its construction.

I had an opportunity to go to the Metropolitan Opera sometimes, where I thought the coloratura sopranos were particularly beautiful. Because they often sang in Italian, there was an electronic translation device on the seat. I watched a Broadway show twice, although those modern musicals did not attract me as much as opera did. We often visited the Metropolitan Museum of Art, where one could go many times and still not ever see all the magnificent art on display. Other museums were enjoyable as well, like the Natural History Museum and the Museum of Modern Art.

After I had been in America for a year, I submitted a request for a "green card" and got it after an additional year. That card was important because it enabled immigrants to stay (and for Ognjen and Vladana, to work) in America without being treated by the government as a foreigner. Especially important to my getting the card was a medical screening for tuberculosis. They were confused by my lung x-ray, which showed tiny calcifications. In my childhood I caught a TB germ from a woman who washed laundry for us. I took fish oil and, I guess, was not inclined to it, so I didn't become ill. My sisters did not have it. Since then, the tiny calcifications remained and Americans, who had strict TB control, and were always afraid of it, analyzed it seriously upon my arrival in America and before giving me a green card.

Three years passed. Ognjen completed his residency training in general internal medicine. He submitted a request for his sub-specialization in critical care medicine and was accepted at the Mayo Clinic. He was very happy about it, because the Mayo Clinic was one of the top American institutions and was not easy to get into. During my work as a doctor, I recognized the Mayo Clinic by its excellent performance, and we used to say, "It was done like they do it in the Mayo Clinic." I was present at his graduation party in Brooklyn, which was formal and rich, and I was particularly happy when his chief told me, "He is really good in all respects."

We moved our things again, Ognjen drove a truck with our belongings and Vladana drove our car. We left New York, and we kept it deep in our hearts. It was a twenty-four-hour drive, and we had to pass through five American states, so we stayed overnight close to Chicago. We came to Rochester, in the State of Minnesota, and changed from the eight-million-person city to the eighty-thousand-person city. But living in America was the same everywhere, and Americans, regardless of their origin, were Americans everywhere, with all their characteristic features.

Rochester was not very densely populated and was a large and spacious city. The neighborhoods were surrounded by thick forests, and the city center—downtown—was interconnected by subway, underground passages, as well as skyways, bridges between buildings. So in wintertime when it was very cold, and especially during a snowstorm, people moved along those corridors. The Mayo Clinic was founded by the brothers Mayo, the surgeons Charles and William, at the beginning of the last century, and it continued to grow thanks to many donations. Today it has two big hospitals and several clinic buildings in Rochester.

We rented a small house, and Ognjen began working immediately. After some time, Vladana got a good part-time job in the medical library. In New York she had worked as a secretary to a doctor who gave her a good recommendation. The children went to school by school bus, but in New York it had been our obligation to take them to and from school. Vladana had taken them to school, and I had picked them up from school, because we lived too close for them to have taken a school bus.

I went to see a doctor for my heart follow-up; first I went to the family practitioner, who sent me to a cardiologist immediately. The cardiologist analyzed my heart ultrasound, and he told me I had a worsening prolapse of my left valves, suggesting that I choose one of two alternatives—to be under his close observation or to have heart surgery. Just before that, I had read in a magazine from the Mayo Clinic that a heart becomes weaker if a prolapse lasts longer, which would indicate that an earlier operation—while the heart is still good—would be better than a later one. I agreed to have an operation, and he said, "I would do the same if I were you." He sent me to a surgeon, a real British gentleman, as Ognjen said, but he was actually Australian. He explained to me the risks of that operation, which were very low, and I replied, "I have performed many operations on children," and with no fear I submitted to the operation. Luckily, he was able to repair my valves without embedding artificial ones and was satisfied with the operation. I spent six days in the hospital. In America, the patients stay in the hospital for a very short time after surgery. I had showers everyday, and a nurse took me to walk while pushing a wheelchair. That hospital reminded me of our hospitals, but it was better technically equipped, and their nurses were very good and highly responsible, like most of them in Bosnia.

During my medical follow-ups over the course of four years, I saw three cardiologists, the family practice doctor, and others, and I was always well received. They all showed real concern for me. In general, they were sensitive to *kalokagatia*, as the Greeks called three of the biggest ideals of mankind—beauty, goodness, and truth. Their care was truly outstanding.

We met some of our countrymen at the Mayo Clinic, too, and some of them were from Sarajevo; we invited each other for dinners and parties. Vladana knew how to cook and learned quickly to prepare new specialties that everybody liked. Both Vladana and Ognjen were very sociable, so we often had our friends paying us weekend visits. I learned how to receive guests and how to easily create a welcoming atmosphere. For me, there were lectures held every Wednesday at the Mayo Clinic about new medical developments, and once a month there was a lecture in the history of medicine. I gave a lecture myself, "Bosnia between the East and the West," supported by slides at the Rochester International Association. The people said afterward, "Thank you, thank you." I also went to the local college and practiced English on a computer, and all the time I remembered the words of Professor Kovačević, "If you organize your free time well, you will have time for everything."

I periodically suggested to Vladana and Ognjen that I should move to a separate apartment for elderly people, but they did not support it, probably thinking it was better for me to stay with them. And Vladana had always wanted to make me happy. I did my best to help them with their children, and with the cooking and cleaning, and I learned how to have good relations with the wider family too. I do not know how they managed it, but I believe in the power of love. Whatever makes us angry or hurt, love solves all problems, and I loved them. I remembered the words of Henry Van de Velde, "Take pride in loving more than you are loved, and never being second in line."

We moved to a bigger house with a big yard—a backyard, as Americans called it. It reminded me of the yard from my childhood behind our old house, only instead of trees of apple, plum, and walnut, there were trees of elm, birch, and pine. We had two cars, so I renewed my driver's license and drove when necessary. I enjoyed walking around our neighborhood, which even had a small llama farm. I enjoyed their little dog, too, the American terrier they bought for their children. I did not know earlier that a dog could be so intelligent, and Ognjen said that by its social intelligence a dog is the closest animal to man. So cute and not bothersome, he liked to play and run, and I used to say, "It is the most joyful creature I ever met."

We went to see the natural beauty of Minnesota, with its many rivers, waterfalls, and lakes, and accordingly, its nickname was "The Land of Ten Thousand Lakes." I especially liked some of its waterfalls. Everything was accessible, and we could find good accommodations for a good price. We often visited the Twin Cities, as they called Minneapolis and St. Paul. The two cities were linked by bridges over the Mississippi River, and they had all the attractions of a big American city. So we went to sport events and concerts, including the unforgettable Luciano Pavarotti concert. Ognjen wanted us to see all those attractions and natural beauty when Vladana's parents as well as my Nedžad and his family visited us. Unfortunately, Hamo, Amra's father, had passed away already, and we missed his jovial spirit and lively mind greatly.

After five years of living in America, I submitted a request for citizenship and I got it. With my American passport, I visited Nedžad in Sarajevo, my sisters in Switzerland, and Zoran, Milorad's son, and his family in The Netherlands. I also visited Dino in Vienna, who I had not seen for seven years. He had completed his composition studies. I felt very good in his small student apartment as well as in the beautiful ride across Vienna.

Ognjen took me many times to medical conferences held in different American states, so I saw much more of America than I had expected to see: San Francisco, Orlando, Atlanta, Chicago, San Diego, and Washington, D.C. Among the most memorable things I saw were the geysers in Yellowstone

National Park. They boiled and spurted forth hot water from the ground, with their surroundings in various colors resulting from algae and bacteria, as we were told. There were buffalo, bears, and fawns around, while wolves were hidden in the forest. Ognjen, Vladana, and the children went by car to see many other attractions and took great photos there. They did not mind long rides, so they often visited their friends living thousands of miles away.

I wanted to see Nedžad and Sarajevo more often, but I started to feel the signs of aging. Activities that used to be normal and easy caused various symptoms, mostly feeling faint and problems with my joints. However, little children grow up, they are clever, that is what is the most important, as Ognjen says. I remembered the nice words my high school teacher wrote in my autograph book, "It seems to me sometimes that life is only a series of various experiences. In that series sometimes only one atom of reason is needed for us to avoid the things that could make us sore and dissatisfied in ourselves. But whatever was our life, hard and arduous, or comfortable and nice, the main thing is, that one can say to himself or herself, 'I am satisfied, my final result is still positive, before my life lays a sign of a plus.' I wish all the best to my dear student."

On my fiftieth birthday

With Nedžad, my older son (Dubrovnik, Croatia - 2006)

With Ognjen, my younger son (San Diego, CA - 2002)